THE NEW TOWN STORY

FRANK SCHAFFER

The New Town Story

With a Foreword by
The Rt. Hon. Lord Silkin, C.H., P.C.

MACGIBBON & KEE

First published 1970 by MacGibbon & Kee Ltd
Reprinted 1970
3 Upper James Street Golden Square London W1
Copyright © Frank Schaffer 1970
Printed in Great Britain by
Richard Clay (The Chaucer Press) Ltd
Bungay, Suffolk

SBN 261 63170 5

ACKNOWLEDGMENTS

MY FIRST thanks are to Lord Silkin for his generous contribution of the foreword.

I am grateful to the Commission for the New Towns for readily agreeing that I might write this book and for allowing me to use for the purpose some of the information and facilities available to the Commission. I must emphasize that the book does not necessarily reflect the views of the Commission or of its individual members.

Among those who at various stages have patiently read all or part of the manuscript are Sir Henry Wells, Chairman of the Commission for the New Towns; Richard McDougall who was for many years General Manager of the Stevenage Development Corporation; Wyndham Thomas, at that time Director of the Town & Country Planning Association and now General Manager of the Peterborough Development Corporation; and my colleagues, Malcolm McKenzie, the Commission's Chief Administrative Officer, and Eric Overstall, Chief Finance Officer of the Commission until his recent retirement. I am grateful to them for the helpful suggestions they made. I accepted most, but not all, of them; and, of course, I take full personal responsibility for the statements and views expressed in the book.

To my colleagues the General Managers of the twenty-six development corporations—the names of those now in post are given in the Appendix—I owe both thanks and apologies. The thanks are due on two counts—first, because they and their staff have helped in the preparation of the Appendix and were good enough to provide information in advance of general publication, thus enabling the statistics to be as up-to-date as possible; second, and perhaps more important, because I have drawn heavily on my recollection of the many talks I have had with them during the years in which we have been closely associated on new towns work. But here apologies are necessary too, because I have not been able to consult them on the numerous references to their towns in the main text and because in a book such as this, which is about all new towns and none in particular, it is not possible to do full justice to any one town. Of the hundreds of general statements in the text there are bound to be some of which at least one town will say 'This doesn't apply to us'. Nor will all the General Managers agree with everything I have written—indeed I would expect lively disagreement and a variety of views on many of the more debatable issues. So I can only ask for indulgence and hope that friendships will survive this publication. If some of my more controversial or critical statements help to stimulate a closer study of the problems still facing the new town movement and if they lead to a wider examination of the opportunities and needs for the future, I shall be content.

Of the many others who have helped in various ways I must mention particularly Jeffrey Kay, now Chief Finance Officer of the Commission for the New Towns, who prepared the financial analysis in Part III of the Appendix; James Darling, F.R.G.S., for twenty-one years a member of the staff at Crawley, who drew the map and graphs; Len White, Liaison Officer at Harlow, with whom I had a long talk about new towns in general and Harlow in particular, and various government officials, who by tradition must remain anonymous, of the Ministry of Housing & Local Government, the Scottish Development Department, the Welsh Office and the Ministry of Development in Northern Ireland, who have answered my queries and helped in my search for material and references. The Ministry of Housing & Local Government compiled the statistics for the tables at Figs. 1 and 2, both of which are crown copyright and are reproduced by permission of the Controller of Her Majesty's Stationery Office.

Finally, a special word of thanks is due to Pauline Wright, my secretary at the Commission, without whose unsparing help the manuscript would never have reached the publisher's desk and seen its way through to publication.

London   F. S.
December, 1969

CONTENTS

CONTENTS

APPENDIX

TABLES AND GRAPHS

FOREWORD

by The Rt. Hon. Lord Silkin, C.H., P.C.

WRITING the story of the new towns is a formidable task. For it is not one story. There are now thirty stories, some nearly finished, some in the opening chapters and all different. They reflect as they must the various problems that had to be overcome, the changing pattern of demand and the personality and imagination of the chairmen and corporation members and of their professional advisers.

The people who live in the new towns are different too. They have different traditions, different interests, different ways of living and organizing their affairs: the Londoners, the Durham and East Fife miners, the Geordies, the Welsh, the steel workers at Corby with their strong Scottish contingent, the people from Birmingham, Merseyside, Manchester, Edinburgh, and Glasgow. New towns must be tailor-made to fit their needs.

Yet there is a common thread, a unity of policy and objective that binds them together. They set out to show that we in Britain could do something better than the soulless suburbia, ribbon development, single industry towns, and one-class housing estates of the '30s; that our big cities need not forever go on expanding until all their people were engulfed in a sea of bricks and mortar, cut off from the open countryside; that our obsolete, overcrowded, slum-ridden, and bomb-stricken towns could be thinned out and transformed from their Victorian squalor into decent centres of living of which we need no longer be ashamed. The new towns were part of a much wider vision of which as yet we have barely touched the fringe.

A backward glance over twenty-five years cannot but invoke a feeling of nostalgia. I count it a great privilege to have been responsible for introducing the New Towns Act into Parliament in 1946 and thus launching this great venture. In some ways it was a leap into the unknown. Despite the pioneering work of Ebenezer Howard and his colleagues we had no real knowledge of the organization and finance required nor could we readily see the social problems that might emerge. Decisions had to be taken quickly and I shall always be grateful to Lord Reith and his committee for the speed and thoroughness with which they framed their advice to me. Their recommendations have stood the test of time.

It has been a turbulent journey, two steps forward, one step back as the state of the economy dictated, but the whole time learning by experience and making progress towards the goal. In 1946 I predicted we would need some twenty new towns. Fifteen of these were started within a year or two, but it took nearly twenty years to get another half a dozen established. But now the road ahead is clear. The organization has been well tried and is a success; the financial results are encouraging; the social problems are better understood. The tremendous strides forward in recent years in the technical aspects of town design could never have been made if we had not had the courage, twenty-three years ago, to make a start. But above all, close on a million people can now bear witness to the fact that 'new towns work'.

Mr Schaffer's book thus comes at a timely moment when more and larger new towns are just getting under way. His detailed account of how the movement has fared so far and his drawing together of the problems, the solutions, the shortcomings and the achievements will be of value to all those who are taking part in this exciting field of public endeavour. And here I do not just mean the teams of corporation members and managerial staff. Nor do I just mean the people living in the towns today. Equally important are the millions of people who will be living in them tomorrow. They, after all, are the clients and they must be ready to play their part in the work ahead.

So I commend this book also to those living in our *old* towns. Most people in Britain have never seen the new towns and have never paused to consider how they may affect them and their children. Yet already these early efforts in large-scale planning and development are leading to a searching and critical examination of our methods in other fields—the expansion of towns, the clearance of slums, the rebuilding of cities. The new town achievements must surely have a profound influence on all future plans for development or redevelopment in Britain. Sooner or later, they will affect us all.

May I conclude by saying that there is no one better qualified by capacity, knowledge, and experience to write this story and I am delighted that Mr Schaffer has done so. Both as an Officer at the Ministry of Housing and Local Government and since then as Secretary of the Commission for the New Towns, Mr Schaffer has been in the thick of the new towns business and his wisdom has been of outstanding value in both capacities. I would suggest that this book be made compulsory reading for all those who are called upon to play some part in the development of the existing and future new towns.

'Yet all experience is an arch wherethro'
Gleams that untravelled world, whose margin fades
For ever and for ever when I move.'

TENNYSON

INTRODUCTION

AT a score of places in Britain a quiet revolution has taken place. From Glenrothes in the north to Crawley in the south, fifteen new towns have been built in less than twenty years, another five are getting under way and more are about to start.

For close on a million people it has meant a new life, new opportunities for themselves and their children and the privilege of taking part in one of the greatest experiments of our time. By the end of this century, according to one estimate, one out of every seven people in Britain will be living in a new town.

The process is a slow one—too slow, many would say. But democracy cannot be hurried. The careful search for a site, consultation with the local authorities, statutory designation of an area, inquiry into objections, appointment of the development corporation, selection of staff, preparation of plans, purchase of land, building of roads and sewers and provision of water supplies—these are just the preliminaries before a single brick can be laid and the first house built.

Then begins the real task of creating a town—jobs, houses, shops, schools, churches, parks, playing fields, pubs—all these and the many other things that make up the physical framework in which thousands of people will find a new life; people with widely differing backgrounds, strangers to the area and strangers to each other, who by their own efforts must come together and create a new community. Only people can make a town.

Other towns have grown up over the centuries through many generations and people, buildings and landscape have mellowed in the process. The new towns must achieve maturity in a few short years. That so many are doing it, and doing it successfully, is one of the most notable achievements of post-war Britain.

The odds against success were formidable. The economic and political consequences of failure could hardly be contemplated. Even the most ardent advocates of new towns had some misgivings at the outset, when they counted the cost and began to think out the intricate organization needed for such a venture.

Unpredictable, too, was the strength of the opposition, even after Parliament had given its blessing. Legal action in the Courts, local resistance or non-co-operation, undermining of industrial confidence and the cries of the Jonahs who insisted that the towns would never be built or would be the biggest white elephant of all time—all these forces combined to try to stifle the idea at birth. The new towns have been called the miracle of the century. The real miracle is that they ever got off the ground.

At any other time the opponents of planning might well have won. But this was the Britain of 1945 that had suffered devastation by bombing and was insistent that the promises of a better world should be honoured. For once, history was on the side of progress. Now, through the determination, devotion to an ideal and the brilliant work of a small band of dedicated enthusiasts, this dream of visionaries and philosophers through the centuries has been achieved.

There have been difficulties, delays and disappointments. There have been mistakes and shortcomings. No new experiment so vast, so intricate and affecting so intimately the lives of so many people could hope to get by without some setbacks. Many of the growing pains could perhaps have been avoided by better co-operation, understanding, and communication. But those days are past. If we are willing to learn from mistakes and take full advantage of the wealth of experience built up over the past two decades the slow march forward into the twenty-first century can take on a new impetus. It is a fresh and exciting chapter in our social history.

The British new towns are famous throughout the world. Tens of thousands of people visit them every year, half of them from overseas. They come in ones and twos, in professional and political delegations, in charter plane-loads even. Almost every country in the world, east and west, has sent official representatives to find out more about them.

They come to see, sometimes to criticize, but mainly to

admire, to envy, and to copy. The success of the new towns needs no demonstrating—the flourishing industry and healthy children are witness enough. But the one question they all ask is—'How is it done?'

It is that question which this book sets out to answer.

The New Towns of the United Kingdom of Great Britain
and Northern Ireland

1. VISION

THE idea of new towns is not new. Philosophers throughout the ages have condemned the living conditions of their time and with reforming zeal have described the society of their dreams—the perfect state, the perfect city, the perfect system of government.

In a way, many of them can claim through an idea here or there to be founding fathers of the new town movement: but the resemblance is superficial. A new society and a better life are not built by visionaries. In this hard modern world the way people live is governed by economics and political power.

Aristotle and Plato both wrote of the perfect town or city, self-supporting and controlled in size to provide a cohesive social unit best suited to the needs of the time. But this was in the context of a military aristocracy where the ruling class spent their lives in the sport of politics and war while the 'producers' were condemned to the menial work of keeping them free from the sordid detail of living.

In Britain, even seven hundred years ago, we were searching for growth points. In 1296 King Edward I ordered twenty-four English towns 'to elect men from among your wisest and ablest who know best how to devise, order and array a new town to the greatest profit of Ourselves and of merchants.'[1]

Thomas More's vision of Utopia in 1515 describes fifty-four towns, each twenty-three miles apart. Of particular interest is his description of the Utopian town of Amaurote

> built on the side of a hill covering some four square miles down to the river's edge, with streets very commodious and handsome, twenty feet broad . . . the houses of fair and gorgeous building . . . joined together in a long row through the whole street without any partition or separation. On the back side of the houses lie large gardens. Every house hath two doors, one into the street and a postern door on the back side into the garden. The houses have three storeys, one over

another, the outsides made of flint, plaster or brick and the inner sides strengthened with timber work and the roofs are plain and flat, covered with a kind of plaster so tempered that no fire can hurt or perish it and able to withstand the violence of the wind. And after supper the people bestow one hour in play, in summer in their gardens, in winter in their common halls where they exercise themselves in music or in honest and wholesome communication.[2]

This was More's vision of how the newly-developing Elizabethan architectural ideas could transform the fourteenth-century hovels of London. It was a very practical vision that could well have been possible within the technical and economic achievements of the era. It was Utopian only because the will and power to accomplish it were lacking. Not until the Great Fire of 1666 did the opportunity arise. But the vision was again lost and Christopher Wren's great comprehensive plan for rebuilding London was buried away in the pigeon-holes. Ownership of land dictated the rebuilding.

There were lessons to be drawn and ideas to be developed. Johnson, Swift, Butler, Bellamy, Buckingham, Morris, Owen, and many others throughout the world all explored in various ways the structure of society and advocated a better organization of our system of living. But it was over two hundred years before the dreams of the philosophers were taken up again. By then the industrial revolution had transformed Britain. The needs of a new system of production, helped on through the enclosures and the virtual destruction of the rural pattern of medieval life, had driven over half the population into the towns. To give them shelter, without which they could neither work nor breed, Victorian Britain was built around the smoke and dirt of factory, pit, and mill.

In its time it was a remarkable effort. In the years from 1832 to 1900 millions of houses were built by hand and brawn, with no mechanical diggers, no tower cranes, no industrialized building methods. This was in a period, too, when the whole railway system was laid down, sewerage, water, and gas supplies provided in every major town, and a massive programme of commercial and industrial development carried through, including the later monumental Victorian achievements of free schools, free libraries, elaborate town halls, and equally elaborate public conveniences.

In quantity the achievement was tremendous. True, the houses for the working people contrasted poorly with the elegance and luxury of the Regency and Victorian squares and terraces. This was a sharply divided class society, with the rich getting richer and the poor kept poor. The mass-production of insanitary and overcrowded jerry-built houses in the first half of the century soon led to demands for better control as a defence against the resulting outbreaks of cholera. With legislation on public health and building standards came the long 'by-law street' of identical two-up-two-down dwellings opening directly on to the road with a tiny space at the back for the closets and to give the prescribed minimum of space between buildings.

A few years later the tighter by-law controls resulted in row after row of almost identical 'tunnel backs'. They can hardly be termed an architectural achievement but most of them were well built by highly skilled craftsmen and with good quality materials. It is significant, too, that many of these houses, particularly in the south, were designed to meet the demands of an increasingly prosperous society with the status symbol of the time—electric bells in the parlour and master bedrooms to summon the maid of all work to do the chores before she retired to her attic bedroom. In the affluence of Victorian Britain even the poorly paid white-collar worker was beginning to demand some of the comforts so long enjoyed by the wealthy and was moving, if he could afford it, into the fashionable new suburbs that were encroaching rapidly on the open country.

Two isolated examples of enlightened housing development for industrial workers in the late nineteenth century are to be found at Bournville, near Birmingham, and at Port Sunlight, near Liverpool. These well-laid-out villages of the cocoa and soap philanthropists—Cadbury and Lever—were a step forward, a sign that the conscience of the nation was beginning to stir and that the link between housing conditions and industrial efficiency was beginning to be recognized. But for most of the working population at that time there was no escape from the congested central core of the industrial towns. It was against this congestion, with its growing squalor, social evils, lack of sun and divorce from the countryside that Ebenezer Howard came forward in 1898 with his famous work *To-morrow: a Peaceful Path to Real Reform*.[3]

Howard's thesis was a simple one—unduly simple for the needs of the more complex society of today—but it was a brave challenge to the philosophy of the time. He saw a town as a complete social and functional structure, limited in size to some 30,000 people with sufficient jobs to make it self-supporting, spaciously laid out to give light, air, and gracious living well away from the smoke and grime of the factories and surrounded by a green belt that would provide both farm produce for the population and opportunity for recreation and relaxation. Growth, design, and density would be strictly controlled through public ownership of the land.

Howard, however, was not content just to sit back and wait for his ideas to be accepted. He was a man of action. Following the publication of his book he founded the Garden Cities Association and four years later—in 1902—established the First Garden City at Letchworth, some thirty miles north of London.

Influential people rallied to his support but the public were slow to invest money in such a novel and speculative venture. Of the £300,000 needed, only £100,000 was subscribed at the end of the first year. Shortage of money meant that standards and building costs of houses to rent had to be kept to a minimum. Internal dissension, financial troubles, and heavy losses led to near-failure and to the sacrifice of many cherished principles. Much of the land was leased for private building and the investors were getting a poor return for their money. Nevertheless, the project went ahead slowly but surely on the lines of the plan for the town prepared by Raymond Unwin. Dividends were limited by the Articles of Association to 5 per cent but it was twenty years before the shareholders received any dividend at all and forty-three years before the arrears were paid in full.

Howard and his supporters were not daunted, however, by the early troubles at Letchworth. In an effort to influence the house-building programme after the First World War they renewed their plea in Frederic Osborn's book *New Towns after the War*,[4] but they were still determined to lead by example. 'If you wait for the authorities to build new towns,' Howard told Osborn, 'you will be older than Methuselah before they start. The only way to get anything done is to do it yourself.'[5]

So in 1920 they launched the Second Garden City at Welwyn in Hertfordshire. In their preliminary announcement—described as 'an invitation to the public to subscribe for a non-profiteering investment'—they quoted from a speech in May 1917 by the then Prime Minister, Lloyd George—a speech that was to find an echo in the speeches of an even more famous Prime Minister a quarter of a century later:

> 'There is no doubt that the present war presents an opportunity for the reconstruction of the industrial and economic conditions of this country, such as has never been presented probably in the life of the world. . . . Immediately after the war . . . I believe the country will be in a more enthusiastic mood, in a more exalted mood for the time being, in a greater mood for doing big things, and unless the opportunity is seized immediately . . . I believe it will pass away, I will not say for ever, but it will pass away far beyond either your time or mine, and perhaps beyond our children's.'

When the war ended in 1918 little heed was given to these words of warning and there was certainly no encouragement for 'big things'. Successive housing Acts allowed the local authorities to resume building 'houses for the working classes' and subsidized the speculative builder. In 1921 a committee under Neville Chamberlain[6] recommended in favour of garden cities and powers to buy land for the purpose were included in various housing Acts. But they never got beyond the talking stage. Ten years later the Greater London Regional Planning Committee, in a special report by Raymond Unwin,[7] recommended the building of satellite towns as a matter of urgency. The Government thereupon set up yet another committee under Lord Marley which after four years of discussion came to the same conclusion;[8] but again the advice was ignored.

Despite the lack of official encouragement and the national economic troubles of the early 1920s, Ebenezer Howard went ahead with his Second Garden City side by side with the rash

5

of unplanned speculative building and ribbon development that spread across the countryside throughout the 1920s and 1930s. As in the case of Letchworth, response to the Welwyn Garden City prospectus was poor. The investing public were not particularly interested in 'non-profiteering' investments. The £90,000 subscribed was less than the cost of the land.

Nevertheless, a plan for a town of 40,000 was prepared by Louis de Soissons. In twenty years it had a population of 18,500 and was well established as a flourishing industrial centre. But financial troubles nearly wrecked the project. The Government came to the aid of the Company with a loan, some £420,000 of the share capital was written off and the limitation on dividends was removed. Fortunes revived and by the end of the thirties quite good progress had been made. In the immediate post-war situation, however, with its shortages of materials and labour, the Government came to the conclusion that the Company would not be able to build with the necessary speed and that Welwyn Garden City ought to be completed as part of the overspill programme for the London area.

At Letchworth, on the other hand, it was left to the Garden City Company to complete the town, but Ebenezer Howard's intention that the local authority should take over the assets almost came to grief a few years later through the sale on the market of most of the Company's shares. A group of people gained control in the 1950s and were all set to take advantage of the post-war rise in land values and sell off the property at a handsome profit. At this point the local authority stepped in and with Government support promoted a Bill in Parliament to enable the shareholders to be bought out compulsorily.[9] A new public corporation was then set up, appointed partly by the local authorities and partly by the Government, which now holds the assets in trust for the town. But it was an expensive operation. The compensation to the shareholders was finally settled by arbitration at over £3 million.[10]

Such were the halting and unpropitious beginnings of the new town movement. It is a classic story of a pioneer who believed passionately in his principles. Although at times Howard's projects seemed near to failure and even nearer to bankruptcy, he never lost faith in them. The Garden Cities

Association which he founded in 1898 kept up a constant campaign throughout the inter-war years under its new name of the Town & Country Planning Association and, when Howard died in 1928, found an equally powerful and determined advocate in Mr—now Sir—Frederic Osborn, the first estate manager of the Welwyn Garden City Company.

Thus, Ebenezer Howard can justly be called the father of the new towns. But his preaching and propaganda achieved far more. It marked the beginning of a slow acceptance of the need for planning control. In 1909 the first timid legislation on urban planning was sponsored by John Burns; in 1919, 1925, and 1932 further modest extensions were made to curb, though not to cure, the worst excesses of suburban sprawl; but it was the wartime devastation that finally brought home to the British people the need for more forthright powers and more positive direction. New towns are but one aspect only of the revolution that culminated in the famous Silkin legislation of 1946-8.

2. FOUNDATIONS

THE new town movement as we know it today started officially when the New Towns Act passed through Parliament in 1946; but for the real beginnings it is necessary to go back to the days of 1940 when the bombs started falling on Britain and the German armies were twenty miles away across the Channel in undisputed control of western Europe.

The mood of the people was unmistakable. With the fall of Chamberlain they rallied behind Winston Churchill in a supreme war effort, but there was none of the flag-waving and jingoism of 1914–18. This was a battle for survival—but survival for what? That question had to be answered.

For this was a generation that had grown up in the hard political school of the twenties and thirties. The economic collapse of the inter-war years had led them to examine critically the whole social and economic fabric of society. Political meetings in the thirties would fill the Albert Hall to overflowing; book clubs gave millions of people for the first time an understanding of political economy; in meeting halls or in their own homes, groups of enthusiasts throughout the country met together to study and understand why the world had failed to tick.

Perhaps never before—or since—in British history has there been such a widespread and informed interest in economic and social affairs among the broad masses of the people of all classes, all ages, and all levels of education. With this political understanding that enabled the nation to be mobilized in an all-out war effort against Fascism went an equal determination that there was to be no return to the unemployment, slums, and planless chaos of the thirties.

The wartime leaders of the nations understood very well the mood of the people. This was a time when Henry Wallace, Vice-President of the U.S.A., could talk of the 'century of the common man', and when Winston Churchill could end a broadcast to Europe with the eloquent peroration:

8

'Long live the forward march of the common people of all lands towards their just and true inheritance, and towards the broader and fuller age.'[1]

Day by day the Forces Educational Services kept up morale by laying stress on post-war problems and opportunities. Discussions in the factories, the air-raid shelters, and the Naafis made it abundantly clear that words and empty phrases were not enough. This was no time for a mere repetition of the 1914–18 promises of Homes for Heroes. The people of Britain would not be sold down the river a second time. Action was needed, concrete proof that preparations were really being made for the day when peace would break through.

So it was that the process of post-war reconstruction started even when the first bombs were still falling on London. When and how the war would end, how much destruction there would be, whether invading armies would reach these shores, and what resources would be available for reconstruction—all these were completely unknown factors. It was a supreme act of faith. In October 1940 Lord Reith was appointed Minister of Works and Buildings, with special responsibility for studying the problems of reconstruction after the war, and he quickly collected together a small band of advisers from the civil service, universities, industry, commerce, and the architectural, planning, surveying, and legal professions. Their job was to plan the future.

A starting-point was ready to hand. The Royal Commission on the Distribution of the Industrial Population, set up in 1938 under the chairmanship of Sir Montague Barlow, had argued for two years without reaching agreed conclusions; but their Report,[2] presented and pigeon-holed at about the outbreak of war, at least pointed the way forward by recommending some form of central planning authority and a further expert examination of the land problem. But there was also a minority report that was much more positive and forthright and indeed much too controversial to have found acceptance in pre-war times. It recommended a central planning Ministry, the building of garden cities or satellite towns and special powers to deal with the redevelopment of overcrowded city areas. This minority report was just the approach needed in the changed

9

political atmosphere of the forties and it had a marked influence on the evolution of policy.

Much more thought and investigation were needed, however, before long-term policy could be framed. Lord Reith accordingly set up two inquiries—one on the land problem under Mr Justice Uthwatt,[3] and the other on the use of land in rural areas under Lord Justice Scott.[4] He also commissioned J. H. Forshaw and Patrick Abercrombie to prepare a new plan for the County of London,[5] which was later supplemented by the Abercrombie Plan for Greater London.[6]

The reports of these committees and the proposals for London contained a penetrating and constructive analysis of the problems of post-war reconstruction. In a matter of a year or two, and at the height of the war, they carried planning thought to a new plane, far removed from the negative and half-hearted level that had dominated the previous thirty years since the first planning legislation of 1909. The purpose of planning, the rights of landowners, the age-old question of land values, the needs and duties of industry, the right of people to live and work in comfort and to enjoy the countryside—all these controversial and politically explosive issues were brought out into the open.

Events moved quickly, however, long before these reports were all received. By February 1941 the wartime Coalition Government had accepted the principle of national planning as a basis for post-war reconstruction.[7] By July 1941 they had accepted the recommendation in the Interim Report of the Uthwatt Committee[8] that, to prevent speculation and profiteering, land values for public acquisition purposes should be frozen at March 1939 level.[9] In the following February Lord Reith in the Lords and Arthur Greenwood in the Commons announced that the Government had agreed to establish a Central Planning Authority,[10] and the Ministry of Works and Planning was set up to take over all planning functions from the Ministry of Health. To the surprise of most people Lord Reith was moved out of the job and Lord Portal was appointed as Minister in his place with Henry Strauss (now Lord Conesford) as Parliamentary Secretary to deal with the planning work. Then in 1943 the new Ministry of Town & Country

Planning was created, with W. S. ('Shakes') Morrison as the first Minister, charged with the duty of 'securing consistency and continuity in the framing and execution of a national policy with respect to the use and development of land throughout England and Wales'.[11]

The new Ministry, despite wartime conditions and a very limited staff, moved swiftly. Within a few months legislation was introduced, as recommended by the Uthwatt Committee, making the planning control of the 1932 Act (hitherto a matter of local option) compulsory throughout the country;[12] and a year later the Town & Country Planning Act 1944, again following a recommendation of the Uthwatt Committee,[13] made new and far-reaching arrangements for post-war reconstruction by enabling areas of severe war damage and obsolete development—blitz and blight—to be bought compulsorily by the local authority, replanned and leased out for rebuilding.

The debates on the 1944 Bill contained the first ideological skirmish. It was a complex measure and by including compulsory powers for dealing with both blitz and blight established the point that the rebuilding of towns and cities was a comprehensive planning process that could only be properly carried out by bringing complete areas into public ownership and replanning them as a whole. All the profitable development was reserved for private enterprise, however. The local authority had to carry out all the unprofitable work with no financial help from the Government on 'blight', and only a modest measure of assistance towards the annual losses incurred in dealing with war-damage, the capital cost of which was estimated at that time to be about £575 million.[14]

Although the Bill went through Parliament without serious opposition, the Government came in for some heavy criticism for failing to deal with the more fundamental question of land reform. The Uthwatt Committee had stressed the need for this in their final report presented in 1942 and had recommended, as an essential minimum, the transfer to the State of all development rights and development values in unbuilt-on land.[15] Four years of study by the Government had produced no more than a half-hearted White Paper[16] recognizing the need for control and for some form of central machinery for balancing compensation payments with the collection of betterment.

Many Members of Parliament accepted this situation as inevitable. The Uthwatt Committee's recommendations were opposed by all the landowners' organizations and the Coalition Government could hardly be expected to reach agreement on them. W. S. Morrison showed considerable courage in producing his White Paper because it contained proposals which many on the Conservative benches would clearly oppose; but the Government side-stepped all requests in the Commons for a full debate on the subject.

By then the end of the war was in sight and when post-war problems were under discussion the differences between the parties on social issues were never far below the surface. There were constant undertones suggesting that the Conservatives, who were the dominant party in the Coalition Government, were refusing to take any decisions that might prejudice the power and the profit of private owners of land and private developers. Indeed there were strong rumours, voiced later in Parliament, that the sudden and unexpected dismissal of Lord Reith in 1942 had been due to anxiety in some quarters that a policy of national planning should *not* be effectively put into operation.[17]

It is particularly interesting, however, to note that throughout all these discussions, there is hardly a mention of new towns, despite the constant lobbying by the Town & Country Planning Association, the recommendations in the Barlow Report and Abercrombie plans, and the clear need to restrict the growth of London and other big cities and to reduce density on rebuilding.

Indeed, in those days the idea of new towns was far from popular. The big local authorities disliked the thought of new rateable value going outside their areas; the small rural authorities held out no welcome to London's overcrowded millions; the farmers and the agricultural community generally opposed any interference with farmland; industrialists stressed the economic necessity of a return to pre-war freedom to build more and more factories on the Great West Road and other urban fringe areas; while some political spokesmen and land value 'experts' ridiculed the idea that the land to be developed should be selected by a Government department instead of by the demand of the market and the index of land values.

Elections are won or lost on broad policies, not details, and the idea of new towns was no vote-catcher. In the rural areas it might well be a vote-loser. The urban electorate and the men and women returning from the Forces wanted houses and jobs, a reshaping of the economy and a new prosperity, but how, when, and where was not in issue. What was in issue was the need for new ideas and the need to carry them through against strongly entrenched interests.

When the fighting in Europe came to an end in 1945 Parliament was dissolved and a few weeks before the election the coalition was broken up to enable the various political parties to resume their separate identities and make their separate appeals to the electorate. To which Party could the people of Britain entrust their hopes for the post-war world? Conservative? Liberal? Labour? Communist?

On 26 July 1945, the first general election after the war gave a decisive answer. The Labour Party led by Clement Attlee was returned with, for the first time in Britain, an absolute majority over all other parties, pledged to carry through to reality the vision of the future that had kept the nation going during the Churchillian days of 'blood, sweat, toil, and tears'.

3. POWERS

DESPITE the limited progress in legislation up to 1945 the Ministry of Town & Country Planning had been making a very thorough examination of all the problems of post-war planning and development. When Lewis Silkin was appointed as the Minister in the Attlee Government he found many important questions awaiting decision. 'Plan boldly and comprehensively' had been the advice given by the Coalition Government to local authorities and others seeking guidance on post-war policy.[1] Now they must be given the tools to do the job. New towns were merely one of many question-marks, and there was no noticeable enthusiasm for them in Parliament or among the general public.

Of first importance was the task of reshaping the planning system. The Town & Country Planning Acts of 1909–1932 were too timid, too negative, too static in their approach. Hundreds of complicated 'planning schemes' submitted by local authorities before the war were still awaiting the long drawn-out process of securing Ministerial approval. Now they were consigned to the vaults as relics of a bygone age.

For the post-war period a new and dynamic machinery was needed: a flexible system that could be quickly adapted to meet changing needs but in particular a system under which a positive programme of development could be carried through, whether it be for the reconstruction of the war-damaged areas, demolishing and rebuilding the outworn areas of towns and cities, opening up new areas for development, building new towns or expanding old ones, controlling the location of new industry, preserving green belts, stopping ribbon development or protecting rural areas for public enjoyment. And as an essential background to all this must come a final and permanent solution of the problem of compensation and betterment which had bedevilled planning for a generation and which had now been so thoroughly analysed by the Uthwatt Committee.

It was only too clear that a Bill to cover all these aspects

14

would be a formidable document. Moreover, the Government had many other important problems to cope with—demobilizing the millions in the armed forces, establishing civilian work to replace the wartime jobs, reorganizing and re-equipping the basic industries of coal, steel, transport, and power, establishing the health services, pulling down the slums and getting going on a programme of house-building to meet the demand flowing from the wartime marriages and the millions of returning servicemen. These were all priority tasks. The legislation programme was clearly going to be heavily congested and many of the projected Bills would be controversial and take up much Parliamentary time.

Priorities had therefore to be established and fitted into the drafting and parliamentary time-tables. On planning matters, the rural areas question was the least urgent, the new planning and compensation-betterment system the most complicated. Both were directed to the long term rather than the immediate future. The wartime system of building licences and rationing of materials was still in operation and this, combined with the newly-established planning control throughout the country, would prevent any seriously prejudicial development and at the same time allow an immediate programme of house-building to get under way. For major works, the reconstruction of the war-damaged areas was of first priority and the Coalition Government's Act of 1944, with its '1939 ceiling' controlling the price of land, was adequate and would check for a time any attempts to profit out of post-war needs by speculation in land.

This left a major gap—the 'overspill' problem. Before any policy could be adopted for reducing congestion in London and preventing further peripheral expansion, some positive alternative had to be available and actually in operation. For this Professor Abercrombie had recommended 'satellite towns' and the new Government quickly accepted his recommendation in principle. It was a self-contained subject that could have an immediate and beneficial impact on the pattern of future development.

Fortunately, an unexpected opportunity occurred in 1946 to introduce some legislation, provided it could be prepared quickly. Lewis Silkin accordingly laid down a three-stage programme for dealing first with new towns, then with planning and compensation-betterment, and finally with the problems of the countryside. This programme was to embrace a complete set of powers covering the whole needs of physical development for the forseeable future. A simpler and more flexible system of planning control was to be applied to the whole country under the overall direction of the Government. Development values were to be vested in the State, with once-for-all compensation to owners. Future building and other changes in the use of land could then be properly planned, with a development charge paid where development was allowed. Local authorities could buy land to carry out or organize comprehensive development, in place of the piecemeal and spasmodic efforts of the past. New towns could be built in areas selected by the Government. Stretches of our most beautiful countryside and coast-line could be protected for the enjoyment of all.

All this, however, was purely a framework for administration—a mechanism through which to implement such policy or objectives as the Government in office at any time or the local authorities in their areas wished to achieve. The actual decisions were to be left to the ordinary democratic processes. Under these powers could be built the New Jerusalem or a new round of slums; under them private enterprise could be allowed to play a major or a minor role; under them owners of land selected for development could reap large profits or could have the profits reduced according to the amount of the development charge. Public purchase of land could be operated on a large or small scale according to the needs of the area and the policies it was desired to secure.

These Bills eventually reached the statute book as the New Towns Act 1946, the Town & Country Planning Act 1947, and the National Parks Act 1948—perhaps the most courageous and far-reaching series of Bills ever to have passed through Parliament in such a short period. This famous trio has earned for Lewis Silkin permanent recognition in the social history of our time.

The first stage of this legislation had to be prepared quickly if it was to get into the Parliamentary programme. New towns had been talked about for years, but much thought was needed before a Bill could be drawn up. Despite the Abercrombie Plan, the long agitation by a few small groups of enthusiasts, and the none too promising experience of Letchworth and Welwyn Garden City, nobody had seriously worked out how new towns could be securely financed, how they could be built quickly enough to serve their full purpose of relieving congestion in London or elsewhere, and what sort of organization should be given the responsibility for building them.

Accordingly, in October 1945, Lewis Silkin, together with Joseph Westwood, the Secretary of State for Scotland (for the Minister of Town & Country Planning had no jurisdiction north of the border) appointed an Advisory Committee under the chairmanship of Lord Reith

'to consider the general questions of the establishment, development, organisation and administration that will arise in the promotion of New Towns in furtherance of a policy of planned decentralisation from congested urban areas; and in accordance therewith to suggest guiding principles on which such Towns should be established and developed as self-contained and balanced communities for work and living.'

Rarely has any Government Committee got down to business so quickly and so effectively. Lord Reith knew that the drafting of legislation was awaiting his Committee's report, and with his customary zeal and hustle produced within three months an interim report[2] on the choice of Agency for building a town. After discussions with representatives of local authorities, private enterprise building organizations, Building Societies, and Housing Associations, the Committee came down very firmly in favour of a Government-appointed public corporation, one for each town, and financed by the Exchequer.

Some local authorities—particularly the London County Council and the City of London—supported the recommendation of Lord Reith's Committee. Others, notably those in likely new town areas, were reluctant to see control pass out of their hands; but many of them recognized that the task of building a complete new town, as a sideline almost to their main statutory functions, was beyond their capacity. If a new agency was to be established they would have preferred to see it appointed by the local authority; but this would inevitably have meant local authority money, and few councils were able to face the financial implications.

Some ten weeks after signing their first report the Reith Committee produced a second report[3] dealing with the matters on which legislation was needed. This covered such questions as the acquisition and disposal of land, the attraction to the towns of industry and commerce, the provision of basic services such as roads, sewers, etc., the speed at which a town could be built, adjustment of local government boundaries, and a number of financial questions.

Finally, in July 1946 the Committee presented their last report[4] dealing in remarkable detail with the principles on which in their view a new town should be planned and with the organization and method for executing the plan. To have produced these invaluable reports in a matter of nine months was a *tour de force* typical of Lord Reith's vitality, perception, and organizing skill.

Meanwhile, even while the Committee were still sitting, legislation was being prepared on the basis of the first two interim reports, and the New Towns Bill was introduced in Parliament on 17 April 1946. It had an easy passage. All parties supported the main principles, and although discussion went on for many hours it was mainly confined to points of detail. The Conservatives tried to carry an amendment prohibiting the development corporation from doing anything if a private enterprise firm was willing to do it, on the lines of the similar prohibition on local authorities in the Town & Country Planning Act 1944, but the Labour Government would not give way on this point for new towns.

In pressing for this restriction on the powers of a new town development corporation some Members of Parliament clearly had in mind the action of the private Welwyn Garden City Company which had set up several subsidiary trading companies and the discussion turned largely on preventing this sort of activity. But the amendment went much further. It would also have made it virtually impossible for the development corporations to build any shops, factories, or houses, even though they used the private enterprise building contractors as agents. Apart from such services as roads and sewers the whole job, or at any rate the profitable parts, would have had to be handed over to the property development companies. This the Government firmly rejected. They agreed that private enterprise would play an important part in building new towns but they refused to tie the hands of the development corporations in the way suggested.

There was pressure to improve the compensation terms to landowners, which the Government met in part by adding a supplement of 60 per cent to the 1939 standard of values for owner-occupied houses;[5] and they accepted the need to include local people on the development corporation.[6] On the ultimate destination of the new town assets all parties agreed that they should eventually be transferred to the local authorities on suitable terms, and the main concern of the Conservatives seemed to be to limit the Treasury's power to prevent it![7]

Many tributes were paid to Lewis Silkin from both sides of the House for his courage in introducing such a valuable and far-reaching Bill. The one lone voice, unsupported by any of his Conservative colleagues, was that of Viscount Hinching-brooke who declared the Bill to be a useless and wicked measure, a dead letter, and predicted that the Minister's policy would soon be on the scrap heap. 'The Bill,' he said, 'will lead us into gigantic schemes of construction which are impossible of attainment in a free society.' He talked of 'mausoleums' and 'the men, women, and children who will be enticed into chromium-plated, soulless homes'. And he gave the warning that there were 'members of Parliament who, with their friends and associates outside Parliament, do not fully understand the Bill and do not like the smell of it. They,' he reminded the House, 'are nevertheless more powerful politically in the long run.'[8] To this Leah Manning gave a spirited reply, recounting her own experiences at a crowded meeting at Harlow where she found 'a great mass of people who looked forward to the day when a new town would arise.'[9]

The Act received royal assent on 11 November 1946. Even before the Bill was put before Parliament Lewis Silkin had announced that the Government accepted the main principles of Professor Abercrombie's Greater London Plan which involved moving a million people into new towns within 20–50 miles of the centre of London,[10] and a week later he announced the proposal to build a new town at Stevenage.[11] This time the Government clearly meant business.

But, as Viscount Hinchingbrooke had warned, there were still battles ahead.

4. DESIGNATION

THE first step in building a new town is the designation by the Minister[1] of a suitable area. It is a lengthy process. Technical examination, local consultations, public inquiry, formal order, possible challenge in the Courts and, in some cases, in Parliament—from start to finish it can easily take several years. From this act of designation flow all the statutory powers—the right to buy land compulsorily, the freezing of land values, the use of Exchequer money and the many other processes involved in building a new town.

There is no easy recipe for selecting a new town site. Whatever area is suggested there will be some who say 'Have a new town of course: but not here.' Farmers and other residents are likely to be uprooted; country towns and villages may find their old-world charm diminished; a century-old way of life may be destroyed. It is little wonder that new town proposals sometimes produce fierce opposition.

This is no new problem. The conflict between old and new, preservation and change, stagnation and progress is the whole drama of history. The conflict between the needs of the community and the rights of the individual is as old as private land-ownership itself and has probably aroused more controversy in Britain during this century than any other topic. To some land means power; to others wealth; but for most people it just means ownership of a house to live in or a farm to work on. Yet all, with their varied interests and their different motives, jealously guard their property and regard it as a breach of a fundamental right if any attempt is made to interfere with their ownership or their ability to do as they like with their land. We are all Naboths where our own vineyards are concerned.

It is little use trying to counter these views with constitutional argument. In theory, all land in Britain is held on tenure from the Crown with the right of the Crown at any time to repossess; but that is just a polite fiction. The theory of 'eminent domain' may be interesting reading in the legal text-books but it is too thin an argument on which to turn a man out of his house or off his land. Solid justification is rightly demanded, and it must have the seal of approval by Parliament.

Yet, despite the political difficulties, Parliament has never flinched from the task of giving powers of compulsory purchase to meet the public need. Scores of Acts were passed in the days of the industrial revolution, when the building of railways, docks, and waterways was vital to the economy, when water supplies, sewerage works, and a whole range of civic action were essential for the public health, and when education, recreation, and housing became accepted as the responsibility of the State. The catalogue of needs and priorities changes through the years but no civilization could function and certainly no modern industrial community could survive on the basis of a system that regarded private land-ownership as sacrosanct and inviolate.

Safeguards there must be against arbitrary action by the executive; compensation there can be on whatever basis or at whatever level the legislature thinks right and proper—and this can vary with historical, economic, and political circumstances. But the right of individual owners to withhold land or hold the community to ransom can never be conceded by any society. Indeed, the more advanced civilization becomes, the more dependent a nation becomes on ever-increasing industrial efficiency, the more prosperous its people become and the more demanding in terms of good living conditions, both for work and leisure, then the more important becomes the need to control and direct the use of land for the benefit of the nation as a whole.

The designation of land for a new town is a part of this process and it has to be based strictly on need and suitability. In the selection of the area there is little room for sentiment or emotion and not much room for manoeuvre except on minor detail. For when it comes to a close examination there are remarkably few places in Britain that fulfil all the many and exacting criteria.

First comes the general policy objective. The aim of most of the new towns is to relieve pressure on overcrowding in the big cities such as London, Birmingham, Liverpool, Manchester, or Glasgow. For social and economic reasons the site of the new town must be within a reasonable distance away—not too near to be in danger of coalescing, destroying green belts, or encouraging commuting; not too far to destroy commercial and industrial ties or split up families too much.

Other new towns have been built to provide housing for workers in particular industries such as Corby, based on the steel works, Peterlee and Glenrothes on the coalfields, Newton Aycliffe on the wartime factory estate, and Cwmbran for the workers in the Monmouth valley. The town must be built near the jobs. These factors settle the general location and limit the area of choice.

Some hold the view that the best site for a new town is a stretch of completely rural land. A virgin site gives better scope for imaginative planning and avoids the difficult problem of integrating new and old populations and possibly destroying established communities. From the cost point of view, it is easier to plan and cheaper to buy and develop. But cost is not the only criterion or necessarily the right one. The social implications and the well-being of the people who live or will be living in the town should be the paramount considerations. Others take the view that it is better to have an established town as a nucleus because it has tradition, local character, a range of amenities, and a social life into which, given goodwill on both sides, the new population can readily be absorbed.

This question has never been resolved. Both types of town have been built and in the long run they are equally successful. There can be friction between new and old inhabitants; on the other hand, in a virgin town before roads are built, buses are running, new shops are opened, and a social and cultural life has been established, the early years can become intolerable for an ex-city dweller accustomed to the bright lights and a long-established pattern of family and other social relationships. Frequently, however, there is no effective choice. The final decision turns on so many other factors and the weighing up of a mass of technical data within a limited area of search.

Water for domestic and industrial use is of first importance and reservoirs and new supply systems may have to be built. A modern town of 60,000 people, with associated industry, will need over four million gallons a day. The post-war policy of grouping small water undertakings has improved the efficiency of the distribution system and steps are being taken through the Water Resources Board to remedy the position in the areas of acute shortage, but there are still some places where sufficient water simply does not exist.

The site selected must also be capable of being drained and sewered at reasonable cost. New sewage works are usually required and facilities for disposing of effluent and surface water to the rivers or sea. The cost of these services is one of the heaviest overheads that a new town has to carry.

Contours, too, are of some importance from other aspects. Steeply sloping land presents problems to architects and engineers no less than to mothers with prams, and can add a lot to the cost. A completely flat area on the other hand, though desirable for industrial development, can lack views and perspective and gives less scope than gentle contours for good design, layout, and landscaping.

Geological factors and subsoil conditions have to be examined, with test-boring where necessary to establish the suitability of the land for building. Several proposals have been rejected because of the depth of peat cover or the danger of subsidence through salt workings or because of valuable deposits of coal or other minerals. Many of our proved mineral resources are none too plentiful and building that would make their future extraction impossible could have serious economic consequences in years to come.

By no means least in importance is the agricultural appraisal. It has long been the established policy of successive governments whenever possible to avoid using top-class agricultural land for development and to avoid splitting up efficient farming units. Much of the opposition to new towns comes, understandably, from the farming community and in the prolonged consultation that precedes any new town proposal the protection of farming interests and food production is always an important element.

All these factors are directed to the inherent qualities of the land itself. Even more important, however, are the economic potentialities. A balanced town must have its own industries able to guarantee continued employment for the whole population. People will go to live where the jobs are, but the jobs can only be provided in areas that are economically viable.

Transport facilities in relation to raw materials and markets are a prime necessity. Main road access, preferably near an existing or proposed motorway, is essential because, outside the heavy industries, so many goods these days are carried by road. In the early new towns much stress was placed on the need for rail communications but, although access was provided to railway sidings, little use is made of them at present. Circumstances may well change in the future, as the rail service to industry is improved by liner trains and other means.

Air services for passengers and freight were thought of little importance in the early days but the new towns already established within reasonable distance of an airport are now beginning to have a pull over those without such facilities. The prosperity of Glenrothes, the most northern of the Scottish towns, received a tremendous fillip when they established an air-strip there, only a short hop from the international airport at Prestwich. Many other new towns not served by a near-by airport are following suit.

The area of land required for a new town depends, of course, on the population intended. For 100,000 people, some seven thousand acres may be needed and the search may take a year or more of intensive examination and discussions among Government departments and local authorities. Only then can a start be made on the long and detailed procedure laid down by Parliament for designating the land as a new town.[2]

The first duty of the Minister is to consult with 'any local authorities who appear to him to be concerned'. These will include the county council for the area and possibly the councils of near-by counties or county boroughs, the district councils—borough, urban, or rural—the parish council or parish meeting and also such bodies as the river or catchment boards or other joint boards. In practice statutory undertakers in the area are also invited to comment.

Some of the authorities will know of the proposal through informal discussion at an earlier stage and may already have expressed their views; but this statutory consultation gives them an opportunity of putting to the Minister their considered conclusions so that he can decide whether to go ahead with the project. The consultation is no mere formality. As Mr Justice Morris put it, 'The Minister with receptive mind must, by such consultation, seek and welcome the aid and advice which those with the local knowledge may be in a position to proffer.'[3]

The decision does not rest with the Minister alone. Many other departments are concerned—notably the Treasury and the Ministries of Agriculture, Transport, Technology, and Education—and much negotiation may go on among officials and Ministers before a final Government decision is taken.

Even then, the decision is a tentative one. When the exact land proposed to be designated has been settled the Minister must publish in the *London Gazette* and one or more local newspapers a notice describing the area and stating where any persons interested can inspect the draft order. He must place on deposit for inspection, too, a map showing the precise boundaries of the area, a statement of the size and character of the proposed new town, and the reasons for making the order. Similar notices must be sent to all the local authorities concerned.

Then follows a period of at least twenty-eight days during which objections may be made, followed by a local inquiry. Because the draft order is made by the Minister it is not thought appropriate for one of the Ministry's own inspectors to hold these inquiries and an independent inspector is usually appointed. The Inquiry is open to the public and a representative of the Minister attends to make a factual statement about the proposals and answer questions. Representatives of other interested Departments may also attend to state the view of their Ministers.

The Inquiry into a controversial order can extend over several days. All objectors can be heard and may be legally represented and witnesses may be cross-examined. All the local authorities, including those in near-by areas, give their views. Every point raised is carefully recorded and considered in the report which the Inspector makes to the Minister. Objectors and other interested parties are entitled to a copy of the report after the Minister has issued a decision.

At this stage the Minister can abandon the project or he can make a Designation Order covering some or all of the land in the draft order. Frequently parts of the area proposed are excluded to meet particular objections, but the Minister cannot add to the area without the consent of 'all persons interested'—a phrase that is not defined and is open to various possible interpretations.

The final order must be in the form of a Statutory Instrument.[4] Notice of it must be given in the *London Gazette* and two local newspapers; copies must be sent to the local authorities; and copies of the Order and map must be deposited for local inspection.

But the Minister is not out of the wood yet. If the local planning authority for the area was one of the objectors, the Order must be laid before Parliament (unless it is an extension of an existing designated area and is less than 500 acres or less than 10 per cent) and may be annulled in either the House of Commons or the House of Lords within forty sitting days. This additional safeguard was the result of a Private Member's Bill, introduced in 1964 by Martin Maddan, then M.P. for Hitchin, following lengthy public discussions about proposals for the expansion of Stevenage.[5] The right was exercised in the case of the designation of Peterborough, where a motion to annul the Order was debated in the House of Commons for nearly two hours—even though the Member of Parliament who put down the motion explained that in fact he had no wish to annul the Order or even obstruct it. His object was to seek assurances on certain financial and other implications affecting the City Council and, having got from the Minister satisfactory answers on these points, he then withdrew the motion.[6]

Finally, comes the ultimate safeguard of appeal to the Courts. Even at this late stage, and after all the procedure has been gone through, the Act enables anybody to challenge the Order by applying to the High Court within six weeks asking for it to be quashed. This can cause serious delay because once such an application is made the Minister can do nothing further until the final answer has been given. He may have to wait a long time while appeals are heard by the Court of Appeal and the House of Lords; and if the Order is quashed, the search for a site and the long procedure may have to start all over again.

The Courts have no power to quash the Order merely because they think the decision is wrong. That is the Minister's sole executive responsibility and the judiciary cannot question it. But the appeal could succeed on points that, on the face of it, might seem trivial. Any failure to operate even one small detail of the procedure laid down by Parliament could be enough. Justice must not only be done but be seen to be done and the Courts come very quickly to the support of an aggrieved objector if the Ministry or the Inspector holding the Inquiry has failed to give him all the opportunities and protection laid down by Parliament.

These technical and legal aspects of designation are unexciting but the first attempts to use the powers developed into heated controversy. Even before the New Towns Act was introduced in Parliament, Lewis Silkin had tried to make a start at Stevenage using the very limited and inadequate powers of the Town & Country Planning Act 1932. Reaction was almost vitriolic. At the meeting in the town to explain the project he was greeted with cries of 'Gestapo!' 'Dictator!' The tyres of his car were let down and sand put in the petrol tank. The name boards on the railway station were replaced with ones marked 'Silkingrad'. A residents' 'protection association' conducted a vigorous and prolonged opposition campaign. A colourful account of these early episodes is given by Harold Orlans in his study of Stevenage.[7]

After a heated local inquiry, the Designation Order was finally made; but it was immediately challenged in the Courts on the grounds that by announcing at the public meeting beforehand that he intended to have a new town at Stevenage the Minister was biased and could not have fairly considered the objections. In the King's Bench Division the objectors won, Mr Justice Henn Collins holding that the Minister was clearly biased. The Court of Appeal took the opposite view and supported the Minister. The objectors then took the case to the House of Lords where they lost the day. The Law Lords went thoroughly into the whole nature of the Minister's actions and obligations and decided that the Minister was not acting in a judicial or quasi-judicial capacity. He was taking a purely administrative decision and had properly complied with all the legal requirements.[8]

Both in the Courts and in the Commons statements made at the stormy public meeting were freely quoted, including a prophecy Lewis Silkin made:

'Stevenage,' said Mr Silkin, 'will in a short time become world famous (*laughter*). People from all over the world will come to see how we here in this country are building for the new way of life.'

It was a particularly striking prophecy. Despite the many troubles, both then and afterwards, within a few years Stevenage opened the first all-pedestrian town centre in Europe and for a long time it was more visited, more talked about, and more photographed by people from all over the world than any other new town feature.

Meanwhile, back at the Ministry, further new town proposals were going forward to designation and were running into equally fierce opposition. The Abercrombie Report had suggested Holmwood and Crowhurst as possible sites to the south of London but after a new technical survey these were rejected. Crawley, a small Sussex town of 5,000 people, was selected instead as the most suitable site south-west of London. By then new towns were news and lively opposition was expected. In his account of the early history of Crawley, Ernest Stanford commented:

'Crawley was invaded by an army of pressmen and photographers covering not only national papers but the international press. Crawley had become the centre of world attraction. There had been an anti-new town campaign in some of the national dailies following the designation of Stevenage. The press boys from London were hoping to stir up some really active opposition in Crawley but they were singularly unsuccessful.'[9]

Nevertheless, the three-day local inquiry produced a good deal of controversy and some novel reasons against the new town project. The whole area was waterlogged and would cause chaos right down to the Thames; there would be a multiplicity of railway bridges because the whole railway system would have to be rebuilt; the gems of architecture in the area would all be destroyed; and there was even one objector—a Mr Oakes, living in Horley some five miles to the north and twenty-five miles from the coast—who complained that the town would intervene between him and the sea. 'If I go to the top of my house or on the railway bridge at Horley,' he said, 'I can get the advantage of the sea breeze. It is the one place in the south where I can get the ozone. . . . The freshness of the area will be vitiated by 50,000 people here and the opportunity I have had of enjoying the sea breezes will cease.'[10]

But not even the eloquence of Mr Oakes could dissuade the Minister from designating the area, although he cut down the acreage. Again, some of the objectors took him to the High Court alleging that he had not given sufficient information to the local authorities, that he had not had proper consultations with them, and that no proper local inquiry was held. The Minister won. The objectors appealed and the Court of Appeal not only supported the Minister but refused them leave to take the case to the House of Lords.[11]

At about the same time there were proposals to designate land at Hemel Hempstead, an ancient borough with a population of 21,000 and royal charters dating back to the early sixteenth century. This town was chosen by the Minister for development as a new town instead of the near-by village of Redbourn recommended by Abercrombie. The Designation Order was made after considerable opposition from the local people and, as in the case of Crawley, was challenged in the Courts on the grounds of inadequate consultation. Mr Justice Morris ruled in the Minister's favour and the case was not taken to appeal.[12] Notice of motion to quash the Harlow order was also served but after the House of Lords decision on Stevenage it was withdrawn.

A battery of legal talent was employed by the opponents of the new towns to conduct these cases. The litigation caused a good deal of uncertainty and for a time effective work had to be held up, but in the end it resulted in a strengthening of the Minister's position. The Court decisions had firmly established that the Minister was entitled—and indeed had a duty under the Act—to satisfy himself *before* designation that the project was a sound one. Provided he supplied the local authorities with sufficient information and gave them sufficient opportunity to state their views, and provided he listened to objections and properly considered them, it was no part of the Court's duty to say whether his decision was right or wrong. Mr Justice Morris, in the Crawley case, very aptly summed up the difficulties of a Minister looking for a new town site. 'The roving inquirer,' he said, 'might find himself perpetually speeded on his way and encouraged to believe that what he sought lay always further on.' Somewhere the buck has to stop.

Some people have criticized the designation procedure as being too long and time-consuming. Certainly it is no quick answer to the politician, social worker, or homeless family desperate to see more houses built. But it has a certain merit. A new town nowadays can cost several hundred million pounds to build and can have a decisive influence far beyond its boundaries. It can affect, for good or ill, many people living in the area itself or the surrounding countryside. It may involve a complete recast of all or most local government and other services. It can involve the disturbance of long-established businesses and change radically the whole economy of a region.

It is right therefore that new town projects should not be hastily conceived and forced through without the most thorough consideration. Local views must not be lightly brushed aside. The two years or more it may take between the first exploration of an area and final designation give time for mature examination, searching analysis and, if necessary, second thoughts; for once an area has been designated and a

31

start has been made on the expensive task of providing the initial services, there is no going back.

Nowadays, when new towns are more readily accepted, local inquiries are perhaps less colourful and less exciting than they were in the late forties. Indeed, to many local authorities and their ratepaying inhabitants, the selection of land in their area to be dealt with under the New Towns Act is a most welcome decision. It ensures rapid and comprehensive expansion with the support of Government money and a team of experienced professional experts. A good part of the proceedings at some of the recent local inquiries has been directed not to objections but to getting explanations and assurances on matters which the authorities and landowners, including the tenant farmers, regard as particularly important. But where the objections are strongly held and are supported by solid argument, the Inquiry can be an effective instrument. Not all objections can be met by compensation or promises of financial help—sometimes it must be all or nothing, as was shown by the Ipswich affair.

The proposal to expand Ipswich from 121,000 to 275,000 population and to make it a focus of economic growth in East Anglia was under discussion for seven years. Following the South-East Study, which suggested it as a possible area for 70,000 'overspill' from London, the Minister commissioned a preliminary report from Leonard Vincent and Raymond Gorbing in 1962, and after much discussion Shankland Cox and Associates were asked in 1967 to make a feasibility study and prepare a Master Plan.[13] The agricultural aspect was already seen to be an important one, and a supplementary study[14] was prepared examining seven alternative ways of expansion. This came down in favour of taking good agricultural land to the west, rather than poorer land to the east, thereby reducing the capital cost of building the town by some £16 a head. The Minister's Draft Designation Order in 1968 was based on this recommendation, but after hearing the strong and well-documented opposition at an eight-day local inquiry the project was abandoned.

Although there were other supporting reasons, it is clear that the agricultural factor was the main one. The almost fanatical pressure in the early post-war years to avoid taking agricultural land at all costs has now given place to a more scientific appraisal of relative merits and relative costs, but experts still disagree about how it should be done. The relative costs of building, the rising agricultural productivity, the long-term future of the balance of payments, and the pressure for housing in particular regions must all be weighed up. Professor Wibberley and Dr Robin Best of the Department of Agricultural Economics at Wye College have shown how difficult it is to assess the true significance of the loss of agricultural production from a few thousand acres.[15] In the national context the loss caused by the new towns has been negligible, and the total development of the post-war years has taken less land out of agricultural use than a comparable amount of virtually unplanned building in the 'thirties.

Nevertheless, the agricultural needs and pressures are still strong. The opposition to the Ipswich proposal was presented as a test case of the Government's *bona fides* in safeguarding agricultural land, and the National Farmers' Union claimed the final decision as a 'total victory for their strategy at the inquiry'. The costs of the initial planning studies was £141,000,[16] and under arrangements made some years ago[17] the Minister paid the costs of the local authorities and the objectors, several of whom were represented by Counsel. So, altogether, it was an expensive exercise.

One of the difficulties of the lengthy process of statutory designation is that until the final decision is taken the Minister cannot appoint the members of the development corporation, no money is available to engage staff or consultants, no Master Plan can be prepared and no land can be bought even though owners may be willing, even anxious, to sell. Meanwhile, virtually all private development proposals have to be turned down and stagnation tends to settle over the area. Nor are the issues resolved by the designation. The process of preparing the Master Plan then starts and another two years or more must usually elapse before the first trench can be dug and the first brick laid.

Some means may have to be found to cut short or telescope these stages. It is interesting to note that when in 1965 the

33

Government of Northern Ireland introduced legislation on new towns, after a close study of the arrangements in Great Britain, they modified the procedure considerably. Before the new towns were started at Craigavon, Antrim, Ballymena, and Londonderry the Northern Irish Government had already selected the area and had even prepared the Outline Plans.

In England, the Minister has recently gone a long way in this direction by engaging consultants to report on the possibilities of development in certain areas and to advise him on the land suitable for a new town. This is an essential part of the designation process. It is expensive, too. The fees for the major investigations carried out during the early 1960s came to over £1 million and were criticized by the Public Accounts Committee.[18] Sir Matthew Stevenson, the Permanent Secretary to the Ministry, assured them that a close watch was kept on the level of fees and the method of calculating and checking them, but, as he pointed out to the Committee, these surveys are the preliminary work for projects that may cost some £400 million per town. It is important that the Government should have thorough and competent advice on which to base their decisions.

In the case of Peterborough and Irvine Ministers took the process a stage further by asking the consultants to prepare an Outline Plan; but, although this falls somewhat short of a full Master Plan, it has not proved popular. Some development corporations feel strongly that they should not be just agents for carrying out a Plan which they have not prepared and with which they may not agree. Each town has its own individuality, derived not only from the physical nature of the area and its surroundings but from the personality of the Board members, the planners, the architect and the rest of the professional team. New towns ought not to be fashioned in Whitehall.

There is no complete answer that would remove the uncertainty and temporary stagnation. The time lost is eventually more than made up by the speed at which new town development can take place once the preliminaries are over and building can start. In the long term that is answer enough. It would be possible to appoint a 'development corporation designate' at a very early stage—as indeed was done in 1947 for the first of the new towns—and to ask them to start recruiting staff and preparing a plan in case it should be wanted. But the Minister might be at risk in the High Court for having anticipated his final decision, and the work and money spent would be wasted if the project fell through.

Expedients of this sort should not now be necessary. In recent years the national planning process has been reorganized so that the needs of development can be seen well ahead and more and more it is being recognized that the land for large-scale development ought to be selected some three to four years before building must start. The needs of the country are too important to be dealt with on a hand-to-mouth basis.

5. CORPORATION

THE organization responsible for building a new town is the development corporation. It is an interesting example of the development in recent years of the new form of public utility undertaking of which the B.B.C. and London Transport were about the first. Much the same pattern was adopted in the 1940s for the nationalized industries and the Post Office—a Government department for well over a century—has now been reconstituted on a similar basis.

The new town corporation comes into being by an order of the Minister, under his seal of office, constituting the corporation for the purpose of developing land specified in a particular designated area, giving it a name and setting out its constitution—a chairman, deputy chairman, and not more than seven other members. The Minister's order does not at that stage appoint the members: it merely creates the corporation as a legal entity able to enter into contracts, hold the title to land, take decisions and carry out the many other functions and legal processes necessary in the course of building a town. The corporation is not a Crown body. It enjoys none of the rights and privileges normally enjoyed by Crown bodies and the members and staff are not civil servants.

Nor is the corporation the local authority.[1] The existing local government administration, through elected members, continues unchanged. The county council, the county district council, and in some rural areas the parish council remain responsible in new town areas for all the normal statutory services. The development corporation has parallel powers to build houses and roads, and can, if necessary, be authorized to provide water and sewerage services. It can also contribute to the local authorities' costs. But it cannot levy rates and in practice, apart from house-building, does not overlap with the general run of local government functions.

The Minister is answerable to Parliament for the activities of the development corporations and for this reason has complete control over what they do and what they spend. The local authorities are consulted on all development proposals and their views are carefully considered but the decision rests with the Minister whose approval carries with it a planning permission.[2] But, although all development projects have to be approved by the Minister, the corporations are given a good deal of freedom in the way they organize their affairs and conduct their business. It is a semi-independence which they appreciate and jealously guard.

The appointments of the chairman and members of a development corporation are made by the Minister and he is free to select whom he likes, up to a maximum of nine. The one statutory qualification is that he must try to find at least one 'local' member. He need not succeed: the Act merely says that he must '*have regard* to the desirability of securing the services of one or more persons resident in or having special knowledge of the locality in which the new town will be situated'.[3] Similarly before making any appointments he must consult the local authorities; but he is free to ignore their views if he wishes. In practice, of course, suitable local men or women are usually found and suggestions by the local authority are welcomed and frequently accepted.

The selection of members is no easy task. When the first corporations were set up their job was to give effect to this important part of the Labour Government's post-war programme. The Act had passed through Parliament with the official blessing of all parties but a strong rear-guard action was being fought in the areas selected for new town development. In these circumstances it was perhaps only natural to include among the corporation members some tried and trusted party supporters who could be relied upon to carry out the job enthusiastically and stop any attempts to sabotage the work. But pressure of this sort has, for the most part, been resisted. Members of known political alignments have been appointed but as often as not it has been a Labour administration which appointed Conservative or Liberal members and Conservative Ministers who appointed Labour sympathizers.

The prevailing political sympathies of the area can, of course, have a strong influence. No Minister would seek to appoint a

37

Board dominated by Conservatives in a Labour stronghold or vice versa. But however carefully and objectively a Minister selects the members, he can never please everybody. If a supporter of the Government is chosen, the murmur of 'jobs for the boys' is heard. If a leading local authority personality is appointed, it is buying off local opposition. If no local authority representative is appointed, it is riding rough-shod over local feelings and ignoring the rules of democracy. If a businessman is appointed by a Labour Minister, it is trying to run socialist policy by capitalist methods. If a Conservative Minister appoints a Labour supporter, it is encouraging the 'thin end of the wedge' that some people seem to fear from any State organization.

In this situation the real social and economic problems the policy is designed to solve could be in danger of getting submerged in a welter of political argument and log rolling; and in many countries this might well happen. But with the British flair for compromise and with the general acceptance of the constitutional channels for influencing or protesting—the deputation, the petition, the parliamentary question or debate —any arguments soon die down once a firm decision is taken.

In carrying out this delicate task, therefore, the only satisfactory course a Minister can adopt is to determine firmly at the outset what objectives or what combination of qualities he looks for in making the appointments, and then, without fear or favour, appoint a corporation that, taken as a whole, measures up in his view to the job in hand. There is no room for passengers. Each member must be there solely because of his ability to contribute something of value to the pool of knowledge or ideas. This is the crucial test Ministers must apply to all appointments. Successive Ministers—and there have been no less than nine in England since 1946—have appointed members of a variety of skills and professions and they have invariably included at least one woman member.

In many ways the corporation members can be likened to a board of directors. True, their work has a social slant and the primary object is not to make a profit; but they are expected to pay proper regard to economic factors, to secure a reasonable return on the Exchequer investment and to organize the building of the town with due regard for economy, public policy, and the particular needs of the people for whom they are building no less than those already living within the designated area.

Above all they must work as a team. They may have different views about many things, different approaches to problems, different political and social philosophies; but they must be capable of discussing and reconciling these differences in the interests of building—as every development corporation is determined to do—the best town ever.

Equally important, they must get—and keep—on good terms with the local people and in particular with the local authority; and good relations between the staff and the local officials is even more vital. In many new towns this has not been easy. There have been clashes of personalities, differences of opinion, professional jealousies or disagreements, resentment by local councillors, fear that the role of the elected representatives might be overshadowed or usurped and impatience by development corporations with local views or with criticisms of their policy, planning, and design. At times open hostility and even downright obstruction has developed, with, in one case, demands to the Minister, as the town grew in size and increased in importance, that the development corporation should be abolished and the job of building the town handed over to the local authority.

In some towns there may well have been faults on both sides and it can often be traced to lack of communication or lack of understanding. Some friction at times is inevitable, but it is important not to exaggerate its effect and to concentrate on finding ways and means of resolving differences without rancour. In recent years more cordial relationships seem to have developed. In most of the towns liaison committees have been set up (if they did not already exist) and Ministers have been appointing more local councillors as members of the development corporation. Some support this on the grounds that 'only local people understand local problems'. Others retort that 'local people only understand local problems'. Neither is true of course; but what is certainly true is that a local member of a corporation can only do the job effectively if he

39

can rise above a purely parochial approach and see beyond the parish pump; and a non-local member can only do justice to his responsibilities if he is able and willing to get to know, and fully understand, the local views and feelings. In combination, they make a team.

The key appointment to a development corporation is the chairman. He must be diplomat, democrat, and administrator rolled into one. He must keep a firm grip on policy and at the same time avoid undue interference with the day-to-day work of the staff. He must be able to understand technical details and settle important issues without trying to do the job of the architect, engineer, or other professional adviser. He must have confidence in the staff and they must have confidence in him.

On the whole, the process of selecting corporation members has been surprisingly successful and it is immensely encouraging to see how quickly a Board, all probably strangers to each other at the outset, settle down to work as a united team and how quickly they sense the feeling of the local people and gain their confidence.

Perhaps the most difficult job is that of the development corporation member who is also a member of the local council. A corporation should benefit greatly by having such a member who understands local feeling and aspirations, but he is not a delegate and wearing two hats is never an easy job. Sometimes it is downright embarrassing. There was an occasion when a development corporation, having collectively decided on a course of action, agreed to meet a deputation from the local authority to discuss their differences. When the deputation arrived the corporation found it was led by one of their own members, firmly—but very successfully—wearing his 'other hat'.

Corporation membership is a part-time appointment, carries a small salary, and disqualifies from membership of the House of Commons.[4] It is not an executive job. Formal meetings may not amount to more than one or two a month, although members frequently participate in the occasional function or joint meeting with the local authority or some town organization and take an interest in the life of the town. The fact that they do not have to stand for election relieves them of the need to canvass popularity and enables them perhaps to take a more detached approach to problems than can the average local councillor. As a matter of law the status in the town of a development corporation does not differ greatly from that of any private building organization carrying out large-scale development or the many other statutory bodies who provide gas, electricity, rail, postal, and other services in the town.

Some Chairmen and Board members make a point of remaining rather in the background, not because they want to be 'shadowy figures' but because they think it right to prevent any misunderstanding in the public mind and avoid any suggestion that they are competing with or duplicating the role of the locally elected representatives. But they must combine this with a readiness to explain to the townspeople what they are doing, consider criticisms or suggestions and encourage public participation. Sir Thomas Bennett, during his thirteen years as Chairman of Crawley Development Corporation, held a meeting once a year, attended by nearly two hundred representatives of the many organizations and authorities in the town, at which he gave a very full progress report and invited discussion. It was always a popular occasion.

Argument about whether a development corporation is the right form of organization has gone on for twenty years, despite the careful examination by the Reith Committee. Some local authorities think they could do a better job or that they should at least have the right to nominate representatives to the Board. There is no one answer appropriate to all circumstances. Ministers have been very concerned to make sure that development corporations and local authorities work closely together; and when announcing the proposal to use the machinery of the New Towns Act for the expansion of Ipswich, Peterborough, and Northampton they said that a new form of 'partnership' organization was being devised to give the local authority a much greater say in the operation and a much greater part in the actual building operations. 'I am making sure right from the beginning,' said Richard Crossman, 'that the relationship between corporation and local authority should be one not of domination but of full and equal partnership.'[5]

Towns such as these, however, are exceptional. They have

existing populations of between 80,000 and 130,000 with an established local authority and a staff with long experience of the technical problems of large-scale building. The setting up of a completely independent development corporation in such circumstances might well have been resented and friction would have been almost unavoidable. On the other hand, a town proposed on a 'green-fields' site or based on a small existing community in a sparsely populated rural district demands a somewhat different approach; but as the town increases in size, possibly with a newly formed urban district council, councillors naturally wish to play a larger part in the development of the town and this clearly should be encouraged. Any fear that the development corporation is a cuckoo in the nest, out to usurp their functions and put them out of business, must be dispe ll ed

Because members are appointed, and not elected locally, it is often said that the corporations are a denial of democracy. But this does not stand up to serious examination. The elected local authorities remain responsible for the normal local government services (with financial help where necessary from the corporation) and levy the rates to pay for them. That is the proper role of local government. But for the building of the town the Minister is answerable to Parliament; and as the corporations are financed entirely from money voted by Parliament the right point at which democratic control should be exercised is at Parliamentary level. Control by Ministers and Parliament is not a lesser form of democracy than control by locally elected councillors. An aggrieved citizen may in fact stand a better chance of getting a legitimate complaint against a development corporation investigated than he would a complaint against a local authority. Direct reference to the Minister, Parliamentary questions or debate, possibly even reference in some circumstances to the Parliamentary Commissioner—the 'Ombudsman'—are available to him, through his M.P. Complaint against a local authority can rarely be taken up at those levels.

But whatever the theory, the very fact that the corporation members are not elected puts them under a greater obligation to take the townspeople into their confidence, tell them by way of Press reports, exhibitions and all other means what is being done and why, explain any difficulties or delays, listen to their complaints, examine their suggestions. This demands supporting staff work of a very high order.

The first job of a development corporation is to appoint the key staff. However able the members, the success or failure of a new town depends in large measure on the quality and enthusiasm of their staff and the ability of the corporation to pick the right people for the job.

All development corporations have substantially the same staff structure. At the head is a General Manager[6] who is the full-time chief executive responsible to the corporation for the whole work of the organization. He has to be *par excellence* an administrator, co-ordinating the views and activities of the professional team, organizing the office, ensuring that the programme of planning and building goes along slickly and on time, with proper economy of staff and money, maintaining liaison and good relations with the local authorities, statutory undertakers, Government departments, churches, social groups, employers' organizations, trade unions, political parties, and a host of others who are concerned in one way or another with the new town. Frequently he has a delicate tight-rope to walk, but most General Managers will admit to enjoying the job immensely. It is probably one of the most stimulating and mentally rewarding jobs in the public service today.

The senior professional staff operate as a team under the General Manager's direction, and usually cover the professions of Planning, Architecture, Engineering, Estate Management, Housing Management, Finance, Law, Administration, Public Relations, and Social Development, each supported by adequate staff of the right quality for the work to be done. At the height of their development programme a corporation may need, all told, a staff of some 300 people, but the number varies, of course, with the size of the town.

Consultants are sometimes engaged to prepare the initial Master Plan or for specific items of work. Outside firms of private architects or engineers may also be brought in for particular projects or housing schemes, thus contributing to variety of design; landscape consultants are sometimes asked to advise on planting schemes or the layout of parks and open spaces or the preservation of trees and woodlands; quantity surveyors are appointed for particular contracts. One development corporation engaged the services of Victor Pasmore, the artist, to work with the team designing a new area of housing in a locality that demanded particularly imaginative treatment.[7] But most of these professions are usually represented on the corporation staff as well, so that the whole range of professional and technical advice needed in the task of building a complete town is available from the corporation's own staff and any consultants engaged for particular projects work in close touch with them.

The importance of teamwork cannot be over-emphasized for it is the essence of the job. Much public authority development suffers from departmentalism, from an approach limited by their statutory duties and from the system of control by numerous committees. One could often be forgiven for asking whether the Planning Department and the Housing Department ever speak to each other. New towns cannot be built in that way. They demand a breadth of view that goes beyond the expertise of any one profession and an ability to apply and adapt professional skill to the overall task. Michael Thorncroft has summed up the point very well in relation to the estates profession in the following terms but it could apply equally well to other professions:

'Estate management of new towns is more than the direction and control of physical assets: it is the moulding of environmental influences in order to achieve economic and social ends, in the widest sense. The skills and experience needed to achieve this comes from a far greater range of experts than is usual even in large-scale estate management.[8]

Landscaping work is a particular feature of the new town organization, not just as an ornamental addition but as an integral feature of design. Existing trees are preserved wherever possible but new planting is carried out on a large scale and many corporations have established their own nurseries. Cumbernauld and Basildon, for example, have planted some half a million trees and other corporations could probably match this figure. Some towns have also arranged for mature trees to be transplanted, now that the technical advances make it possible almost to guarantee success.

Most of the actual work of building is by contractors through the ordinary process of competitive tendering, though one corporation (Newton Aycliffe) has its own direct labour force that has carried out much of the building in the town and has been complimented for its high standard of quality and achievement. Many corporations have their own maintenance organizations. As the number of houses and other buildings owned by a corporation increases, it becomes very important to have ready and efficient means of carrying out both routine maintenance and emergency repairs. Some towns rely on the jobbing builders in the area but others have found it more effective and more economical to run their own labour organizations for this purpose.

New town salaries and the general level of staffing are controlled by the Government but the appointments are the sole responsibility of the corporations. This semi-independence in fact runs through the whole new town system. The salaries of General Managers and chief officers are related to posts of comparable responsibility in the Civil Service. Other salaries are negotiated through the Whitley Council for New Town Staff and are influenced by the level of pay in local government and other comparable service. Posts are pensionable either through a suitable local government pension fund or through a separate new towns pension fund which is run jointly by all the corporations.

The corporations are responsible to the Minister and are subject to his direction. Formal directions are very rare—in fact there is only one recorded instance and that was made because the corporation were doubtful of their legal position and asked to be covered.[9] There is however a steady stream of guidance or instructions from the Ministry on current policy issues, and each town has to submit an annual budget. But even within the limits of an approved budget there is not complete freedom to operate. In theory the corporations can plan and develop the town according to their own ideas, but for every major item of expenditure and every development proposal they have to get the Ministry's approval and the Ministry must get the consent of the Treasury. This close financial control has long been a bone of contention.[10]

However strong the desire of a corporation to be independent and free to get on with the job, they have to accept that there are many other people who may be affected by the new town and who have a very real interest in what is going on. Consultation and co-ordination is an essential part of any building operation on this scale. The development corporations do not have to apply for planning permission—that is taken care of by the Minister when he approves their proposals—but the various local authorities must first be consulted and the corporations have to get approval under the building regulations. Discussions can take a long time. Many Government departments, statutory undertakers and other bodies are involved on such questions as roads, schools, churches, industrial development, electricity, gas, and other services, river control, hospitals, and health centres, and it is no easy task to negotiate proposals with all the bodies concerned.

In the early days, the corporations were disturbed at the amount of talk that had to go on before any progress could be made. Sir Ernest Gowers described the machinery as 'cumbrous beyond belief' and deplored the 'tangled thicket of controls and overlapping duties';[11] Sir Thomas Bennett commented laconically 'they consume a great deal of time and effort';[12] but there is no satisfactory short-cut. To their other virtues, corporations and their staff must add patience and tolerance.

Side by side with the desire of the various development corporations for freedom and independence goes the need to recognize that they are all part of one new town 'movement' and must make arrangements to co-ordinate ideas among themselves. Many corporations face similar problems and it is a waste of staff time if each town has to make a separate investigation. The experience of one should be available to all.

The Reith Committee had this point very much in mind and suggested the appointment of a Central Advisory Commission.[13] This was never done. In the early days Lewis Silkin held frequent meetings of Chairmen to hammer out the many points of principle that cropped up while the corporations were finding their feet; but this practice stopped when Hugh Dalton became Minister in 1950. Since then the Chairmen have arranged this co-ordination themselves by meeting regularly as a Standing Conference—a proposal which the Reith Committee considered and rejected—and they have set up a substructure of a General Managers' Committee and sub-committees of the various professions. It is a somewhat informal arrangement that makes the minimum demands on the time of busy people but it is a reasonably effective means of exchanging ideas and co-ordinating experience. Thus it is not true, as is sometimes alleged, that each corporation works in a sort of splendid isolation. They have achieved co-ordination without sacrificing independence.

There have been suggestions in some quarters that a newly established development corporation has to start from scratch and is not able to draw on past new town experience. Barry Cullingworth voiced this view at a conference on social development in new towns.[14] There is a little substance in the point, but not very much. The Ministry issue a digest explaining the powers of a corporation and the current policy governing all aspects of their work and the first move of a newly-appointed corporation is usually to visit one or more of the established towns to see at first hand how the organization works. Experienced senior staff are often ready to accept appointment to a new corporation and as a town is usually complete in some fifteen to twenty years it is important to see that the staff have the opportunity to move—otherwise they might become redundant in the middle of their careers and much valuable experience would be wasted.

Finally, there are now many firms of professional consultants who have a wide experience of new town problems. The consultants engaged by the Minister to advise on the designation are usually available to guide a newly-appointed corporation through some of the initial stages, including the preparation of the Master Plan and advising on the many planning applications submitted for comment during this period.

Nevertheless, it must be admitted that more could and should

C

have been done to co-ordinate research and documentation of new towns experience. In 1948 the Ministry set up a small research unit to do this work but in the drive in 1952 for staff economies in the civil service the team was disbanded. Ten years later when another programme of new towns was started an attempt was made to pick up the threads but it is not easy to recapture so many years of experience. It needs to be a continuous process. Demographic information and advice is however now available from a central point in the Ministry; numerous factual investigations have been made on questions of interest to all new towns; and a detailed analysis has been made of certain aspects of estate management experience. New towns are a fruitful field for research by universities and the Centre for Environmental Studies and Social Science Research Council will certainly include some aspects of new town work in their programmes.

With the greatly extended field of new town activity—and the scope for large-scale development is bound to increase—some changes may be needed if the organization is to be able to play its full part in the years ahead. Better co-ordination, exchange of technical information, wider use of house designs, better use of experienced staff, security of employment, central financing and central services for legal and technical problems —all these aspects could usefully be examined. They point to the need for a measure of centralization, possibly by joining the corporations into a federation or advisory body, possibly even by creating a national corporation or council that could act as the executive arm of the regional and national planning machines. But if this were done it would be important to preserve the local touch, the local involvement, and the independence of ideas.

Whatever changes there may be in the future, the present arrangements have worked remarkably well. Fifteen new towns are almost finished, all different, each with its own special characteristics and certainly not suffering from a drab uniformity. Many hundreds of people in the various corporations have played a part in the process and some of Britain's most distinguished architects and planners have been engaged in new town work at some time in their careers and it is still attracting the young and talented recruits from these and other professions.

There are no private fortunes to be made, no speculative profits, no inflated salaries or large expense accounts. It is just another job of public service, quietly and efficiently done, but one which captures the imagination and devotion of a dedicated body of men and women who give their time, their ability, and their enthusiasm to an exacting but exciting task.

6. PLAN

A NEW town gets off to a slow start. Even with over twenty years of experience to call upon there is much to be done before building can begin, but in 1948 every move had to be thought out from scratch. The late General ('Dagger') Rees used to tell how, when he was appointed as General Manager of Cwmbran, he went off to the area, borrowed a small room in the town hall and sat down wondering just where to start. A pencil and a copy of the New Towns Act were the sole assets of the corporation; his instructions—to build a town for 30,000 people!

There is, of course, by way of background the Minister's statement of intentions, giving the total population proposed and the acreage of land designated, but this must be followed up by a detailed land survey and the preparation of a Master Plan for the whole town. This is a statement of general policy rather than a detailed blueprint and a great number of facts and figures have to be got together before the main structure of the town can be determined.

Nowadays, the technique has become well established. A study of the Master Plans for any of the towns recently designated[1] will demonstrate, much better than any general account, the amount of research needed before the outline of the town begins to take shape. Contours, geology, condition and function of buildings, ownerships, farm boundaries, communications, population structure, climatic conditions, landscape or other features, buildings to be protected or preserved, water and power supplies and other services, drainage and sewerage problems, and the economic and social structure of the area as it is—these are some of the basic facts from which a start must be made. The concept of the town to be built, its economic function in the region of which it forms part, its possibilities and limitations, must then be hammered out and welded together into a framework that covers every aspect of development and life in the town.

Calculations must be made of the likely build-up of population, with age and household structure, future birth, death, and marriage rates. At this stage it can only be a statistical exercise based on carefully considered assumptions about such factors as the rate of industrial and commercial development, the build-up of service industry, the density of employment, and the distribution between male and female employment. On any one of these questions, estimates may prove in the event to be wrong. Changes in the economic climate, both national and international, can happen quickly and unexpectedly and the Plan must be sufficiently flexible to enable it to be readily adapted or modified to cope with some new situation. Perhaps the most difficult change of all is a decision, many years after a Plan has been settled, to increase the size of the town, because so many aspects of a Plan are calculated by reference to the projected population. Yet almost all the first of the new towns have by now been told by the Minister to build for a larger population. This has meant a very close re-examination, in the light of experience, of the structure of the town and its capacity to cope with current or increased levels of demand and, so far, all the early plans have been found capable of absorbing substantial increases in population.

Traffic circulation is of particular importance. No Master Plan can be drawn up without extensive study of the traffic flow the town will generate at various stages of its growth and the road pattern must be adequate for the long-term future; for once the roads are put down there is little chance for second thoughts. Yet sometimes the second thoughts are forced on a development corporation by actions outside their control—as when Harlow found that the Ministry of Transport had suddenly decided to switch the route of a motor-road from the east side of the town to the west. Sir Frederick Gibbard, the consultant planner for the town, commented that it was 'as though he had designed a sea-side town and then somebody moved the sea!'

The land needed for industrial development to provide work for the people of the towns can be calculated with reasonable certainty at present, but the rate of future mechanization and its effect on both the jobs and the factory space needed is not readily predictable. Long-term calculations can therefore only be guarded estimates. So, too, with shops. Changes in shopping habits, the development of supermarkets, the reduction in house delivery services, all have their effect not only on the number and type of shops needed for a given population but also on such matters as car parks and access.

The amount of land wanted for schools, open spaces, parks, sports and recreation grounds has to be worked out—there are reasonably safe yardsticks for this, although some of them, particularly the traditional 'six acres per 1,000 people' for open space, could well be reviewed. A new and detailed examination of current needs by a Working Party appointed by the Sports Council[2] will certainly affect all future plans. Hospitals, civic buildings, police, fire, ambulance and welfare services, churches, pubs, offices, community halls, have to be provided for; and most important of all come the decisions on housing —numbers, types, densities—with the related questions of garages and gardens and the degree of segregation of pedestrians from road traffic. The detailed design comes later but the main principles governing housing layout must be established at this stage.

Finally comes the programme. The rate at which the town will develop depends on many unknowns, but assumptions must be made and the programme adapted as time goes on to meet changing circumstances. The building labour force available in the area will place a limit on the speed of construction; the attraction to the town of industry will settle the number of jobs and therefore the number of houses and shops needed each year; the economic climate will determine the amount of capital available. It will be some fifteen years or more before the programme is finished and that is a long time ahead for predictions that are so dependent on unpredictable facts.

The planner must look, too, to the final stage of growth. He must try to estimate the age of the population that will be living in the town fifteen or more years ahead, the number and ages of the children they will have, how many people will move away from the town, and how many will stay, need jobs, marry and have more children. For these, the second and third generations, he must leave room. It will be a slower rate of development, going on possibly for thirty years or more before the population has settled down to a normal age distribution, but he must work out the amount of land that will be needed for this 'natural increase' and make sure that it is reserved.

These are just the bare facts. From the assembly and close study of the data the creative work of the planner begins. The relationship of these uses to each other, and the weaving together of all these facets of daily life into a coherent pattern of living for a busy and thriving community—this is the true meaning of the science of planning. For above all, the town has got to *work*. It must be capable of running with the ease of a complicated piece of precision machinery; but whereas the properties of metal are known to the engineer and stresses and strains can be calculated with the utmost accuracy, the reactions of people and the stresses and strains that arise from human relationships defy scientific prediction. The planner must understand people and anticipate their every need.

In the past, towns just grew up under the pressure of industrial and housing demand and nobody was much concerned to examine the social pattern that emerged. It was a branch of planning science of which the profession in pre-war Britain had little or no first-hand experience and which there was certainly no opportunity of using. Densities, road widths, industrial needs, open space formulae and other such routine data were enough to make sure that people could eat, sleep, work, and play; but what made a town tick in terms of social life and human relationships had no place in the complicated pre-war planning schemes under the 1932 Act.

The need to prepare for rebuilding after the war gave the profession the opportunity to analyse questions such as these and inject a more decisive social content. In the County of London Plan, for example, Forshaw and Abercrombie pointed out that the apparently great sprawling mass of London was not so incoherent as some people thought. It had grown over the centuries from a series of villages and, although they had now coalesced into one continuous built-up area, the old communities were still discernible. Clapham was still Clapham; Stepney was still Stepney. The people over the border at Battersea, Brixton, Bethnal Green, or Bow were different

53

people, almost foreigners. London in fact was not just one big city; it was a collection of separate communities. They did not exist in isolation, of course, but each had its own traditions and loyalties. And this, he said, was the one thing it was essential to preserve when London was being replanned and rebuilt.

How could this experience and analysis of past growth be harnessed to the planning and development of a new town? It was not going to be easy to weld some sixty thousand people into a community. It was too big a unit in which to create quickly any satisfactory social cohesion. But if it could be broken down into a number of smaller and more intimate neighbourhoods, a satisfactory social life could emerge in a short time.

This conception of 'neighbourhood units' was not new. Ebenezer Howard's book in 1898 had envisaged towns of 30,000 people divided into six 'wards', each with its own school and shops; and in 1929 an American, Clarence Perry, had advocated traffic-free neighbourhood units large enough to support a primary school. Neighbourhoods were recommended, too, by the Reith Committee,[3] supported by the Ministry of Town & Country Planning[4] and for many years dominated new town thinking. Each neighbourhood was planned to have its own small shopping centre catering for day-to-day needs and within a short walking distance of the houses; each had its own primary school and its own meeting hall, pub, and church that would be the focus of community life; and in some towns each was given an attractive name, often derived from some local source or tradition, such as Langley Green, Little Parndon, Broadwater, Priestwood, Langdon Hills, which gave it an immediate separate identity and local pride.

The theory seems to have worked out, but only up to a point. It has come under attack in recent years on the grounds that it detracts from the unity of the town as a whole and limits the degree of support for all-town activities. There is much truth in this. Indeed, the Reith Committee, while generally supporting the neighbourhood idea as a 'natural and useful conception', added a warning that 'the neighbourhood should not be thought of as a self-contained community of which the inhabitants are more conscious than they are of the town as a whole.'[5]

The emphasis that has been placed in some quarters on the 'social unity' of a neighbourhood is probably misplaced. Basically, the justification is much more down to earth. The distance a small child can walk to school and the number of people needed to support a local shopping centre are much more vital considerations. Contours, too, can impose a geographical limitation. Neighbourhoods have varied from 3,000 to 10,000 population and success or failure in social terms certainly does not seem to depend on size.

Nor does it depend on density. The drive towards higher housing densities in the new towns—strongly opposed by the garden city enthusiasts and many of the local authorities—was supported in some quarters on the view that a close-knit urban huddle was necessary to create a sense of 'togetherness', avoid the loneliness and separation of twelve-to-the-acre suburbia and thus create a sense of belonging to a community. So far, there is no conclusive evidence either way. The people of Britain show a delightful obstinacy in refusing to conform to any one theory. Some like one thing, some like another. But analogy with the big cities can be dangerously misleading. They may have their Chelsea sets and the camaraderie of the slums but to a newcomer London, with all its teeming and crowded millions, can be the loneliest place on earth.

One's neighbours are important, of course, but mainly the near ones. The small close or cul-de-sac will have a neighbourliness of its own—not unlike the camaraderie of regular travellers in a commuter train. It's part of the day-to-day business of living and being pleasant to the fellow one sees most of. But this is little more than peace over the garden hedge. A 'community life' depends on identity of interest and desire to take part with others in enjoying that interest, whether it be sport, drama, pottery, social work, or the other hundred and one things people enjoy doing together and for which opportunity and encouragement must be given. This cannot be confined to a planner's neighbourhood ring-fence; and nobody would contemplate so organizing activity on a strictly geographical basis that a visitor from over the neighbourhood border felt like an interloper in a Bateman cartoon. With the increase in car ownership people are more mobile than they were twenty years ago, their circle of friends is not limited to close neighbours, and they are able to support activities anywhere in the town.

This is not to say that facilities for meetings and other functions within the neighbourhood are not important. In most areas the small community halls are in constant use and are particularly valuable where distance from home is important— as for nursery schools, a meeting place for old people or for wives with little time to spare, for clubs for the younger children and indeed for any adult function for which there is a strictly local demand. They are particularly important, too, in the early days of a new town when people need to get to know each other and set up their own local organizations. The truth is that central and neighbourhood buildings and functions serve different purposes. Both are needed. The job of the planner is to provide the right sort of buildings in the right places and at the right time to cater for reasonable demand and changing tastes and fashions.

Many of the older new towns have been criticized for not paying sufficient attention to social aspects and Master Plans are expected nowadays to include a 'social development plan and programme'. This was one of the recommendations of a Committee under Barry Cullingworth's chairmanship.[6] Social aspects are just as much an integral part of the plan as the technical needs of a sewerage system or the analysis of shopping demand.

The first breach with the 'neighbourhood' idea came with the plan for Cumbernauld which was designated in 1955. There, aided by a hill-top site, the development corporation and their chief architect, Hugh Wilson, planned the town as one unit, with a multi-level town centre to be built along the ridge on the top of the hill that would include all the main shops, civic and cultural buildings. The surrounding houses are at a high density, with none more than a few minutes' walk away and the whole life of the town is focused on the centre.[7] Only time will tell whether the planning concept will prove acceptable to the people who live there but so far, at any rate, a survey in

1967 by the University of Strathclyde has come to the conclusion that 'the general picture of Cumbernauld is of a community that is largely satisfied with its conditions'.[8]

Skelmersdale, where the planning consultant was also Hugh Wilson, is based on much the same idea—a strong and imaginative centre, within easy access from the surrounding high-density housing. But now the plans are coming out for the third round of new towns. 'Neighbourhoods' are back in fashion but once again the pattern is changing in other ways. 'Linear towns' is the current phrase—that is to say, towns in which houses are concentrated on either side of a central traffic road with shops and other facilities at about half-mile intervals.[9] This is the answer suggested to the problem of central congestion and to the difficulties posed by a 'finite' town. Everybody can be within five minutes' walking distance of the local shops and of fast public transport to other parts of the town. The traffic load on the public transport service evens out to give more economic running costs and the neighbourhood unit is capable of almost indefinite cell reproduction as and when expansion is necessary. In a way it is a modern type of ribbon development, with a series of neighbourhoods strung out end to end.

The linear idea is not new. Thomas Sharp, writing about it in 1940,[10] recalled that it was first put forward in Spain in 1882. He regarded it as a somewhat eccentric way of planning for an age of communications and added that a town 'cut into slices like an overgrown cucumber' would mean a regrettable remoteness of most of its parts from any recognizable centre. Not only the civic administration but also the civic loyalty of the linear-citizens would be affected.

This perhaps implies a much too literal interpretation. The linear conception is really no more than a basic structural idea, a set of fundamental principles, from which the planner then weaves his design. In the plan for Runcorn, for example, Arthur Ling translates the straight line into a figure of eight, with special lanes reserved for buses that serve all the neighbourhoods and the town centre, a fast traffic road enclosing the whole area and continuous open space within everybody's reach. At Washington in County Durham nineteen new villages, each with a population of about 4,500, will be grouped around a highly sophisticated traffic system. The new city of Milton Keynes adopts a flexible grid pattern of fast roads about a kilometre apart within which the numerous towns and villages will expand and eventually link up into a coherent city equipped for the needs of the motor age.

At the root of all urban planning today is the need to get a proper balance between the parts of a town that generate traffic and the means of coping with it. The Buchanan Report on *Traffic in Towns*[11] did not say anything much that wasn't already known in planning circles but the skilled and vivid presentation forced the point home in many other quarters and helped to loosen the official purse-strings for more effective solutions of the traffic problem.

The more recent new towns have made a notable contribution in this field. Cumbernauld, so planned that there are no traffic lights, no right-hand turns, no traffic policemen and no pedestrian crossings, claims to be Britain's safest town, with a road accident record only 22 per cent of the national average. Later towns are also designing sophisticated systems of express, distribution and feeder roads with grade separated junctions and full segregation of pedestrians from traffic. But they are also placing particular emphasis on the future role of public transport by providing—as some of the tramways did, though possibly for other reasons, half a century ago—a special public transport route, closed to other traffic, linking the whole of the town and guaranteeing a quick journey at peak travelling times. The Redditch Plan likens this to 'a necklace, the beads of varying shape and size representing the districts and the string the public transport system.'[12] Runcorn terms it 'a planned balance between the use of the private car and public transport'.[13] Special cycle ways—a popular feature of some of the earlier towns—are now thought to be unnecessary except perhaps, say Corby,[14] for school-children, for whom safe and convenient cycling facilities can be provided as part of the system of green ways and local footpaths. But Stevenage and Harlow both report that their cycle ways are still extensively used.[15]

But a plan nowadays must look beyond the traditional methods of transport and must consider the new forms that are just round the corner—monorails, automatic buses and various other methods of mass transit that are the subject of close study.[16] One or other of the larger new cities is almost certain eventually to become a pioneer in this complicated field, but it will be many years ahead. In preparing the interim report on the planning of Milton Keynes[17] the consultants considered no less than forty-six public transport equipment types and came to the conclusion that at the outset at any rate a 'small bus' service, provided it was of high quality, would give the best value for money. But the plan contemplates the reservation of land along the major roads so that some form of fixed track or automatic guided system can, if necessary, be introduced later.

These new plans represent a big technical advance. Planning, like all science, takes cautious steps forward. One man builds on the work of another. Experiments are made and the results analysed. New ideas are opened up, new solutions found for old problems. In a changing world there is no such thing as perfection but each step is a move towards a better service to the people who are to live in the environment which the plan creates.

The 'Mark I'[18] new towns of the fifties, it is said, are old-fashioned now; but there are still plenty of people old-fashioned enough to prefer them. They were designed with plenty of open space, green wedges and well spaced-out houses, very much on the lines advocated by the garden city enthusiasts as a revolt from the congestion of our cities. But the tide of opinion turned in planning circles and the 'Mark II' towns aimed at higher densities to provide a more compact way of urban life, a unified, instead of a dispersed town. They, too, will give place to the 'Mark IIIs' of tomorrow. Already densities are being lowered and some of the traditional features thought now to be fundamental truths may have to be discarded.

By general consent the conception of a single industrial area in the lee of the town has been abandoned. The disadvantage of a one-way night and morning traffic surge needs no demonstrating. Modern production methods no longer pour out smoke and dust. Good design and landscaping make factory buildings acceptable even in residential areas and many people, particularly housewives, want employment close to their homes.

The concept of a central shopping area may be the next to go. For how much longer can we expect the whole population of a town to surge towards a central point at peak shopping time, walking or driving through a densely built-up area to get there and creating such congestion that the use of cars may eventually have to be banned? The thought of out-of-town shopping centres—beyond the built-up boundaries but readily accessible from the main road system and well provided with car parks—shocks the traditionalists to the core and would upset the current pattern of land-values. But other countries are more and more being driven to such solutions and it may not be long before we see a complete revolution not only in the technique and economics of retail trading but also in the function of a town centre. To ban the car or limit its use to avoid central congestion is as bad as solving a water shortage by prohibiting baths. But the alternative, in our traditional thinking, may well be a town centre surrounded by a sea of tarmac or ringed with multi-storey car parks costing millions to build and involving substantial charges for their use.

Towns are built to last a long time. They must cater not only for what people want today but for what they are likely to want tomorrow; and the planner must provide for both. He must understand the science of social change and be ready to adapt his ideas to meet the needs of a new generation. In his stimulating and highly controversial Reith lectures for 1967,[19] Dr Edmund Leach suggested that the whole pattern of family relationships was likely to undergo radical change within another generation or so, that the inward-looking dependence on the family unit would be replaced by a wider communal concept. If he is right the towns we are now building might well be obsolete, in terms of a pattern for living, long before the buildings have finished their useful life.

Yet, in a way, it is perhaps a recognition of this very trend, an understanding of a growing need for wider contacts and wider social relationships, however highly we rate the family as the essential basis of our current society, that has led the new towns to place such importance on the creation of a community unit with a central focus. The group round the piano in a Victorian parlour has now been replaced by the nightly cluster round the television set but we still have the groups of youths on the street corners desperately in need of something constructive to do in the increased leisure time that now has to be filled. They are not peculiar to new towns.

There are no stereotyped sets of rules for Master Plans. Each new town has its own problems and each planner has his own individual approach. His ideas are subject to the closest scrutiny and he has plenty of opportunities to explain them. He must carry with him the development corporation, the local authorities and the statutory undertakers, he must give the general public the chance of criticizing or objecting and he must satisfy the Minister at a public inquiry. Most development corporations stage an exhibition before the plan is submitted to the Minister, with screens, models, and maps as an aid to understanding and with members of their staff available to answer questions. Some hold public meetings. Any points of substance raised can often be dealt with before the document is finally complete.

Perhaps the oddest thing about the Master Plan is that it is not required by statute. It has no legal significance and is not mentioned in the New Towns Act. The Minister requires it to be prepared, purely as an administrative necessity, and he studies it and may comment on it; but he never formally approves it.

Yet it is the most important document in the new town process. It is the foundation stone on which the whole town rests. Most people think of it as just a map, with colours showing where the houses, shops, factories, and schools will be built. But it is much more than that. It is, in truth, a way of life for thousands of men and women and for their children yet to be born.

7. LAND

THE designation of a new town area settles in principle that the land can be bought for the purpose of building the town. Land outside the area can also be bought for roads, sewerage, and other related purposes. Corporations are free to buy by agreement but no compulsory purchase can be made without the Minister's express approval and, once more, objections can be made and a local inquiry will be held before the Minister reaches a decision.[1]

In practice, most owners agree to sell; but whether it be by agreement or compulsion inevitably it means disturbing people. However tactfully the process is handled there are bound to be some hard words spoken and even a few hard cases that do not seem to be quite covered by the rules. All development corporations recognize the need for sympathetic negotiations during which the owner's particular problems can be discussed and, so far as possible, met. If houses, shops, or business premises are bought, suitable alternative accommodation has to be offered and it must be offered on terms that take account of the price being paid to the displaced owner.[2] The corporations must therefore work to a carefully prepared programme that gives time and opportunity for solving the many personal difficulties that arise on any projects of this magnitude.

'It is the clear intention, when an area is designated, to acquire all the land,' Lewis Silkin told the House of Commons in 1946; 'the only doubt is about *when* the land will be bought.'[3] In fact, purchase is usually spread over many years and experience now shows that some parts of the area may never need to be purchased at all unless the owner wants to sell. For the initiative does not lie solely with the corporation. An owner can ask to be bought out at a time that suits his convenience, so that he can move or start a new business elsewhere. The corporation will usually be willing at any time to buy land they will eventually need, but after seven years from designation an owner has a right to serve a notice on the development corporation requiring them to buy his land.[4] He is then entitled to exactly the same compensation, including payment for disturbance and certain legal fees, as under a compulsory purchase order. It is questionable, however, whether the section as drafted in 1946 is appropriate now that designations include large urban areas, much of which will not need to be redeveloped in the foreseeable future and which the development corporation will not need to buy for their own purposes. It could mean spending a great deal of public money on which there will be little return and which ought in any case to be spent on new development. It may be that few owners in these areas will want to sell to the corporation because they will lose any increase in value due to the new town. On the other hand, if the new town has caused a decrease in the value of any property the owner ought not to be deprived of his right to sell to the corporation at a price that disregards the decrease.[5]

Land owned by public authorities, statutory undertakings, railways and the like normally remains unaffected unless reorganization of their services is needed in the course of building the town; and churches, public or historic buildings and any modern houses, factories or shops in the area will usually be retained in the new plan. The Minister has a statutory duty to give the corporations directions for preserving features of architectural or historic interest.[6]

Shops sometimes present a problem, because the effect of the new development on established shopping values is not fully predictable. On the one hand, the addition of a large new population can increase trade enormously; on the other, the building of a new modern shopping centre some distance away can spell near-ruin for the older shops. Difficulties of this sort are usually solved amicably. Corporations are able to buy the older shops at a price that disregards any loss of value due to the new town and this gives the owner the opportunity of transferring his business to the new centre if he wishes. By taking early advantage of the improved trading opportunities many small shopkeepers have been able to build up very flourishing businesses in modern shop premises.

In towns where the value of the older shopping centre is

likely to increase substantially as a result of the new town a strong case can be made for allowing the development corporation to buy these shops early on and thus recover their proper share of these increased land values. At Crawley, for example, the development corporation bought most of the property in the old High Street, including some attractive buildings dating back to the sixteenth century which have now been renovated at considerable cost with the objects of preserving the character of the High Street and maintaining its importance as a main shopping area.

In Hemel Hempstead, most of the leading stores moved into the new shopping centre and many of the old High Street shops now provide services of a different character—antique furniture, boutiques, etc.—not often found in a new town. For a time the old High Street developed a rather run-down appearance but it has now been given a 'face lift' in collaboration with the Civic Trust; several of the ancient buildings, some of them hundreds of years old, have been restored and there is every hope that it will flourish again as an important commercial area of the town.

Corby village, too, has been restored and renovated under the guidance of Professor Misha Black. Old buildings have been restored, others modernized, and new houses and garages have been built as part of a comprehensive village improvement scheme.

In some of the other towns, the older shopping areas have been left untouched, the traders carrying on business as before and usually benefiting by the increased population; but occasionally, as for example at Bracknell, the decision to increase the size of the town made it necessary to buy most of the old shops and pull them down in order to make way for a new town centre. Every town has its different problems.

Buying farmland has its special difficulties because so many farms are on yearly agricultural tenancies. The value of the land is, of course, paid to the owner and the development corporation then becomes the landlord with the right of any such landlord to give the tenant farmer a year's notice to quit and to pay him merely the amounts required by law.[7] They rarely have farmland available to offer to a displaced farmer, though temporary arrangements can be made where farmland comes into the corporation's possession some years before it is needed for development.

This hardship to tenant farmers has long been a bone of contention. Corporations were sometimes able to give longer notice and since 1963 have been able to make small additional payments at their discretion.[8] It was not until 1968 that the law was amended—following protests at Milton Keynes where about sixty tenant-farmers were affected—giving payments equal to at least five years' rent.[9]

The procedure by which development corporations buy land compulsorily in a new town is something of an oddity, purely through historical accident. They still have to operate the procedure devised in 1944 primarily for the purchase of war-damaged land,[10] even though for all other public purchase a slightly different streamlined procedure was introduced in 1946.[11] One advantage of the 1944 procedure was that it included arrangements for 'expedited completion'—changed in 1967 to the 'vesting declaration' of the Land Commission Act —by which full ownership of land could be transferred to a development corporation without waiting for investigation of title, formal conveyance and settlement of compensation.[12] The power to ensure rapid transfer of title is of particular importance where a resale is contemplated. Essential development might be held up for a long time if legal complications had first to be sorted out and ownership rights established. In practice the procedure has been little used in the new towns, mainly because the planned programme of purchase has given adequate time for investigation of title and if the owner cannot be traced an alternative procedure can be used of paying the compensation into Court.[13]

On the whole, the land purchase side of new towns has gone very smoothly; but there have been occasional difficulties and upsets. The development corporation at Basildon faced a particularly acute problem because the main object of the designation was to deal with the five thousand shacks in the area. This was one of several parts of Essex where in the 1920s and early thirties, when farming prosperity was at its lowest ebb and before planning control was imposed, farmers had sold off small plots of land. There were many takers in those days, mainly from the overcrowded East End of London, and hundreds of converted railway coaches, wooden shacks and the occasional self-built bungalow had been put up—all without electricity, sewerage, or properly made roads. To protests that the country-side was being ruined, one farmer at the time replied 'I'm a public benefactor. I'm giving people in the slums the only chance they will ever have of getting some sun and air. Just look at the children. They've never had such colour in their cheeks.' In a way he was right. Even a rural slum is that much better than a crowded town slum. But he little knew that Harold Macmillan as Prime Minister would echo the very words thirty years later in the very different context of the new town being built on the very same spot.

It has cost the Basildon Development Corporation over £4 million to buy and demolish these shacks, but they put off disturbing the occupants for as long as possible and when finally demolition had to start they were given a priority alloca-tion of the new modern houses being built. Only one owner steadfastly refused to move and he was allowed to stay even though it seriously disrupted the building programme. 'I'm the only one who stuck up for my rights,' he said, 'it will take more than a £2 million housing estate to get rid of me.' And Charles Boniface, the new town General Manager, commented 'He's a grand old chap and we respect his desire not to be moved at his time of life. It will only mean building a few houses less.' When he died, still in his own home, at the age of ninety-three, the new development had been built all round him to within a few feet of the timber bungalow he cherished.

Sometimes it can be very costly to put off buying. At Hemel Hempstead the Corporation left an elderly woman in possession of her cottage and some little while later, when she lay dying, they suspended work on the new town centre at a cost of several thousand pounds a week to avoid causing her distress. At Hemel Hempstead, again, there was a farmer who con-sistently resisted all attempts to buy his land by agreement and threatened any 'trespasser' with a shot-gun. But then he would look at his watch and say cheerfully, 'Eleven o'clock: come in and have a glass of sherry.' It was many years before he decided the time had come to sell and retire to the seaside.

There is Farmer Lee, too, at Crawley, who in 1952 asked the development corporation to buy his farm and received the full compensation then provided by law. The land was not required for building for some years, however, and at his own request he was granted a tenancy so that he could go on farming until the land was wanted. When the compensation law was later changed and particularly when the land, by then provided with roads, sewers and other services, was sold by the corporation for private house building at full development value, he regretted his decision to sell. For years he has been a well-known figure in the town, protesting against what he felt to be an injustice, campaigning whenever any Minister or other public figure visited the town, and driving a placarded tractor from Crawley to Buckingham Palace in an effort to get royal support for his case.

More drastic was the determined stand at Bracknell of a county councillor and former chairman of the Rural District Council. His house was the last one left standing after an area had been cleared to make way for the £9 million new town centre; but still he refused to move and barricaded himself in with his family. When finally police and bailiffs had to break down the door and escort them out he said, 'I have made my protest. The residents of the old town have been getting a raw deal.'

Incidents such as these are few and far between. A generous view of compensation within the limits allowed by law, reinstatement wherever possible, a disturbance allowance to cover the cost of removal and other such expenses, payment of professional fees and legal costs and, perhaps even more important, sympathetic personal discussion—all these have combined to enable the difficult but critical programme of land purchase to be achieved with the minimum of trouble. In all, some 70,000 acres have been bought and not more than a handful of cases have had to be referred to the Lands Tribunal to settle a dispute over the price to be paid.

To the owner, of course, the price he gets is most important. The valuation has to be made according to general principles laid down by Parliament but there have been major changes in these principles in the years since new towns started. Even in the simple case of buying a house there can be differences of opinion about what the value should be; and where 'development value' is concerned—that is to say the additional value land would fetch if sold for some new purpose such as building houses or factories on farmland—the argument has gone back and forth for many years.

The general principle is that the owner must be paid what the property is worth in the market; but in land, as in other things, that depends on who wants to buy it and for what purpose. The professional valuers have to make a number of assumptions and can usually negotiate a fair price without difficulty, but important questions sometimes have to be settled or prescribed by law before a basis of valuation can be established.

The code laid down in the middle of last century[14] said that compensation should be based on the value as between willing buyers and sellers. The code worked well for many years. It was customary—although there was no statutory authority for it—to add 10 per cent because the purchase was compulsory; but in 1919 new rules came into force[15] which excluded any such addition and also made it clear that the special value to the purchaser—for example where land was being bought by a local authority to build a reservoir—was to be excluded.

By the time the New Towns Act was passed in 1946 another problem had arisen. In the early days of the war it was realized that the long-established pattern of values was going to be seriously upset and there was a danger that speculators would buy up land, particularly in war-damaged areas, in the hope of making large profits when the war was over. Indeed, there was clear evidence that it was happening and, following the Uthwatt Committee's recommendation, the Town & Country Planning Act 1944 had accordingly 'frozen' compensation for land bought by public authorities for five years at the 1939 level of values.[16] But by the end of the war house prices had begun to rise sharply. The 1939 value no longer gave an owner enough money to buy another house and after much pressure the Government agreed in 1944 to increase the compensation by

30 per cent and then, in 1946, by 60 per cent.[17] This increase applied only to owner-occupiers of houses and was applied to new town purchases by the 1946 Act; but before any property was bought the basis was changed by the Town & Country Planning Act 1947.

This Act, the second of the famous Silkin trio, was of fundamental importance not only to new towns but to the whole post-war reconstruction programme. It laid down a completely new system for controlling and directing development and as an essential background transferred all development values to the State. There was little controversy about the need for a new planning system. All parties accepted it in principle. The most difficult and controversial aspect was the financial effect on the landowners.

The subject of land-values was by no means new to the British Parliament but this was the first time that it had been raised in the context of planning policy. Half a century earlier Henry George had advocated the taxation of land-values and the Liberals had raised the slogan 'God gave the land to the people'; but it never really meant what it said. It was the taxation of values, not ownership, that the Campbell–Bannerman and Lloyd George Governments of 1906–10 were after and to secure it they went to the lengths of curbing the powers of the House of Lords by the Parliament Act of 1911. The Valuation Office of the Board of Inland Revenue—which still exists today —was set up for the express purpose of making the valuations, but the outbreak of war in 1914 delayed the work and in 1920 the post-war Coalition Government repealed the Act and the little money that had been collected was repaid. The old slogan arouses no passions today and the Liberal Party have long since abandoned it as part of their political philosophy.

Just twenty years after the Lloyd George legislation a Labour Government made another attempt. In 1930 Philip Snowden brought in a Land Valuation Bill but withdrew it in the face of opposition from the House of Lords. The same provisions were included in the Finance Act of the following year, which the Parliament Act of 1911 prevented the House of Lords from rejecting. It provided for a modest enough tax of 1d. in the pound on the capital value of land or the development value of farmland; but with the fall of the Labour Government in 1931 the valuation work was stopped and a year or two later, before any money had been collected, the tax was repealed.

Another twenty years further on, a Labour Government once again had to face this issue, not in the context of the old political controversy about the ethics of land-values or unearned increment but because of the need for a land system under which a national planning policy for the use and development of land could be carried out. In the past, owners who were not allowed to do what they liked with their land had, with a few small exceptions, been entitled to compensation for the loss of value; but despite some brave words in the Town & Country Planning Act 1932 about collecting increases in value—'betterment'—from those who gained as a result of planning policy, it had never been found possible to collect any money. As a result most local authorities had been careful to frame their planning schemes so that no restrictions were imposed that might lead to a compensation claim.

The Barlow Commission had realized even in pre-war days that effective planning would be impossible unless this problem was solved and after hearing evidence from the Ministry of Health (the Ministry responsible at that time for town and country planning) one of the members of the Commission had suggested that the transfer of all development values to the State on payment of a 'global sum' might be a possible solution. The Barlow Commission did not feel able to examine this proposal in detail and they accordingly recommended further study by experts.[18] This was the main purpose for which Lord Reith appointed the Uthwatt Committee in 1940.

The final report of the Uthwatt Committee contained a closely reasoned analysis of the problems of land-values and the philosophy of compensation. It explained with almost brutal clarity the reasons the compensation to landowners as a class was always in excess of the true loss of value, and why 'betterment' could rarely be collected. Development value, said the Committee, is a floating value spread over many more acres than are ever likely to be developed so that the compensation to each member of a group of individual owners, separately assessed, greatly exceeds the real loss of the group as a whole.

If development is not allowed in one area the value shifts to land elsewhere, but it is impossible to say with certainty whether and to what extent a given land-value is attributable to a given cause.[19]

After considering evidence by nearly fifty organizations the Committee came down in favour of the main principles of the scheme suggested to the Barlow Commission. They recommended a general prohibition on development, with immediate compensation for loss of development value on the basis of a fair global sum, and thereafter purchase by the State at existing use value of all land required for development, whether public or private, followed by a lease of the land to the developer. For built-on land they proposed an annual tax on increases in value.[20]

Despite the good progress made by the Coalition Government since setting up the new Ministry of Town & Country Planning, four years of study of these controversial and far-reaching recommendations had produced nothing more than a White Paper[21] and the inadequate Planning Act of 1932 was still in force. The new Government now had to frame a planning system that matched the future needs of the country. It had to be fair to the public authorities by precluding excessive compensation and it had to avoid the challenge of 'confiscation' by preserving the rights of owners in values already accrued. As between one owner and another, it had to ensure that they were treated alike. One should not gain by getting a planning permission and the other lose by getting a refusal. The development programme demanded that decisions should be objective, and not influenced by considerations of individual losses or gains. Good administration demanded that there should be no possibility or suspicion of bribery or behind-the-scenes wire pulling because of the profits to be made. Economics demanded that large amounts of unearned increment should not be paid out to individuals to add to the very real danger of post-war inflation.

In the event, the Uthwatt Committee's recommendation for a tax on the value of built-on land was not accepted but the main principles of the 'development rights scheme' were adopted and applied by the Town & Country Planning Act

1947 to both unbuilt-on land and built-on land. Thus all landowners retained the value of their land for its existing use which then became the price to be paid on compulsory purchase. The '1939 standard' was repealed so that an owner could be assured of enough compensation to buy another comparable property elsewhere. If development or more intensive redevelopment (with a 10 per cent margin of tolerance) was allowed, the development value would be paid to the Central Land Board and the existing use value would be retained by the owner. No compensation would be paid on refusal of permission to develop unless 'existing use rights' were infringed but landowners as a class were to receive a once-for-all payment for the loss of any development value that had accrued by 1948. For this purpose a central government fund of £300 million was provided, to be distributed *pro rata* when all claims had been received and all the valuations had been made. Actually the £300 million was not a bad estimate. It took about three years to make all the valuations, which added up to about £350 million, and it is tolerably certain that this total, made up as it was of about a million separate valuations,[22] contained a substantial element of what the Uthwatt Committee called 'floating value'; but the addition of another £50 million to the £300 million would have made it possible to pay everybody in full at the assessed figure. It would have been a generous—even over-generous—settlement but well worth while to secure a permanent solution of the compensation-betterment problem.

This was the position when the first land was bought for new town development. In their Second Report the Stevenage Development Corporation reported 'some reluctance to sell at existing use value' but they did not mention it again and the corporations do not seem to have had any serious difficulty in buying at existing use value. Nor did the local authorities up and down the country have any trouble in buying at existing use value the land they needed for housing and other functions. Where land was changing hands for private development it was expected that the price would be at or around existing use value because the development value was payable to the Central Land Board and the buyer clearly would not pay twice. As a reserve power, the Board were able to buy land compulsorily so that

they could take action if a landowner held up important development by deliberately keeping his land off the market or demanded a price greatly in excess of the value for existing use.
One of their early attempts to exercise these powers over land
belonging to Earl Fitzwilliam was, however, challenged in the
Courts. The case was taken to the Court of Appeal and finally
to the House of Lords before the legality of the Central Land
Board's action was confirmed.[23]

But by then a couple of years had gone by during which the
powers were in doubt and it was possible to mobilize pressure for a repeal of the development charge. The report
of the Ministry of Town & Country Planning published
in April 1951 records that during 1950 (when the Act had been
in force for only two years) memoranda were produced by the
Royal Institution of Chartered Surveyors, the Chartered
Auctioneers' and Estate Agents' Institute, the Council of the
Law Society, the Federation of British Industries, the Association of Chambers of Commerce, and the Country Landowners'
Association, all suggesting that the liability to development
charge was putting a severe brake on development. The
Ministry did not accept this view. They pointed out that
development was proceeding within the limits of the available
resources; that the limiting factor in the building of houses,
factories, and schools was not liability to development charge
but shortage of building labour and materials; and that a great
deal of land covered by private planning permissions was
exempt from development charge—enough for over 100,000
houses plus 3,800 acres of factory and commercial development. Development charge, said the Ministry, had not so far
shown itself as a deterrent to development.[24]

Difficulties were however arising because some landowners
were said to be demanding a development value on a private
sale, thus imposing a double burden on the developer. Despite
intensive Press publicity and other warnings, some purchasers
were paying twice; but as Sir Robert Fraser, the Secretary of
the Central Land Board, told the Public Accounts Committee,[25]
the real cause lay in the fact that a building licence was necessary in those days. They were not easy to obtain because of the
shortages of labour and materials, and land with the benefit of

the building licence was temporarily commanding a greatly enhanced scarcity value which the Central Land Board decided as a matter of policy should not be included in the calculation of development charge.

There was no sure way of overcoming this problem except by widespread use of the Central Land Board's compulsory purchase powers. The Uthwatt Committee had indeed foreseen this situation and had recommended that, except where a man was building on his own land, all land on which development was allowed should first be bought from the owner by the central authority at existing use value and then leased to the developer. This the Government was clearly unwilling to do. Compulsory purchase is never popular and with the Fitzwilliam case awaiting decision by the Courts their hands were somewhat tied. Matters came to a head when a Mr Pilgrim committed suicide, allegedly because he had, in ignorance, paid development value to a landowner and then found, when the land was bought from him by the local authority, that he received in compensation only the value for existing use.[26]

Six months after the publication of the Ministry's report in April 1951, the Conservatives won the election, and the next report of the Ministry records that 'by that time the difficulties associated with the financial provisions [of the 1947 Act] had become formidable ... they were acceptable neither to landowners nor to developers.... The Government ... after exhaustive examination of the possible alternatives, decided that development charge must go.'[27] By 1953 the financial structure of the 1947 Act had been dismantled, payment of the £300 million was suspended and development charge was repealed.[28] For a time existing use value plus 1948 development value (as established by a claim on the £300 million) remained the basis of compensation for compulsory purchase. This, it was said, was the 'sheet anchor' that would stop land-values drifting back into chaos. But, predictably, a 'two-price' system of land-values soon ran into difficulties and this too was abolished, together with the Central Land Board, when the Town & Country Planning Act 1959 re-established 'open market values' as the basis of compensation. This is not such a simple conception as it was before effective planning control was imposed.

Value now depends entirely on what development would be permitted and the Act therefore includes a complicated system for certifying what permissions would have been granted if the land were not being bought for some other purpose. [29]

Only in new towns, it seems, had things been running reasonably smoothly under the compensation code of the 1947 Act. Although they were about the biggest single building projects in the country, covering almost all forms of development, no real difficulties had arisen despite the very high development values that had been created by the selection of the areas for development, by the building of roads and services and by the rising demand for houses, shops, and factories. All development values result from the public need in one form or another, but in the case of new towns it was the direct result of Government action. Even the landowning interests did not seriously dispute that it would be over-generous to hand over these values to those who still owned land in the area. The 1959 Act accordingly provided that any *increases or decreases* in value attributable to the carrying out, or to the prospects of carrying out, new town development on *other* land, were to be disregarded.[30]

This is very different from the 'existing use' value of the 1947 Act. It does not necessarily mean that an owner of farmland receives only farming value. If the corporation are buying for the purpose of housing or shops or industry, the owner receives the value appropriate to that use on the assumption that the surrounding conditions were as they might have been if the new town had not been designated. The complicated provisions for certificates of alternative development also apply, so that where land is being bought for, say, an open space or a road, the planning authority has to decide what the land might have been used for if there had been no new town and if some other land had been selected for the open space or road. In the result, instead of paying a farm value of about £200 an acre, some development corporations are having now to pay £20,000 an acre or more for farmland they need for housing or roads, etc., and even higher prices for land they need for other purposes. Sometimes they even have to buy back at these sort of prices land they have already sold. It does not happen often but an acre and a half of land sold by a development corporation in the early days for open space purposes at a nominal value of £1 was valued under the new law at £36,000 when it had to be bought back a few years later to round off a site for commercial development.

At about the time the 1959 Bill was before Parliament some of the new towns were being enlarged and it was asked whether this exclusion of value ought to apply to extensions of a designated area. Would not this be depriving owners of values already established? Henry Brooke, the Minister then in charge, decided that the right course would be to allow owners of extension land to retain the benefit of values created by the new town. They had every reason to regard themselves as outside the new town, he argued; and if such land had changed hands privately it would have done so at ordinary market value.[31]

On the face of it, this sounded reasonable enough—until some of the valuations began to emerge. Land just outside the boundary of a new town is normally accepted as a necessary green belt area and is thus never likely to receive planning permission for development. In some cases such land had been deliberately excluded from the designated area because of high agricultural quality or objections by the farmer and was fetching perhaps £100-£200 an acre on sale to another farmer. If, through an extension of the new town, this land were now brought within the designated area for, say, an extension of the housing or industrial areas, with the benefit of roads, services, and other near-by development, the value would immediately go up to thousands of pounds an acre. The farmer who a year or two earlier had bought, say, a 50-acre farm for £5,000–£10,000 suddenly found himself the owner of compensation to the tune of a cool quarter or half million pounds.

With amounts of this order—and the figures are not purely imaginary—it was clear that if a few such cases became known there might well be a public scandal. When the Labour Government took office they accordingly changed the law by excluding from compensation the new town value where extensions of the designated area were made after 13 December 1966, the date their new Act came into force. But the Act still leaves full new town values to be paid where extension land was designated before that date.[32]

This wider historical background is important for an under-standing of the law now governing the purchase of land in new towns but the problem of land-values is by no means confined to new towns. Nowadays almost any owner of farmland who manages to get a planning permission for development can make a fortune overnight. The disparity of treatment between those who get a planning permission and those who are refused is difficult enough to justify but the economic effects are also serious. So once more, with another twenty years gone by since Lewis Silkin's 1947 Act—the 20-year cycle is becoming almost monotonous—the Wilson Government passed the Land Com-mission Act 1967, which provides for a levy—initially 40 per cent but to be raised some day to 50 per cent—on the develop-ment value realized on disposal or development of land and gives the Land Commission powers to buy compulsorily at a price that is reduced by the levy. The Conservative Opposition have said they will repeal the Act and abolish the Land Com-mission if and when they get back to power; and there is pressure from some quarters to pay compensation for 'worsen-ment' to owners who are not allowed to build,[33] thus putting the clock further back even than 1932.

So the political see-saw goes on. Fortunes have been made or lost on the turn of a planning permission, on the date of a notice to treat, on the timing of royal assent to a new Bill. Some landowners have reaped high profits; their neighbours, who have seen the prize snatched from their grasp or who have seen the prize reinstated too late for them to share in it, suffer a permanent sense of grievance to which there is no satisfactory answer. Farmer Lee of Crawley has protested to everybody from the Queen downwards because he was one of the prize-losers; and who can blame him?

Yet the national economy is the real loser in the battle over development values. Where owners themselves have spent money on roads and services, whether it be a private developer, a local authority or a new town development corporation, they are entitled to a commensurate benefit: it is part of the cost of building. But most development values cannot be justified on these grounds. They arise purely because of the spread of towns, public expenditure on services and the national need for more houses or jobs. They represent no past effort or expenditure by the owner. Nothing can be more inflationary than to pay, whether in land prices or compensation, vast sums—and they are vast—which at best are merely the over-generously assessed reflection of the frustrated hope of sharing in the profits of future production.

In so far as compensation represents the current value of land or buildings for their existing use, the payments must be accepted. An owner-occupier who is displaced needs to buy another comparable property, whether it be a house, farm, shop, or factory. The landlord of rented property, too, can reasonably be entitled to replace his investment and thus continue to draw an equivalent income from some other source, whether it be from other land, equity shares, or Government securities. When it comes to the elusive element of development value, however (and most current building is on land where the development value is the major part of the price) the picture is different. Development value is merely the capitalized value of the additional income the owner might hope to get at some unpredictable future date if and when he were able to let his land for a more profitable use. It represents nothing in terms of current assets or current production and the payment of compensation for this hypothetical future loss pumps millions of pounds of paper money into the economy. It can only be a matter for regret that the economic aspects of this problem get submerged in the oft-repeated phrases of political argument or prejudice.

Some idea of the increasing sums of money involved can be gained from the papers submitted to Parliament. In 1947 the eventual amount of new development value to be collected by the Central Land Board was conservatively estimated at £9 million a year—enough at that time to service the £300 million compensation fund.[34] In 1967, the Government indicated that a levy of only 40 per cent of realized values was expected eventually to yield some £80 million a year.[35] The remaining 60 per cent—£120 million: enough in public hands to build a complete new town every two years—remains with the landowner.

Other statistics published by the Government[36] show that in England and Wales every new house being built by a local authority in 1966 was costing, on average, £420 for land. On a density of, say, fifteen to the acre, that works out at over £6,000 an acre, and prices have gone up considerably since then. For private housing the figure in 1967 was nearer £1,000 per house[37] and choice sites for expensive houses, even forty miles away from London, were fetching nearly £18,000 an acre[38] and prices are still rising. In the cities the figures have reached staggering proportions. Central sites can fetch fantastic sums for office development and as Oliver Marriott's book has shown,[39] the repeal of Lewis Silkin's 1947 Act enabled millionaires to be created almost overnight, with negligible risk of their own money. Even in a working class housing area such as Stepney–Poplar, the land still needed for the Lansbury estate, started in 1945 and still only half built after twenty-five years, is expected to cost some £300,000 an acre, if the Greater London Council can ever contemplate buying at that price.

Taking housing alone, an average cost of £800 for the land for each house would probably be a low figure. The housing programme is now running at around 450,000 dwellings a year so that land costs alone must be in the region of £360 million a year. In the ten years since 'market value' was re-established some £3,000 million or so must have been paid out in land costs. In the next thirty years the figure could well add up to another £12,000 million. If to these figures is added the cost of land for schools, roads, factories, shops, offices, playing-fields, and public buildings and other services, the figure could be almost doubled. The land system has run amok and prices are now completely out of hand. Unfortunately there are no published statistics from which the total burden can be accurately calculated but even though part will now be taken by the Land Commission by way of levy, the initial cost—some twenty to thirty thousand million pounds in half a generation—still has to be carried on the economy and borne mainly by the taxpayer or by the tenants or purchasers of new houses.

Some of the capital so created may eventually reach the Treasury by way of taxes or death-duties but that is not a complete answer to the economic problem and does not help the would-be house-owner. Nor does the answer lie, as is sometimes rather glibly suggested, in making more land available for development or abolishing the planning system. Land prices do not respond to the same economic laws as cabbages, and the rate of release of land for development needs to be tightened rather than loosened if the programme of development in the future is to match the social needs of the time.

Whether and to what extent the Land Commission Act of 1967 will help to solve this problem remains to be seen. It adopts a completely different approach from that of Lewis Silkin's 1947 Act, which sought to prevent development values attaching to land in the market and gave the Central Land Board a flexible instrument by which development charge could be tempered to the needs of the time or adjusted to achieve any given policy objectives. The 1967 Act, by contrast, leaves all the market forces to operate, including the effect of the levy itself, and then charges by results. It is a taxation instrument with no other social content. It does nothing to relieve the distorting pressures on the planning system, which was a primary object of Lewis Silkin's Act, it mitigates but does not solve the inflationary effect of these high payments for development value and it can do nothing to reduce the high price or rents of houses. In a century in which Britain can pride herself on steady progress in the sphere of social legislation it is a major tragedy that the land reforms of 1947, broadly accepted then by all parties as the essential minimum for the post-war reconstruction and the proper ordering of our economy, were so hastily swept away under pressure from the professional and other interested landowning organizations, to open the way for one of the most fantastic property booms in our history.

Although new towns have been insulated up to a point from the more drastic effects, these changes in compensation law have nevertheless made a substantial difference to the finances of the new towns now starting. The high prices they are having to pay for land can easily add £100 million or more to the capital costs of building even a small town, on which loan charges—some £9 million a year—have to be carried for sixty years. Higher rents are thus inevitable and a much longer period must elapse before the newer towns become financially self-supporting.

8. HOMES

SOME people who have never seen and explored the new towns visualize them as vast council estates with rows of houses all stamped in the same mould and devoid of any individuality. Nothing could be further from the truth. Scores of architects have been engaged to ensure variety of design and treatment and in some towns architectural competitions have been held which have produced some striking entries. There are literally hundreds of different house types and each new scheme of building adds to the number. It was the high quality of planning, design, and execution in the new towns that led the way to the greatly improved standards that are now being seen throughout the country.

Tastes vary, of course. The houses that are praised by some can be criticized by others. Professional journals, the 'glossies', the quality papers, and the popular Press all carry from time to time articles, letters, or comments on one aspect or another of new towns. Mostly, even when critical, they are fair and objective. Sometimes they are provocative, as when a professional journal talked in vague terms of the 'anonymity of many new town plans'—a comment that produced a sharp reaction in the correspondence columns. Occasionally they seem so distorted and inaccurate that one wonders whether the writer has ever been to a new town.

The spotlight is bound to be on these towns, partly because they are new, partly because they are a Government enterprise, and inevitably, anything that goes wrong is news. But the sweeping condemnations of a few commentators would find precious little support among those who live in them. They need hardly be taken seriously, were it not for the fact that they colour the views of so many people who have never been to a new town to judge for themselves. At a time when visitors from all over the world have paid tribute to the achievements of these towns in creating a pattern of living that avoids the very features alleged by some of these critics, it is perhaps a little surprising that ill-judged and ill-informed comments can find a platform.

New towns are not all good or all bad. There are variations in quality of design and layout; standards were frequently held down for financial reasons; ideas have changed over the years. There are some people who dislike the current architectural idiom and long for a return to the speculative builder's paradise of the thirties. Yet right from the early days new towns produced some delightful examples of co-ordinated design and have received many awards or commendations. Indeed, when the Ministry of Health, who were then responsible for housing, resumed the system of housing awards that had been suspended during the war, the entries from the new towns almost swept the board. Both local authorities and private enterprise builders were being rapidly outclassed.

Even today when so much advance has been made in housing standards throughout the country, new towns are continuing to attract highly competent professional talent. In 1967 the Royal Institute of British Architects organized a competition for designing a 'perfect family house costing no more than £3,750 excluding the site'. The first and second awards went to young new town architects; and at the presentation Professor Simey of Liverpool University commented: 'Most of the designs of the speculative builder are dreadful beyond belief. Why don't they attain the same sort of standards as the new town development corporations?'[1]

The simple truth is that the new towns are a product of our time. A study tour of them reveals a history in miniature of the post-war years—the development of architectural and planning thought, the progress made in the use of new materials, new methods of building, new approaches to design and layout, the impact of shortages, financial crises and credit squeezes, the rapidly changing background to the way people live and the things they want.

There are fashions in architecture and planning as in most other creative professions. Not all succeed; but new towns are a place for experiment, an opportunity for the profession to express the restless needs of successive generations, new ways of living, new standards in society. The danger is that they can become out of date just as quickly as a hemline.

Houses must last sixty years or more and the pace of change must be moderated. The architect must build for everybody, not just the 10 per cent who can appreciate and afford his quick strides into the future. He must build what people want, not what he thinks they ought to have. He can and should lead with new ideas but if he gets more than one step ahead of public taste he is at peril.

Most of the houses built in Britain in the year or two after the war were poor by current standards. There had been no design work for ten years and once the emergency programme of pre-fabs was completed many a builder started where he left off in 1939. This was particularly so in the private enterprise field where the system of individual licences and the restrictions on size, material, and cost resulted in the building throughout the country of thousands of single houses, particularly bungalows, to designs of the thirties, and with little or no regard to what was built or being built on adjoining or near-by sites.

By the end of the 1940s this phase was passing but the first houses built in the new towns were still subject to all the pressures of the period. The size was limited, the amount of timber to be used was restricted, steel was rationed, cement and bricks were scarce, labour was hard to get. To some extent this was a challenge to the architect to make maximum use of space and alternative materials and to the building contractors to devise improved methods of construction. The first types of 'industrialized' building were established in those years, such as the Wimpey 'no-fines' and the Cornish unit house made from the waste from the china-clay workings.

Not all the experiments and bright ideas succeeded. An aluminium house was designed for the Government at that time to overcome the shortage of traditional materials and housing authorities were required to take a quota. But they all had to be demolished after a few years because of corrosion and the Government arranged to meet the outstanding loan charges.[2] Somehow most of the new towns managed to avoid taking these temporary aluminium bungalows and some were saved from taking them by the credit squeeze of 1948. But a number were built in a few towns and these, too, were demolished in 1964.

It was 1951 before the housing programme in the new towns got under way. In the economic crisis of 1948 most corporations were allowed to make a start only on preliminary roads and sewers and the whole of the London new towns were 'rationed' to a total of 300 building workers between them, whereas the Reith Committee had estimated that each town would need 5,000 men for fifteen to twenty years.[3] At the end of three years only just over 1,000 houses had been built, with another 3,000 under construction. But the preparatory design work had gone on and in the next three years the number rose to 37,000. The housing situation in the country, however, was desperate and the drive for an increase in numbers led in 1952, when Harold Macmillan was Minister of Housing, to the adoption of the 'People's House' of no more than 900 sq ft for a three-bedroom house limited to essentials in equipment. This saved £150 a house. Ten houses could be built where nine were built before. New town corporations were for a time required to build many of their houses to this reduced standard.[4]

Even the houses built to more normal space standards were subject to the closest scrutiny. There was a 'price ceiling' on all new houses built by the local authorities and this applied also to new towns. The efforts of the architects to produce new designs and better layouts were frequently frustrated because they cost too much. Specifications were combed through by the Ministry to see what savings could be made. Standards were lowered, designs modified, and fittings reduced or excluded until the price was down to the pre-ordained figure.

It was a frustrating period. All the development corporations who suffered in that difficult time look back on it with regret. Some call it a disaster. Politically and economically it was no doubt necessary. The homeless had become a burning issue. In the short term it spread money, labour, and materials over more houses and made it possible to achieve Macmillan's target of 300,000 houses in 1953. But it meant that the new town stock of houses now includes many that are much below the

85

standards that are generally acceptable today and the savings on capital cost have since been more than outweighed by the heavier maintenance charges.

One former General Manager tells the story of the day, a year or two afterwards, on which he took some visiting V.I.P.s from the Ministry around Stevenage. He showed them a newly built house and they were suitably impressed. He then took them along to another empty house. They looked puzzled. 'Why are there no cupboard doors in the kitchen?' 'Why does the staircase banister go only half-way?' and so on until some half-dozen criticisms had been voiced.

'You've covered the lot now,' he commented with a wry smile. 'They were all the result of "savings" to keep down to the Ministry's price limit. Now, when one of these houses is empty, we can't let it until we've put things right. And, of course, it costs twice as much now.'

Some of the blocks of flats built in those years also suffered from decisions that now, with hindsight, seem particularly short-sighted. To take but two examples, the Harlow Development Corporation were not allowed to install central heating in a new and attractive block of flats; and at Basildon the Ministry refused to sanction the few extra pounds for a communal TV wiring system.[5] Nowadays, one hopes, they would refuse to approve designs that did *not* incorporate both these features.

Certainly the successive financial crises throughout the fifties and sixties have left their mark. The restrictions tightened up quickly at the first sign of a credit squeeze and loosened up slowly when it was over; but gradually standards improved. It became recognized that cost is not the only important factor and that capital savings at the expense of higher maintenance costs is a false economy. Moreover, some people are able and willing to pay for quality and must be catered for. A wide variety of standards, design, and price must not merely be permitted but should be positively encouraged. Development corporations were soon able to demonstrate that a few hundred pounds spent on so-called 'luxuries' such as better finishes and furnishings in the entrance hall and lifts of a block of flats gave an atmosphere of quality that is more than repaid by the satisfaction of the tenants and the additional rent obtainable.

By the time the 1952 restrictions were eased, however, much more fundamental questions were being raised. In the context in which new towns were started it was inevitable that the first of them should be designed very much to garden city concepts with plenty of space around buildings, factories well away from homes, adequate open space and playing-fields and with green wedges coming right into the centre to marry town with country. To many planners at the time and to many of the people who were moving to the new towns this was the ideal solution. It was a necessary and laudable reaction against crowded city conditions, lack of open space, the monotony of inter-war suburbia, and the tedium of some of the big single-class local authority estates.

But the opportunity to plan a whole urban environment was a challenge to the profession and soon stimulated much discussion and controversy. As early as 1953, when a number of Master Plans had been prepared and the first few houses built, some members of the architectural and planning professions began to express disappointment at the results and to question the basic philosophy. Gordon Cullen of the *Architectural Review* invented the term 'prairie planning' to describe his dislike of the spacious layout and low-density housing. He translated it into 'footsore housewives and cycle-weary workers' and, while admitting that the house plans were an improvement on the past, decided that 'in spite of all the energy, publicity, and cash, what should have been a great adventure has come to nothing.'[6]

J. M. Richards of the same journal, while admitting the advantages of cleaner air, up-to-date kitchens, and space for children to play, decided that 'the great disappointment is on the architectural side'. A town, he said, is a sociable place for people who want to live close together, and expresses itself through compactness, layout, and a sense of enclosure. . . . Towns should be planned as towns, with the cheerful life of the street, the corner pub, the market-place gossip and easy access to the country which suburban sprawl prevents.[7]

87

These were early days for such sweeping judgements and not everybody accepted them. There was controversy in the later columns of the journal, the Town & County Planning Association made a spirited counter-attack[8] and most local authorities in new town areas registered strong opposition to any suggestion of increased density. Much of the argument was based on emotion rather than fact. A few years later Robin Best of Wye College made a fully documented study and concluded that 'there are no low density new towns'. They had been criticized, he said, for an openness which did not exist: if anything they could be faulted for not attaining the spacious standards which the Reith Committee had recommended and which they were supposed to have adopted.[9] The key however, did not just lie in grouping houses closer together, making frontages shorter, gardens smaller, or reducing the size of school playing-fields. This controversy stimulated a complete re-examination of the problem of urban design.

About that time, too, the sociologists suddenly found merit in the close-knit family relationships of the crowded slum and near-slum areas of the metropolis;[10] the agriculturists supported any move that would limit the encroachment on farmland; and the menace of the motor-car with its traffic jams and rising toll of road accidents injected a new element into the needs of urban communities. Privacy, safety, and urbanity became the watchwords of the time.

These many pressures led to significant changes in design and layout. Influences from abroad, particularly Scandinavia and the United States, became marked and in their search for a better pattern architects and planners quickly moved away from the tradition of terraces of houses, each with a front door, a back door, and a strip of garden all too often enclosed for cheapness by chestnut paling and having a perpetual Monday-morning look with rows of washing visible down the road.

Ten years before the war at Radburn in New Jersey a layout had been designed that kept pedestrians separate from motor traffic. The houses were grouped together facing gardens and were accessible from the front only by footpaths. Access to garages and traffic roads was from the rear. This scheme was never completely finished and little was heard of it until these events of the 1950s brought it back into favour. Many countries then began to follow its basic principles. The new towns of Britain were quick to adopt and adapt the ideas of the Radburn layout, partially in some places, wholly in others. Now, in most of the newer housing areas, there is segregation of pedestrians from road traffic and the Master Plans of recent years carry the principle through to the planning of the whole town.

This new approach to layout and its use in high-density schemes brought with it other changes. Privacy demanded new forms of grouping and in a few schemes the traditional garden gave way to the smaller but well-screened paved patio—an outdoor extension of living space rather than a garden. It is capable of a limited amount of colourful flower and plant growing and is adequate as a play space for small children, for airing the laundry, and for secluded relaxation out of view of the neighbours. Despite considerable opposition to the higher density from many local authorities and other organizations, the patio house has proved popular, although the demand is limited and this type of layout is found in a few towns only. It needs particularly careful design but it does meet the needs of those who prefer a house to a flat and who like their outdoor pleasures in the countryside a few minutes' walk or drive away. Design must reflect the changes in social habits. People are no longer slaves to the garden. The car and television have taken its place. Most new town houses still have some garden space but the demand for large gardens seems now to be limited to a few enthusiasts.[11]

Now, of course, standards for all types of housing are very much higher than before. The Parker Morris Report[12] recommended certain minimum standards of space, heating, and other facilities and since 1967 all houses built by development corporations have been at least up to those standards. In 1969 they became compulsory for all houses built by public authorities but ceiling prices or 'yardsticks' had again been imposed following the Housing Subsidies Act 1967. Ostensibly this was for the purpose of holding at reasonable levels the new subsidy based on the excess cost over a 4 per cent borrowing rate:[13] but it coincided with yet another credit squeeze. The need to restrict capital expenditure and at the same time reach the new target of up to 500,000 houses a year were clearly important factors.

The 'yardstick' is not a fixed price applicable to every house. The figure varies with density and percentage additions or deductions are made to allow for variations in the level of building costs in different parts of the country. Up to a point it operates as a useful cost discipline on both architects and contractors. In practice, however, many specifications have had to be modified, plans redrawn or densities increased to get within the prescribed figure. One architect advised that a scheme of two-storey flats would have to be turned into three-storey flats to come within the yardstick; but as the flats were intended for elderly people the solution was thought to be singularly inappropriate! One quite serious aspect, however, has been the amount of redesigning necessary before schemes can be approved. Apart from the delay, which itself can be costly, it means a significant addition to the time or fees of professional staff or advisers.

Provided standards are not lowered below the Parker Morris minima, provided the yardstick figures are realistic and provided it is recognized that cutting capital costs at the expense of maintenance charges is a folly, the danger is not perhaps too serious. But there is an uneasy feeling in many new towns that the rigid price control may result in too much uniformity and that the figures, which are based on average costs of a year or so earlier, are not reviewed often enough to reflect the rising cost of labour and materials. Sir Matthew Stevenson, Permanent Secretary of the Ministry, told the Public Accounts Committee that he thought a yearly review would probably be necessary.[14] The first review did not take place for two years, but in 1969 the yardstick figures were increased by about 6 per cent and other adjustments were made to allow more flexibility of design. In announcing them the Minister officially endorsed the view that it was a false economy to reduce standards if the likely result was an increase in maintenance costs.[15]

Theoretically, the 'yardstick' applies to all houses and flats built since July 1967 but the Ministry still recognize the need for new towns to build a much wider variety of houses than the local authorities. Development corporations are thus allowed to build a few rented houses at prices above the yardstick but the excess cost does not qualify for subsidy and has to be fully covered by the rents.

Design and layout have been greatly influenced in recent years by the drive towards 'industrialized' methods of building. Many development corporations started looking into these new methods because the shortage of building labour in their areas, particularly in the finishing trades, was making it impossible to build enough houses to meet demand. The more they started, the fewer they completed and they were faced with contracts running over time, houses nearly but not quite finished and heavy expenses meanwhile in interest charges and loss of rent.

Most industrialized systems depend mainly on prefabrication in specially built factories. The cost of transport is high and large contracts near by, with the hope of extensions, are essential if the initial overheads are to be covered. New towns were thus particularly suited to make use of the many systems being developed both in Britain and elsewhere. There are now well over one hundred systems in various stages and the National Building Agency, one of whose tasks is to examine these new systems, has issued 'appraisal certificates' of which about 50 remained valid in 1969.

It doesn't follow that they will prove commercially successful. This is a new industry in which the growing pains are likely to be particularly severe. Architects do not always welcome the limitations they impose on design; tenants and purchasers tend to be wary of innovation; and the cost is often higher. In 1968 the Comptroller and Auditor-General pointed out that the average cost per house in two contracts was £200 above traditional building and questioned the need for these expensive methods.[16] The Public Accounts Committee examined the Permanent Secretaries of the Ministries and the Chairmen of the development corporations very closely about the delay in completing these contracts and recommended much firmer use of the clauses in building contracts under which damages can be claimed for unreasonable delay.[17]

Yet there is no doubt that new methods must be widely

adopted if the nation's housing need is to be met. Private enterprise house-builders are still, in the main, using traditional methods and the encouragement and development of the industrialized systems is bound, for a time, to fall largely on the public authorities. Some 21 per cent of all dwellings built by local authorities and new town corporations in 1964 were by these new methods. By 1967 this had risen to 42 per cent. The Ministry say that in future at least 100,000 dwellings a year will have to be 'non-traditional'. Eventually, no doubt, they will be competitive in price but some of the less viable systems will have to be withdrawn.

Cleeve Barr, the Managing Director of the National Building Agency, puts the figure at 165,000 a year if the Government's programme is to be achieved[18] and says that may be too low unless there is greatly improved productivity in the building industry. With the labour force in the construction industry not likely to exceed 350,000 and the present figure of 2,000 man-hours needed to build a traditional house, the industrialized methods, with a labour content of around 1,200 building man-hours, are the key to the future. So far, however, progress has been mainly in the methods of building tall blocks of flats and there was a severe set-back in terms of public opinion when the Newham Borough Council's building at Ronan Point collapsed.[19] In new towns at any rate the future will lie largely with the systems being developed for two-storey housing, of which perhaps the most promise is offered by the various timber frame methods and the on-site casting techniques. The 2,000 houses built by Mowlems at Stevenage, using light-weight concrete piped into steel shuttering, show what can be done by way of different external finishes to produce variety in houses of the same basic construction.

Even within the traditional forms, however, there is scope for improved techniques, rationalization of processes and the standardization of components which the spur of competition should encourage. But with it all there must still be variety. If the present drive for more and cheaper houses should lead to monotony and uniformity we would be no better off than we were in the thirties—or last century in the nineties—when the endless repetition of the same designs produced the row after row of almost identical dwellings to be found in every town and suburb.

The task of the development corporation is to build a complete town to meet the needs of all the people who work there. One of their important achievements has been a wide variety of choice. The corporations build houses detached, semi-detached, and in terraces; two-storey, three-storey, or sometimes four-storey combining a separate flat suitable for an elderly parent; dwellings with one, two, three, or four bedrooms—occasionally more; houses with garages attached, houses with separate garages that can be rented only if needed; houses with a traditional interior design or with a new-fashioned layout of rooms. They build bed-sitters, old people's bungalows and flats of varying sizes, some in two- or three- or four-storey design, some—though very few—in tower blocks.

There are houses to let at a wide range of rents; there are houses for sale; land can be bought on which the purchaser can himself arrange for a house to be built to his own design; self-build groups can buy land to build houses themselves; housing associations and charitable organizations are catered for; and, of course, the ordinary speculative builder can buy land to build houses for sale to people living or working in the town. The development corporations insist on high standards when they build for sale themselves or lease land for private-enterprise building, and all such houses are subject to the guarantees of the National House Builders' Registration Council. Local authorities also continue to build subsidized houses to meet the housing needs of the original population of the area.

The new towns cater for the factory worker, the office worker, the single, the married, the widow and widower, the executive director, the professional experts, the teacher, policeman, doctor and dentist, the young and the old. The whole range of types, incomes, and tastes that make up a community can, if they wish, find a home to suit them.

The needs of the elderly are not overlooked. The aim is to have 15 per cent of dwellings suitable for old people, either in

ground-floor or first-floor flats or in specially designed houses
or bungalows near the shops and bus routes. In the early days
of a new town these are frequently occupied by young couples
but the parents whose children have moved to a new town
sometimes decide to move there too when they reach retiring
age and the development corporations try to cater for these
needs within the narrow limits of their programme; but they
have rarely managed to match demand, and from time to time
they have had to close the list of applicants. When, in 1969,
the Commission for the New Towns announced that the list
at Crawley was to be reopened they were besieged by people
anxious to get the names of their parents at the head of the list.
Within hours some 650 new names had been registered and the
list had again to be closed.

For those who need special care there are specially designed
old people's dwellings with a warden in charge. Sometimes
they are built by the development corporation, sometimes by
the local welfare authority. One such project at Stevenage was
specially designed by the Research and Development Group
of the Ministry of Housing and Local Government.

Private and charitable institutions are also encouraged in the
new towns. The Hanover Housing Association, for example,
have already built a hundred flats in the new towns, and the
Y.M.C.A. and Y.W.C.A. have put up some very fine buildings.
At Crawley a Housing Association has been formed to build a
£40,000 project to provide homes for 'twenty lonely folk'—not
necessarily old folk: they have in mind also the students and
apprentices who find themselves strangers in the town.

New town people are no different from people anywhere
else. They have their preferences and their prejudices. The
initial demand is mainly for houses with three bedrooms at a
moderate rent, and both the programme and the letting policy
have to be carefully controlled in order to meet the needs of
incoming industry and the wage levels of people moving into
the town. Admittedly the 'higher income groups' were slow in
coming[20] but as the town begins to take shape the demand for
higher priced houses increases. The corporations build to let or
to sell to suit the market and they offer plots on which a purchaser can have his own house designed and built. This phase

comes rather late in the programme and the demand is mainly for owner-occupation except in the case of flats, where renting seems socially more acceptable.

Flats, particularly tall blocks, have been a controversial subject. The new towns, it was argued in some quarters, were intended to measure up to the ideals of the garden city concept. People wanted houses and gardens. Flat-living was an unfortunate necessity in the large cities where land was scarce and expensive but should not be inflicted on those who had escaped from these conditions. In Britain flats in tall blocks also cost more to build and carry a higher Exchequer subsidy. Why should this money be paid out in areas where land is plentiful?

The arguments are not conclusive. Although the main demand is for a family house—and most people agree that tall blocks of flats are not suitable for children—there is a small but growing demand for flats from the bachelor, the single woman, the widow, the working couple without children and those who have neither time nor inclination for gardening. Working wives, washing-machines, television, and car ownership are gradually changing the pattern of demand. Flats do not always have to be built in tall blocks. Deerswood Court, for example, the attractive award-winning flats at Crawley built around some lovely old trees, is no more than three–four storeys. A few flats are often incorporated, too, in a low-rise housing scheme. But the occasional tall block set in properly landscaped surroundings or in the midst of the town centre can be a welcome alternative to some and can give variety and architectural distinction to the town.

The corporations did not find it easy to judge either the number of flats needed or when the demand would arise. The first block at Stevenage was probably built too early. It was some two or three years before all the flats were let, and most of the towns over-estimated the demand. Crawley started off expecting 15 per cent of the population to want flats but by 1957 had brought the figure down to $2\frac{1}{2}$ per cent.[21] Harlow, on the other hand, started off with 20 per cent; in 1956 they were still aiming at 15 per cent, and in 1965 reported that half their flats were occupied by retired people and they wished they had more.[22]

Despite the additional subsidy, the rents of flats are usually higher than the rents of houses with similar accommodation. Building costs are the main reason, but there are other factors. Flats are particularly convenient to people likely to be moved around the country in their jobs and to young couples who will want to move into a house when a family arrives. This means a more frequent turnover, higher management and maintenance costs and losses of rent through voids. Moreover, staircases, lifts, halls, communal garden space, and landscaping have to be looked after, and all these expenses have to be covered in the rent.

Garages are rather a sore point because some development corporations feel they are sometimes unjustly blamed for the shortage in the first of the housing areas. In 1948 most people were still looking hopefully over their shoulders at the halcyon days before the war, when about one in every ten or twelve families owned a car, and were wondering how long it would take to get back to such a standard of luxury. But the increase in car ownership in America was already well known and some of the new town planners claim to have forecast a similar increase in Britain. The extent of car ownership is vital to any plan. It affects not only garages but traffic flows, road systems, and parking space. The corporations, however, were bound by standards laid down by the Government. Immediately after the war the street by-laws were suspended and the Ministry stipulated 13 ft, 16 ft, and 22 ft as the maximum widths for the various types of estate road. Garage provision in the new towns was at first limited to one garage for every twelve dwellings. In 1956 the Ministry allowed corporations to increase this in new schemes to 1 in 8 and to leave space for an eventual 1 in 4. Later this was again increased to 1 in 3 and to 1 in 1 for the more expensive houses. Now, of course, it is recognized that 1 in 1 is inadequate. When the children grow up there are many two-car or even three-car families, though this will reduce again as the children marry and take houses of their own. There will never be a figure that is right for all time. In their new development most corporations now plan, on average, for about 1·3 cars per family with additional parking space for visitors' cars.

The earlier restrictions were no doubt due in part to lack of foresight, but they were partly the result of the early credit squeezes and shortages of materials. There is little doubt, too, that there still lingered in the Whitehall corridors the old pre-war philosophy that tenants of subsidized houses shouldn't own cars. But whatever the reason, the lack of garages to meet today's demand is causing a serious problem in some of the new towns. In terms of numbers the position is no worse—indeed it is a good deal better—than in most other towns and cities, but the day and night kerbside parking in the rather narrow residential roads is causing not only traffic problems but also a fear that in an emergency the ambulance or fire engine might not get through.

Where there is land to spare in these areas, more garages, car-ports or hard-standings are being built, even at the expense of sacrificing the carefully planned landscaping. Eventually, houses may have to be pulled down to make room for the cars, but no corporation, so far, has been prepared to take this drastic step and it wouldn't necessarily be the right answer. The car-owner is generally reluctant to rent a garage unless it is close to his house and he much prefers to leave the car in the road outside his front gate, where he can keep an eye on it, than put it in an open parking area a minute's walk away where it is not only less available but in danger of pilfering or vandalism. In some places, even where garages are built, people are not prepared to pay the rent. The Cwmbran Development Corporation, for example, are providing parking lots in future schemes because garages are too expensive.[23]

In most new towns, areas are set aside for owner-occupied houses. The extent of the demand is difficult to estimate in advance and private builders are usually reluctant to accept a restriction against selling to people not working in the town. Yet to impose no such restriction, particularly in the towns a mere thirty miles from London, would mean inevitably that many of the houses would be sold to people from outside the town, including 'commuters', resulting in a shortage of houses for the townspeople themselves and an eventual growth of the town beyond the original intentions on which the whole planning conception of the Master Plan was based.

This is not to say that a new town must always be a closed community. People change their jobs, sell houses, and at some stage—when, it is not easy to predict—the town has to stop being a 'new town' and become just a 'town'. Although it will always be predominantly a town in which most of the people both live and work there can be no doubt that, over the years, circumstances will force some modifications. Even in the mid-fifties the Ministry allowed corporations to sell some houses to people working outside the town, as a step in the process of securing a balanced community.

The aim in the newer new towns is to have about half the houses to let and the other half owner-occupied; and the older corporations, who have built a much higher proportion of houses to let, are being encouraged to sell some of their rented houses in order to achieve eventually something like this same 50–50 balance. For a time, particularly where there is a long list of applicants waiting for houses, sales may have to be restricted. Many corporations impose a pre-emption covenant under which the purchaser, if he decides to sell, is bound to give the development corporation the opportunity of buying back the house so that it can become available for an applicant on the waiting list; but a new town cannot be insulated forever against the outside world and gradually the controls and special treatment will have to be relaxed.[24] The process will need great skill and care, otherwise the very attractiveness of the new towns could wreck the carefully balanced planning on which their success depends.

Whether the aim of 50 per cent owner-occupation will be achieved depends very much on the future level of interest rates and the degree of assistance given by the Government. As the figures in Chapter 14 show, even people with reasonably average incomes have difficulty in raising a sufficient mortgage at today's high cost and high interest rates. In a very detailed report prepared for the Ministry, Barry Cullingworth reaches the conclusion that 'the potential demand for owner-occupation in the new towns is held back by the level of house prices. Unlike existing towns, new towns lack a supply of low-cost houses for purchase. A significant increase in owner-occupation can only be achieved if some way is found of bridging the gap between current costs and financial ability to meet them.'[25] In several new towns many of the tenants are being given the opportunity of buying the houses they are renting, but sales are expected to be slow.

With ten to fifteen thousand rented houses in most of the new towns, repairs, external painting, and other maintenance work is a sizeable problem. Internal decoration is usually the responsibility of the tenant—though help is often given to the elderly or incapacitated—but the outside painting and general repair work is the responsibility of the development corporation. It involves keeping to a strict time-table so that whole areas are dealt with together, thus maintaining the unity inherent in the architectural design. This unity of treatment is a particularly striking feature of the more successful housing areas. Even where types and sizes of houses are much the same they are usually designed in a setting that lends itself to the use of colour and in which landscaping, tree planting, screen walls, and street furniture are all part of an integrated whole. Reasonable economy in building combines with quality in environment.

The need to maintain this quality is one of the reasons many corporations are reluctant to give all tenants the option of buying their houses. 'Pepper-potting' of ownership would inevitably result in varying standards and timing of maintenance and could well spoil the well-kept appearance of an area. Whether this is a sufficiently strong reason is perhaps debatable. The difficulty is that so many people are apt to want freedom for themselves but control over everybody else. Where houses are built for sale, covenants are imposed in the leases to ensure proper maintenance but the architect will normally design to a pattern that is less dependent on unified treatment and gives greater scope for free choice in colour schemes and timing.

The question of freehold or leasehold sales was, for a time, somewhat controversial. The Reith Committee had emphasized the importance of retaining the freehold of land[26] and the 1946 Act expressly forbade the sale of freeholds or of leases of more than ninety-nine years except with the Minister's express consent in exceptional cases.[27] In 1952 the Conservative Government removed the restriction in the case of houses,[28] and from then on there were some freehold sales; but most of the houses built for sale were still sold leasehold, mainly because this enabled covenants to be imposed to ensure proper use and maintenance but partly because the corporations felt they had a duty to look ahead to the time when redevelopment will become necessary and when public ownership of the whole area will again be essential to any satisfactory rebuilding programme.

Now, however, the Leasehold Reform Act 1967 allows leaseholders to buy the freehold if they have lived in the house for five years; but development corporations were able, if they wished, to apply to the High Court for a 'scheme of management' under which important covenants could be retained.[29] In towns where such schemes come into force all future sales of houses will probably be on a freehold basis under the umbrella of the scheme. Legislation has also been promised on the enforcement of positive covenants[30] and this may lead to other significant changes of policy.

A generation of housing history is behind us. In terms of quantity the contribution of the new towns has been relatively small but the experience gained of large-scale building within a comprehensive social pattern has opened up great new possibilities for the future.

Any assessment of the achievements of new town housing must be made against the background of history, and even now it is too early for a final judgement. Some of the openness so criticized in the early days is fast disappearing as land reserved for other services becomes built on. The rawness is wearing off as trees and shrubs grow to maturity and bricks and stone weather. The milling crowds of people, which the critics once found so lacking, are now there. They, the people of the town, are the real judges, and for the most part they are well satisfied.

The future is unpredictable. Some of the older houses are already out of date. Those now being built will be out of date within another twenty years. The Parker Morris standards provide no more than the minimum which people of today have a right to expect, but, as David Eversley has pointed out,[31] they are not luxurious. They leave little or no margin for a spare bedroom, sickness, quiet or study or for a teenager to invite his friends in for a record session without involving the whole family. Shean McConnell goes even further and asserts that in our present egalitarian society everybody will soon be demanding the standards at present enjoyed by the professional classes. 'Thus,' he says, 'this generation has no ultimate justification for building houses that will be rejected by the next generation but one.'[32]

He may well be right, but it is a counsel of perfection. The trouble is that it is this generation, not the next generation but one, that has to foot the bill.

9. JOBS

IT was fundamental to the idea of new towns that they should be 'self-contained and balanced communities for work and living'. This phrase was written into the terms of reference of the Reith Committee[1] and has been repeated in all the explanatory documents issued from the Ministry when the towns were designated. 'Self-contained' meant that people who lived there would have jobs there and all the necessary shops and other facilities. 'Balanced communities' meant that all sorts of people would live in the town, from managers to unskilled labourers.

The pre-war experience of the large out-county housing estates, from which many people were expected to travel back to London to work, had long since been recognized as a mistake. The additional rents and fares—small though they seem by today's levels—forced many to give up their new houses and move back into the crowded cities. In those days local authorities built just houses and the occasional shop, with little or no provision for employment. The huge pre-war L.C.C. estate at Dagenham was rescued almost at the eleventh hour by Ford's decision to open a car factory.

Single industry towns, too, were no longer acceptable. The lesson of the thirties, with extensive unemployment in the basic industries in times of slump, had shown the need for variety and stability of employment and this was the aim of all the new towns. Even Corby, built primarily to serve the needs of the rapidly growing steel industry which Stewarts & Lloyds established in 1930, and Peterlee where the object was to provide better living and social conditions for the miners in the surrounding decaying villages, were planned from the outset to provide other types of work for women and for those no longer able to work in heavy industry or in the pits or who chose other employment. But these were special cases because the major industry was already there. The 'overspill' towns were starting from scratch and had to provide new jobs for the new population, with variety and a suitable balance for men and women.

In practice, the conception was much too tight. Jobs are not kept specially for new town people. A man who takes a job does not have to live in the town. Nor does he lose his job if he moves away or lose his house if he changes his job. Many of the new towns have become regional centres of employment and some of them have a great deal of other employment within easy travelling distance. The returns for the 1961 census and the 1966 sample census show a somewhat complicated pattern of cross-journeys. They vary with each town but in most of the towns there is a certain amount of travelling in and out to work; yet despite the good railway services the number who go back to work in London is very small.[2]

No development corporation can predict the extent to which this cross-movement will arise. At the outset they can only assume that it will be marginal—as in fact it has so far proved to be—and that the basic objects will be achieved if there are at least enough jobs to match the population's need for employment and enough houses for all who choose to live in the town.

The paper calculations to achieve this balance are carefully made. In a town of a given number of people of average family size there will eventually be a need for so many jobs for men and so many jobs for women. About one-third of these, particularly for women, will be in the shops and services but the main employment will be in manufacturing industry. An average density of employment inside factories, shops or offices can be assumed and after allowance has been made for roads, landscaping, car parks, and other services an estimate can be made of the number of workers per acre. From this data a decision can be taken about the amount of land needed for employment and the rate at which building should take place to keep in line with the growth of population. A suitable area is then selected, preferably on reasonably level land, with good access to road and rail facilities, sufficiently away from the housing areas to avoid nuisance but sufficiently near for easy travel from home to work.

This, at any rate, is the basic theory. In practice there are several local factors to be taken into account. In a town where industry is already established on a substantial scale, either in the town or near by, the estimates have to be adjusted. Density of employment is difficult to predict. It varies with each industry and at the outset the corporations do not know what firms will come. They have to work on averages. Some years ago 200 sq ft of factory space per worker and employment of fifty workers per acre were reasonable assumptions but nowadays it is thought safer to take about 300 sq ft per worker and 20–30 persons per acre. These figures are a startling comparison with the four hundred workers an acre common in many an old factory area. They reflect the effect of automation, the need for more car parking and the preference these days for single-storey factories which are usually more economical in terms of production but need far more land. Some corporations have built 'flatted' factories which have proved satisfactory for certain small firms. Future developments in these and other fields may well have a greater effect in years to come and the development corporations must therefore allow a margin in their calculations, erring on the safe side by reserving too much land for industry rather than too little.

The next step is to get the industry; and here some of the development corporations ran into difficulties. In the early days few industrialists really believed in new towns; and even when a firm began to show an interest the Board of Trade immediately tried to persuade them to go elsewhere—to the north-east, South Wales, Scotland, Northern Ireland, anywhere but the south-east where there were no unemployment problems looming up.

As in so many other aspects of post-war policy, both these difficulties were rooted, in their different ways, in memories of the thirties. From the industrialists' point of view, business was highly competitive. Distribution costs were an important factor and with London the main market for consumer goods new industries in pre-war days had been stringing out along the Great West Road and other main traffic arteries. Many held the view that it was economic ruin to prevent building on land worth thousands an acre for industrial use and any firm foolish enough to open a factory in the middle of the green fields of

Sussex, Berkshire, Hertfordshire, or Essex, with all the capital expenditure involved, was flying in the face of hallowed economic laws. Transport costs would rocket, labour would be unobtainable, bankruptcy would result. New towns would never be built; they were just another crazy groundnuts scheme.

To the Board of Trade, memory of the unemployment in the thirties was uppermost. The Barlow Commission[3] had taken volumes of evidence on the subject of the pre-war surge from the depressed areas to the south and Midlands in search of work and had stressed the importance of control over the location of industry. One of the first steps taken by the post-war Labour Government was to pass the Location of Industry Act 1946, under which new factory building of more than five thousand square feet can be prevented by the Board of Trade if in their view it is not consistent with employment needs. A planning application to build a factory is invalid unless the Board of Trade (now the Ministry of Technology) have first issued an Industrial Development Certificate.[4]

This, however, was the purely negative side. The task of getting industry to go to areas of unemployment was much more difficult and delicate. There were no powers of direction —only persuasion, financial inducement, and the threat of withholding permission entirely for anywhere but an acceptable site. To be allowed to build in London or the south-east an applicant had first to convince the Board of Trade that it would be quite impossible for him to operate in any of the areas of existing or threatened unemployment. But then the wider planning issues came into the picture. The size of a town or city depends on the jobs it provides and if the spread of London was to be halted, a green belt preserved, and overcrowding eliminated, industrial development could not be allowed to go on spreading out on the fringes. The object of the eight new towns near London was to provide an alternative and the industrial sites on offer there were about the only places within forty miles of London for which both a planning permission and, in suitable circumstances, an industrial development certificate could be obtained.

It was not a popular process. There were the usual

protests about red tape and stifling controls. The more enlightened industrialists, however, recognized the simple fact that socially, economically, and politically, a return to pre-war conditions would hold for them dangers far more serious than the gentle but firm control over industrial location.

The Board of Trade have operated the controls with remarkable success. Since 1946 close on a million jobs have been provided in the development areas and in the Board of Trade's Industrial Estates in the north of England and in Scotland and Wales. But to the new towns in the Midlands and south of England there have been frustrating moments when they were desperately in need of more industrial development and found, as it appeared to them, the Board of Trade working against them. Harlow, among others, protested at this 'grievous handicap'.[5] The whole building programme of a new town must be geared to the rate of industrial growth and millions of pounds can be wasted if roads, water, sewerage, houses, schools, shops, and services are built and are not then fully used. The overheads quickly mount up if the land they make available for development cannot be brought quickly into profitable use.

The Public Accounts Committee were very concerned about the financial effect of this rigid policy and in 1950, after examining the Board of Trade representative, expressed the hope that favourable consideration would be given to applications from firms willing to go to new towns and thus help to create a sound basis for their future development.[6] The subsequent Treasury minute assured the Committee that every effort was made to find suitable industrial undertakings able and willing to go to the new towns[7] and for a time it seems that policy was relaxed somewhat. At any rate, the industrial areas of most of the new towns near London began to develop at a healthy rate and the corporations were soon able to be very selective in their choice of firms.

More recently it seemed the policy was again tightening up, although officially there was no change and Government spokesmen consistently gave the same answer. In November 1967 Robert Mellish told the House of Commons that the development areas were still the first priority and that new towns ranked second.[8] He added encouragingly that 'as long as there is a population requiring jobs, jobs will no doubt be available and industrial development certificates will no doubt be available as required.' But this was little help to a development corporation that must build the houses for the people who will come to fill the jobs when the industry is there. Sir Harmar Nicholls, the Member of Parliament for Peterborough, raised the question again in the debates of 1969, but received from the Minister exactly the same answer and the usual vague assurances that 'new town considerations are taken fully into account.'[9]

A much more positive assurance was given, however, after the Hunt Committee's Report[10] had been considered by the Government. This committee was set up to consider certain aspects of industrial policy, and their report recommended that control should be discontinued over moves of industry to overspill towns. This the Government felt unable to accept. They said again that the development areas and the new 'intermediate areas' set up in the light of the report would still have general priority; but they went a good deal further than before by adding 'we do see the need for a more flexible policy for such moves where planned development may be held up if the flow of industry to overspill towns from an exporting area is impeded. It certainly is our intention,' Peter Shore assured the House, 'that all approved schemes for new and expanding towns should be properly supported by employment opportunities.'[11]

This seems to go a long way towards accepting the oft-repeated argument that a Government decision to build a new town should carry with it the obligation to grant a steady flow of industrial development certificates to ensure that the programme of building can match houses with jobs. On the other hand, it is clearly important to give priority to those in immediate need of work in preference to those who merely want to move house or change jobs. This conflict can never be resolved so long as the volume of national industrial expansion is insufficient to meet both needs. Some argue that it is unsound policy to force firms to go to areas that are unattractive in order to provide work and that it would be better to bring the unemployed to the jobs.

Fortunately for the London new towns, they were started at a time when new industries were beginning to emerge, when new firms were being established to exploit for peacetime purposes the technical advances of the war years, and when old-established industries were having to modernize their methods, re-equip with new machinery, find larger premises, and rebuild their labour force. The rearmament programme of the early fifties also involved large defence contracts for which new factories were needed and many of these went to the new towns.

The men and women returning from the Forces provided just the types needed. During the war many of them had gained valuable experience in electronics and other new fields. They were also foot-loose and those living in overcrowded conditions were only too anxious to move anywhere that offered a good job and a decent house.

To those setting up in business for the first time the new towns were particularly attractive. Factory costs were very much cheaper than elsewhere. A lease could be taken of land if they wished to build their own factory but the development corporation were willing to bear the cost of building and a new modern factory could be rented for a very moderate sum, thus leaving the available capital for production equipment. Room could be left to enlarge the factory when the need arose or a start could be made in a small factory with the intention of arranging for a new building on a selected site later on if and when the business flourished.

Frequently it was found that small industrial concerns were willing to come to the town if immediate possession of a factory could be offered but would not wait twelve months or more for a purpose-built factory. The development corporations therefore built small standard factories as a speculation, capable of subdivision or amalgamation to give whatever size an applicant needed. By building in advance of demand the corporations run the risk of finding no takers and gambling with public money is always open to criticism if it doesn't come off. In 1969 the

Comptroller and Auditor General drew attention to a deficit at Cumbernauld, where half a million square feet of factory space remained unlet for some time.[12] In the early days, however, it certainly proved a wise move. Many now highly successful industrial concerns started in one of these standard factories.

Room to modernize and expand was equally important for some of the old-established firms that were operating in out-of-date premises in London, hemmed in by other buildings and, because of the housing shortage, unable to recruit new work-people. In the new towns—and indeed only in the new towns—both problems could be solved.

Gradually, therefore, demand increased. The reassurance given by the publication of the Master Plans, the building of the first houses, the laying-out of the industrial area and the start of factory building—these added up to an encouraging picture even for hard-headed businessmen. The first response came from firms needing room to expand or reorganize who moved to a new town lock, stock, and barrel with most of their employees. The distinction of being the first falls to the Central Tool & Equipment Company, which moved from London to Hemel Hempstead in October 1950. W. C. Young-man Ltd. and A.P.V. Co. Ltd. from Wandsworth opened their new factories at Crawley in 1951; and Harold Mac-millan laid a commemorative stone when the Bay Tree Press moved to Stevenage in July 1952.

They were small beginnings, but from then on the pace quickened. It was by no means a flood, but it was adequate. Some towns got off to a slower start than others, but by the end of 1954 nearly six million square feet of factory space was either built or being built for two hundred different firms and the towns were by then attracting some large and important national concerns. No less than six hundred firms showed an interest in Crawley in the first few years but many were unable to get the support of the Board of Trade and the building licensing authorities. In some cases protracted negotiations re-sulted in an agreement that the firm would also open a new works in an area of unemployment as the price of allowing them to open in a new town. Ford's tractor factory at Basildon and their large new works at Halewood on Merseyside were one such package deal.

Almost without exception the new town industries flourished and each year the firms gave to the development corporations their estimate of the number of additional workpeople they expected to engage so that the house-building programme could keep in step. But the 'little slump' of 1956 upset most of the calculations. New workers were not needed on the scale expected and many of the houses built remained unlet. In Crawley, particularly, several hundred houses were vacant through lack of jobs in the town. Fortunately Gatwick Airport was being built close by and although Crawley was not intended to cater for these needs arrangements were made to let or sell the surplus of houses to airport employees. Other towns cut back their housing programmes.

Then, quite suddenly, the economic situation improved and industry was once more clamouring for houses for their workers. But once a housing programme has lost its momentum it takes many months to recover. The development corporations, too, were now casting a wary eye at the unduly optimistic estimates of some of the industrialists and for some years afterwards the supply of houses was, in most towns, running behind the number of jobs available. It meant a waiting period of several months before a new employee could move into the town. Meanwhile he had to live in digs or travel to the town each day. This had some advantages, however. The waiting period demonstrated serious intention to stay in the job and prevented people from taking a new job for a few weeks in order to qualify for a house and then going back to their old job. But there was no serious danger of this. With the exception perhaps of a few specialist trades, rates of pay in London are not appreciably higher than in the new towns. Travelling is expensive and takes up a lot of time. It holds no attractions whatever compared with the advantages of living close to the job in a new house at a moderate rent and working in a modern building in well-laid-out and landscaped surroundings.

There were some set-backs, of course, notably when the cancellation in the early sixties of the Government contracts on 'Blue Water' and 'Blue Streak' gave rise to fears of widespread redundancies at Stevenage and Bracknell. As it turned out, there was no shortage of jobs in the area and those affected were soon absorbed into other work. But quite a few took jobs at that time in the motor industry at Luton, some miles away, and no longer work in the town in which they live.

The early provincial new towns were in a different position from the 'overspill' towns because they were designed to serve established industrial centres. Some other industry was needed to give wider choice of jobs and to provide work for women but this was not so urgent and the success or failure of the town did not turn, as it did for the London new towns, on whether industry chose to go there.

At Corby, for example, almost the only employment in the town in 1948 was in the Stewarts & Lloyds steel works. The heavy industries are usually the first to be hit by a trade recession and the possibility of a slump in steel production led to suggestions on more than one occasion that the town ought to be greatly increased in size, with a much wider variety of industry to act as a cushion against unemployment in steel. But for this to be effective the size of the town would have to be increased fourfold. Two practical reasons made this impossible. First, the town was surrounded by reserves of ironstone-bearing land and if this were taken for building, the steel works themselves would cease production. Second, the road and rail connections made Corby relatively unattractive at that time to the general run of light industry. From the national economic view it was not a place into which to pour much additional capacity. The most that Corby could hope for was a modest amount of light industry to provide some employment for women.

By 1964, however, Corby had successfully attracted a number of industrial concerns and was thought sufficiently near London to take some of London's overspill. Moreover, the setting up of the Ironstone Restoration Fund[13] had made it possible to insist that the land should be levelled after ironstone working, instead of being left in the hill-and-dale state which Hugh Dalton described as 'resembling the mountains of the moon'. Experiments had shown that the restored land could

E

be used for building after a suitable period and this opened up big new opportunities for arranging a carefully phased programme of excavation, restoration, consolidation, and building. It was therefore decided to increase the size of the town and the new plan now envisages an eventual population of at least 80,000 and several thousand additional jobs.

Peterlee, based on the Durham coalfields, was in a similar position. It is a smaller town and off the main traffic routes. Other industry has been very slow to come but more land has now been made available and latest reports from the corporation are more optimistic.

Aycliffe, also in County Durham, adjoins the Board of Trade's Industrial Estate, which was a royal ordnance factory built during the war. When the war was over it was decided to convert it for peacetime production and the object of the new town was to provide houses for the employees. The industrial estate has grown considerably in recent years and the town is now being increased to cater for a total population of 45,000.

Glenrothes, too, had to adopt a completely new industrial policy when in 1959, ten years after it was designated, the £14 million coal-mine built to work the Rothes coal seams, had to be abandoned and the town was given the changed role of helping to take overspill from Glasgow. The development corporation had to set out to attract industry on a large scale, which they have now done with considerable success; but one of the projects they encouraged to the town was the ill-fated pig breeding establishment which it had been hoped would provide substantial employment openings as well as a new outlet for Scotland's farm produce. The project collapsed unfortunately before it had started, but not before the development corporation had spent three-quarters of a million pounds building the factory.[14] Fortunately, the corporation were able to convert the piggeries into twenty small factory units and eventually let them for ordinary industrial purposes.

In the areas of high unemployment special Government grants or allowances are given to industrialists in order to encourage new industries[15] and the new towns in the north of England and in Scotland and Wales that come within these areas, or take overspill from them,[16] are managing to get a reasonably steady flow of industry. But some of the new towns now starting outside the development areas are finding it difficult to get any new industry that meets with the Board of Trade's approval and a situation is developing very similar to the position in 1951. The programme at Telford, for example, has been badly hit, though Redditch, also a Birmingham overspill town, is faring better. At Cwmbran, the chances of getting industry into the town were for a time said to be negligible, even though industrial sites were on offer, because the boundary of the development area stopped short at the new town boundary. Now the town is within one of the new 'intermediate areas' and prospects have improved. Most of the London new towns, of course, have become very lively growth points and for many years have had to turn away applicants. Some firms have expanded to the limit of the space available and when they seek to build larger factories on a new site in the town the Board of Trade now try to persuade *them* to move 'up north'.

In all the towns there are the usual jobs available in the shops, local government, and public or private services. The other possible field of employment is office work. Most factories have a small number of office staff but the large office organizations were slow to come for the very simple reason that they need substantial clerical, typing, and secretarial staff, and for many years these were just not available. Most of the children in the town were born there and until they reached school-leaving age almost the only demand for office employment was from wives, most of whom had family ties.

The long-term needs spelt caution. The statisticians had been busy assembling information about age-grouping and birth-rates and it soon became clear that a steady flow of jobs would be wanted for many years ahead as the children grew up and the population increased. In a typical new town near London there were only a few score of children leaving school each year in the fifties, but by the sixties this number would rise sharply, and it was estimated that over a thousand boys and girls would be looking for jobs each year for many years to come. Some of these would go on to university, some would enter the professions, but the great majority would be wanting jobs in the town. Not all would opt to go into industry. The education standards in the new towns are high, the percentage who stay on after the age of fifteen is well above the national average, and many of the children who do leave at fifteen are taking advanced courses in the new technical colleges. In industry there are still far too few training or apprenticeship schemes. Efforts are now being made to improve the position but if these youngsters are to be encouraged to enter industry they must be offered something much better than an unskilled or semi-skilled job with few prospects.

Anticipating this need for more office employment in the later years, the development corporations earmarked some key sites. The demand coincided too with the drive to limit the amount of office building in London. The Location of Offices Bureau was set up in 1963 to encourage organizations to move away and in 1965 the Labour Government made new office building in congested areas subject to an Office Development Permit from the Board of Trade.[17] Permits for offices in new towns were usually readily given, and from less than half a million square feet in the first ten years a further three million were built in the second decade. One of the largest single firms to move from London is probably Kodak who, in addition to a million square feet of factory and warehouse space, are moving their head office into a new 350,000 sq ft nineteen-storey building at Hemel Hempstead. Several branches of Government departments have also moved out into the new towns as part of the programme of decentralization. The office building programme will need to go on for many years yet, side by side with further industrial building, as the new generation grows up.

An employer is free to employ whom he likes. Jobs are not kept specially for new town people. The only limitation is on the allocation of houses. In the towns near London rented houses are normally available only to people working in the town who come from London, preference being given to those in housing need. Exceptions are made for employees of large concerns with branches in various parts of the country where interchange of staff must clearly be allowed. So, too, with public servants who are transferred to work in the town, such as teachers, local government employees, civil servants, and hospital staff. An exception is also made for specialist staff or key workers needed for particular jobs. They can be offered houses in the new town but only if a suitable recruit cannot be found in the London area. The same principles apply to the other 'overspill' towns such as Skelmersdale and Runcorn, which are designed to relieve overcrowding in the Liverpool area, Telford and Redditch near Birmingham, and Cumbernauld and East Kilbride near Glasgow.

These arrangements for ensuring that a town fulfils its function of relieving congestion in the overcrowded cities are made through the Department of Employment and Productivity who are in close touch with the various housing authorities. Lists are kept of people, with their qualifications, who have said they would like a job in a new town. Employers notify the Department of Employment of vacancies they are unable to fill from local sources and are given names of suitable candidates from the lists, with priority for those in housing need. Although these arrangements—called Industrial Selection Schemes—sound complicated they do in fact work smoothly.[18]

However expertly the calculations are made, the future is not fully predictable. Automation, computer services, intensified use of plant, doubling or trebling of shifts—these and many other factors, quite apart from changes in the pattern of world trade, can quickly upset the carefully prepared time-table, and adjustments must be made to meet changing needs. The planned development of a new town is just as important in the later period of growth as in the early days—indeed more important because, though the pace is slower, it will go on for so much longer. It may well be another thirty years before age-distribution settles down to something approaching the national pattern and the town has finally achieved the objective of a self-contained and balanced community. Until then it will be neither 'normal' nor 'complete'.

Looking back over the years at some of the early difficulties it is perhaps fair comment to say that the new towns have been luckier than they deserved. They were set up as an act of faith, in the hope rather than the expectation that jobs would follow, that the economy would expand, and that industry would move on a sufficient scale from its old-established areas. A dozen or more large and flourishing industrial and commercial centres have now come into being without any national economic strategy to point the way and without any serious analysis of the overall production needs or potential.

Whether the luck will hold for later new towns, and the many other growth points now to be established, remains to be seen. It is sometimes said that people will go where there are jobs and jobs will go where there are people, but it is not quite so simple as that. Much of our stock of industrial equipment is tied to fixed points and must continue to be manned. And even though the population is increasing in numbers, it is also ageing and the working population may soon be declining.

Here, then, we must pause and take stock. The scope for new industry in new centres is not unlimited. The Department of Local Government and Regional Planning and the various Regional Advisory Committees are now tackling these problems seriously and the South-East Economic Planning Council is urging the need for a policy that places less emphasis on the development areas and more emphasis on the overall distribution of industry to meet national employment needs. Slowly—far too slowly some would say—we are moving towards a national organization of our productive resources that must form the essential basis for the much needed improvement in both our standards of living and our industrial efficiency. In this the new-towns programme is playing an important part; but to build new homes for another twenty million people without planning also the national economic future would be pushing the luck too far.

10. SHOPS

THE best-known features of the new towns are their main shopping centres. The first all-pedestrian centre in Europe was built at Stevenage and immediately hit the world headlines. It was a particularly courageous step because it represented a complete break with tradition and was carried through in the face of strong opposition from retailers and dire warnings from estate management experts. In fact, it rapidly became a success both commercially and financially and was hailed as a significant advance in planning thought. The main principles have since been followed in countless development or redevelopment schemes both in Britain and abroad.

The new town development corporations can plan and build shops but they cannot sell goods. Retail trade in Britain is essentially a field for private enterprise, although there is also a strong co-operative movement which has shops in most towns. Retailing is also a very specialized and highly competitive business in which tradition dies hard. The new towns must therefore rely for their success on attracting the main national retail organizations. If the plan for the shopping centre does not match up to their needs and they refuse to come, the public will suffer through inadequate service and the centre will fail in its purpose.

In pre-war times, the shopping areas of the old towns had just grown over the years. As population increased it became profitable to open new shops—often by converting a house— and the shopping area gradually extended in each direction along the main road to make up the traditional 'high street' of the smaller towns. They are flourishing trading centres but the congestion of both people and traffic today has given rise to problems that can only be solved—if they can be solved at all— at enormous expense.

A new town cannot be built in that way. The right variety of shops must be provided and the right number the population at any given time can support. They must be distributed around the town in a way that best serves the convenience of the people. The facilities needed to attract the customers and enable them to shop in comfort must be thought out in advance. There must be enough competition to ensure choice for the shopper and efficient service; but if there are too many shops, or too many of any one trade, it may lead to bankruptcies and loss of rent.

As a first step, therefore, a development corporation must make an estimate of the total sales space and storage space that will be needed when the town is fully built. There may be competing centres near by—even those up to twenty miles away can have an effect—and allowance must be made for this. On the other hand, a new shopping centre will be used by people living well outside the town and this 'catchment area' must be carefully examined and taken into account. These estimates demand a close knowledge of modern retail methods, the special problems of each type of trade, and the changing shopping habits of the public. All types of business must be encouraged into the centre—the national firms with branches throughout the country, the supermarkets, the co-ops, the small trader, and the type of shop that gives a valuable service but cannot afford the high rents of the key shopping positions.

This is a highly complicated technique. Detailed formulae, such as Reilly's Law of Retail Gravitation,[1] have been in use for many years for measuring the pull of rival shopping centres and calculating the amount of shopping space a given population can support; and most of the large retail organizations have their own standards and their own methods for judging trading possibilities and selecting sites before opening new branches. But these are directed in the main to areas of existing population and to the individual shop. In a new town the calculations must be made before the population arrives and they have to be based on predictions of what the situation will be many years ahead. A major error could lead to serious losses.

Pre-war experience was a dangerous guide in these matters because retailing methods and shopping habits were rapidly changing. The Reith Committee had suggested that one shop would be needed for every 100–150 persons[2] but this begged a lot of questions and the estate advisers in the new towns had to devise a new technique. In the early days there was little to go on, apart from professional judgement based on past experience, but a lot of valuable data has now been assembled, including studies of hundreds of older towns, and the Master Plans now being drawn up have a much more sophisticated approach.

Conditions vary from place to place. There is no one accepted method or formula that can be applied to all new towns. Reliable information is however available about how much people earn and how they spend their money, and the total amount of retail sales to be expected from a given population in a given area can be calculated with some precision. Estimates can thus be made of the sales per square foot of shop floor space and the amount of space required for each main branch of retail trade. Decisions can then be taken on the distribution of shops in the town and the amount of land to be reserved.

In addition to the central shopping area, most of the towns have provided a small shopping centre in each neighbourhood—sometimes more than one—consisting of some fifteen or twenty shops that cater for day-to-day needs: the butcher, baker, grocer, chemist, newsagent–tobacconist–confectioner, and so on. The number and types of shop are carefully controlled. These small centres usually have a pub as well, sometimes a church and a community hall.

Some corporations were attracted by the idea of 'round-the-corner' shops at various places in the town—the general store that not only sells almost everything and is often open for long hours but also knows everything that is going on. They act as a sort of social focus. There is one in every village and there is one in most of the older areas of every town and city community. The difficulty in a new town is that if there are too many of them there is not enough trade left for the group of neighbourhood shops that serve a wider area. So most development corporations have preferred to concentrate on the shops in the neighbourhood centre, planning them so that they are within reasonably easy reach of all the houses they are designed to serve and limiting the range of goods they sell to avoid duplicating the more extensive service provided by the town centre.

Provision must be made, too, for the many other trades and services that may not need ordinary shop premises such as the small builder and decorator, shoe repairer, carpenter and joiner, furniture remover, garage repair workshop, and taxi service. They do not need expensive central sites or prominent positions but they have to be readily accessible to customers and not too close to houses to cause disturbance.

The central shopping area caters mainly, but not entirely, for the durable goods. Here, in key positions, are to be found most of the nationally famous stores such as Boots, Woolworths, Littlewoods, Sainsbury, W. H. Smith, the multiple tailoring, footwear, fashion, and furnishing trades, the local co-operative society and one or two of the supermarket chains. But the small trader is also catered for, including particularly the trader who was in business before the new town started. Many of them had to leave their old shops to make room for new development or chose to move into the new centre and take advantage of the greatly increased trading possibilities.

It was the design and layout, rather than the amount of shopping space in new towns, that gave rise to most of the early discussion and controversy. Back in the thirties and forties the narrow shopping street, with shops on both sides and milling traffic and people, was regarded as the ideal. This is what traders wanted and shoppers were used to. Delivery vans and shoppers with cars must be able to pull up outside and the best sites were by the bus stops. This indeed is what the Reith Committee in effect recommended. But they added that 'the objections to wide streets and squares might not necessarily apply in a properly planned town', that 'shopping streets for pedestrians only are a possibility' and that a rear access road should be provided.[3] Here was a broad hint that changes ought at least to be considered. But the pressure to continue the traditional pattern was strong. The retail trade interests at that time were very emphatic that the traditional shopping street must stay, with continuous shops on both sides, and that local traffic and buses must not be excluded. Shopping arcades with pedestrian access only and the grouping of shops round open spaces or squares were severely frowned on. Even continuous canopies to protect shoppers from the weather found no favour.[4]

But by this time the planners were beginning to question some of the old tenets. Delivery of goods through the main public entrance of a shop was clearly absurd. The old shopping streets rarely had more than one access but in a new town all loading and unloading could readily be arranged from the rear. Space could also be provided for parking delivery vans and perhaps the cars of the shop manager and his staff. In many an old shopping street these latter take up all the kerbside parking space before the shops even open.

The traditional concentration of value by the bus stops was also open to question. It arose only because people had to congregate round them from necessity, not from choice, and so long as the buses could bring people into a central bus station there was no reason for having stopping places outside any one shop.

Shopping by car was a growing habit, particularly as home delivery was becoming more and more uneconomic. But in the old shopping streets cars were already causing such congestion that shoppers were going away because there was nowhere to stop. They would be encouraged to use the new town centres only if they could be sure of a place to park. The Reith Committee had said that shoppers 'will naturally wish to drive to the shop door and not to a car park'[3] but it soon became clear that this would rarely be possible. Large numbers of cars prowling round a shopping area looking for a spare place at the kerbside only add to the congestion. In a busy centre with mothers and children and prams the ordinary pavements are quite inadequate and to have cars and buses stopping and starting is a particularly dangerous hazard.

A central shopping area that concentrates particularly on 'comparison' goods, rather than the day-to-day needs, requires plenty of display space, an opportunity for 'window shopping' and time for the shopper to walk round at leisure, protected by canopies against the weather, in order to compare goods and prices before making a choice. The mile-long shopping street is ill-suited to these needs and traffic is a distraction rather than a help. The piazza, the town square, or the market place used to be so much more efficient and compact, with all the shops within easy reach and the people mixing together. It focused attention on the important central feature of a town in a way that a street can never do.

Slowly and hesitantly, therefore, new ideas took shape. But the opposition was strong. The first town to get off the mark was Hemel Hempstead where two alternative outline plans were prepared for the new centre, one straddling the valley in a compact square, the other down the valley in a long street. After much discussion and pressure from the Ministry—at that time among the strongest supporters of the Multiple Shops Federation in their opposition to any serious departure from tradition—the long street won and the opportunity to build a really modern centre at Hemel Hempstead was lost for ever. Admittedly there were other difficulties. The topography made the long street easier and cheaper. A lot of occupied houses and other property had to be demolished and the corporation were anxious not to disturb more people than was absolutely necessary. Local opinion at that time was generally in favour of a new High Street like the old one they were used to. The Hemel Hempstead centre is redeemed by the small squares running off the main street, by the Bank Close and in particular by the now famous water gardens. This pleasant stretch of water, with shrubs, trees, and nesting swans a few steps from the shops and the traffic, was made from the narrow stream that runs through the valley. It was designed by G. A. Jellicoe and owes much to the imagination of Sir Henry Wells who was for many years chairman of the development corporation.

Some of the other London towns, fearful of driving away the big national retail organizations, compromised by combining traffic roads with squares and some all-pedestrian shopping ways running off them. Crawley is a good example of this, with traffic and parking places along one side of the large open area of Queen's Square. The whole square could easily be made all-pedestrian and this is being tried as an experiment for a day or two a week, but it is not welcomed by the traders or indeed by all the shoppers because it means closing some very convenient parking places. To alter the design of a centre after it has been built is bound to give rise to problems.

At Harlow and Basildon, too, similar compromises were

made, combining traffic roads with pedestrian streets and concourses. But all these new centres were a departure from tradition and paved the way for further progress elsewhere.

To Stevenage goes the proud distinction of forcing the change. Their all-pedestrian main shopping centre was for many years one of the most photographed places in Britain and it marked the turning-point in the long battle of ideas. But it was touch and go. The opposition was strong and the project was at one time abandoned. 'Many enquiries were made of experts,' the corporation said in their Seventh Annual Report, 'and it seemed to be the general view that the exclusion of vehicular traffic from the shopping centre might well depress the letting value of sites in the early years. Reluctantly, therefore, the corporation decided in favour of a vehicular centre.'[5]

But local opinion then took a hand. The County Council, Urban District Council and local bodies representing residents all came out strongly in favour of keeping vehicles out of the shopping centre. Only the retail trades organizations were against it. With the appointment as chairman in 1953 of Sir Royden Dash, who had been the Government's Chief Valuer for many years, the corporation had second thoughts and eventually came down in favour of a pedestrian centre, despite the possible loss of rent. Even more surprisingly the Ministry, despite the continued opposition of the retailers' organizations, gave their approval. By 1958, with the first hundred shops built, the corporation were able to report that 'traders had overcome any qualms they may have had over the trading prospects of a pedestrian shopping centre. The rents obtained show that a pedestrian precinct does not adversely affect values.'[6]

In some of the older new towns the decision to increase the population targets has given an opportunity to redesign the centre on more modern lines. Bracknell, for example, when building for a population of only 25,000 had retained the old high street and merely built an additional street of modern shops, linking the two with a pedestrian way. The new plan for a population of 60,000 involves demolition of all the old shops and the creation of a centre that will probably be one of the best current examples of new town planning and design. A similar opportunity arose at Corby when the decision to expand the population to 80,000 made it possible to plan a larger shopping centre on up-to-date lines. A model of the new centre was tested in a wind tunnel to make sure of maximum protection from wind and rain.

There is an immense variety of ideas in the new towns and the central areas are all different. There is no fixed pattern but they have all in their way contributed something of value to this new field of planning thought. It is the town centre of Cumbernauld, however, that has really become a second focus of world-wide interest. This Scottish town on a windswept hill, designed for 70,000 people from Glasgow, brought a new dimension to town centre planning. Apart from a few 'round-the-corner' shops—one per three hundred persons—all facilities are to be concentrated in a £15 million multi-deck building reminiscent of a luxury liner. The buses and cars are stowed away at ground level, where there are also facilities for goods deliveries; and from there escalators, lifts, stairs, and ramps lead up to the several decks with shops, restaurant, bars, hotel, offices, library, health centre, community hall, eventually a swimming pool and possibly an indoor sports hall. On the top sun deck, with views over the surrounding countryside, are a number of two-room flats.

It is, of course, much more than a shopping centre—as indeed are all the new town central areas. The whole range of town facilities and local government services will be concentrated on this mammoth half-mile-long structure, with the object, as the corporation explained, of 'maintaining a lively atmosphere when the shops and offices close'. It won the Reynold's Memorial Award in 1967 for community architecture and was described as the 'town centre designed for the millennium'.[7]

So far, only the first part of this ambitious and controversial project has been built and it will take many years to complete; but already it has been acclaimed in professional circles the world over. Whether it will fulfil its high promise in terms of a better community life, whether mothers will take kindly to pushing prams up the long ramps, whether, with its rough grey concrete and lack of trees and grass, it will bear comparison with the lively colouring of other town centres and, above all, whether the high cost of building and maintenance will ever be fully met from rents—all these are questions that will not be answered for many years. But it is certainly a fascinating and inspiring achievement and if the number of people milling around, particularly in the evening, is any guide, it is already proving successful as a social focus.

Short of the millennium—and perhaps not even then—the Cumbernauld experiment is unlikely to be followed elsewhere. It was partly determined by topography but more important it represented a revolt against the whole idea of separate 'neighbourhood planning'. Towns need unifying, not splitting up. But this does not necessarily mean a complicated, expensive, and somewhat bewildering structure; and the high-density housing to ensure that no family is more than three-quarters of a mile from the shops—an unduly long way by most new town standards—would not be readily accepted in the south. Other new towns will draw on the Cumbernauld experience and may well adopt some of the philosophy, but the plans for the towns now starting suggest that a more simple approach is likely. But simple is a relative word. Any new town centre nowadays is bound to be a complex affair. For example, the £8 million shopping and commercial centre at Runcorn, designed by Arthur Ling and Lloyd Roche, and being built in co-operation with Grosvenor Estates Ltd., will be wholly under cover, with a pedestrian shopping deck across the valley served by a rapid public transport service. The comprehensive design includes civic, entertainment, and office buildings. Indeed, the emphasis now is on comprehensive design of a complete and integral centre covering far more than shops. The proposals at Skelmersdale are for a £17 million centre with covered walks and internal squares, half a million square feet of shopping space, offices, and a sports and leisure hall linked to the civic library and county college.

Most development corporations have been anxious to encourage the 'department store' but in this they have not met with much success. The multi-storey building with numerous departments selling a wide variety of goods normally needs a much wider field of custom than a population of seventy thousand or so and even in the new towns with a catchment area of a quarter of a million people or more, the leading firms have so far shown no eagerness to open. The popular Marks and Spencer's store also for many years resisted all attempts to persuade them to open branches in the new towns, but they changed their policy in 1968 and arranged to build in several of the London new towns.

At the other end of the scale, the open-stall 'market' on one or two days of the week has proved popular and adds life and gaiety to the town. Although the local authorities have power to establish permanent markets[8] it has usually been left to the development corporations to provide stalls and other equipment on a temporary basis. This helps in the early days before all the shops are built and the markets usually remain popular long after the new centre is finished. But they need careful management to avoid the untidiness—almost squalor—of the litter left behind at the end of the day in most street markets for somebody else to clear up.

A development corporation has to be wary, however, before setting up any stalls. Markets of this sort are a long-standing tradition in Britain and in many of the older towns they were originally started under special charters granted by the King centuries ago. Often the document itself cannot now be traced and is merely presumed because the market has been going for as long as anybody can remember. These charters, however, gave protection from rivals and if, within about seven miles of a new town, there is such a market—even though it be only a fair held once a year—a development corporation can find themselves in trouble if they set up any form of street trading. The reason for the seven miles is lost in the mists of history, and some authorities say the right distance is $6\frac{2}{3}$ miles, 5 miles, or even less. Before the present statute mile was introduced in the sixteenth century there was the English mile of 6,600 feet and the London mile of only 5,000 feet. Bracton, who wrote his learned legal treatises in the thirteenth century, sought to justify $6\frac{2}{3}$ London miles as being one-third of a day's journey, which he put at 20 miles. This left a third of the day for business and the other third for getting home.[9] But it seems rather thin and specious, and there is just as likely to be some more colourful justification, such as the distance a farmer's wife could drive a goose to the fair.

As long ago as 1884 one of the Law Lords commented that 'these market franchises, however wise and suitable they may have been centuries ago, are unsuited to modern times and exigencies'.[10] They are even more irrelevant today, but they can still prevent a market from being set up in a new town.

In some of the new towns themselves there are ancient charters granting the right to hold fairs, and the development corporations and local authorities encourage their use, even if only as a social occasion. But inheriting a fair has its problems too. It was 400 years ago that Elizabeth I granted to Corby, then a tiny village, the right to have a one-day fair once every twenty years, to exact a toll from the people entering the parish on that day, and to clap in the stocks any refusing to pay. When the fair was last held in 1962 ten thousand people came along, and the real difficulty foreseen for the next time in 1982 is to find a site large enough.

Another feature sometimes found in the early days of a new town is the 'travelling shop'. It is usually welcomed by the housewife, particularly as shops cannot be opened until there are enough people in the area to give a worthwhile trade. The development corporations have mixed feelings about them. They can carry only a limited range of goods and can never provide the full service of a neighbourhood shopping centre, but if they become too popular they capture enough of the custom to discourage the ordinary trader and it is then even longer before proper shops can be opened. Some development corporations have solved this problem by arranging with a trader that he will take a tenancy of a shop when it is built and will operate a travelling shop until then. In this way he builds up a goodwill in the area which helps when he comes to establish his permanent business.

A criticism sometimes made of the new town shopping centres is that there are few 'high quality' shops. This comment is heard mainly in the towns near London and generally from those in the higher income groups.[11] It is true that there are no

Savile Row tailors, no Fortnum & Mason, no Heals, and indeed rarely anything in the range between those exceptionally high standards and the mass-produced products of the chain stores. Some of the smaller shops offer a wider range and more personal service and firms such as Boots and W. H. Smith offer the same goods as can be bought in any of their branches; but apart from these, the general tone and character of the shopping is much the same as that found in any industrial town throughout the country. The retail trading organizations are very skilled at judging their markets, estimating the amount people are willing and able to spend and the type of goods they want. They have to cater for the bulk of these predominantly young populations. The relatively few customers who demand specialized products can get them in the big cities or sometimes in the old-established towns near by.

What the future holds for new town shopping centres is difficult to say. Gillian Pain asserted even as late as 1967 that the 'methods of assessing shopping needs in this country are as yet primitive and unscientific'.[12] This may be fair comment; but for good or ill the development corporations had to work within the best advice then available from their professional staff and consultants. If the rising income from rents, the popularity of the shopping centres and the few trading failures are any guide to results, the new towns can reasonably claim a high degree of success. Most of them attract custom from many miles around. If anything the towns have too few shops rather than too many for the volume of trade and the catchment area served. This can be adjusted in the central areas, as and when the need for more shops is proved, because space has been left for further building as the population increases. The neighbourhood centres, on the other hand, designed to serve a known number of families, are fully built up. Tenancies change from time to time, new trades can be brought in if necessary and sometimes shops can be increased in size by rear extensions. But requests for more shops can rarely be met because there is now just not room.

Although, architecturally, the shopping centres of the early new towns are not particularly outstanding, they have the important merit of being built as a comprehensive unit.

Some of the shops were built by the development corporations and some were built by the traders themselves, but they all fit in with an overall design. The size and style of shop-fronts and fascia boards are not necessarily uniform. They allow for the special needs of traders, some of whom have a distinctive style that is well known throughout the country; but at the same time care is taken to see the overall impression is one of harmony and not of discord.

Inside the shop and in his display windows the trader has complete freedom.[13] This has at times been criticized on the grounds that the new trends in advertising can produce a garish effect on an otherwise colourful and attractive shopping area. Shops are not built to glorify the architects but it can drive them near to distraction—and some of the customers too—to see the carefully designed elevations plastered with large notices of sixpence off this or fourpence off that. Whether this is a necessary feature of supermarket retailing is open to argument. The convenience of shoppers, efficient and economic management and a suitable profit margin are the dominant factors. Towns must learn to accommodate themselves to these changes in retailing methods; and in time, perhaps, retailers themselves will find their name and reputation advertisement enough.

It is barely ten years since the all-pedestrian shopping centre was hailed as a revolution, but already new philosophies are emerging. Towns will be bigger. Transport problems are being examined in much greater detail. The shopping pattern for a city region or linear town of the future may well be completely different again. The former emphasis on the centre, where trade and values would be concentrated, is losing its force under the impact of traffic needs. More and better neighbourhood shops are now seen as a means of reducing central congestion. If the out-of-town shopping precinct, on the American pattern, is adopted in Britain, the town centres of the future, instead of being primarily devoted to retail trade, may become just a focal point for civic, cultural, and entertainment activities and with many more people living in the centre than is possible now. In the world of today the one certain thing is that ideas do not stand still.

11. SERVICES

A HOUSE to live in, a job of work, shops for daily needs—these are the basic elements. But a score of supporting services must be woven into the fabric of a town to create a full pattern of living. The development corporations can provide very few of these. They do not usurp the functions of the local authorities, hospital boards, water, gas, electricity, railway, postal, telephone, and other public bodies who all remain responsible for providing their numerous services. But the development corporation must make land available, negotiate with the organizations concerned and, because timing is all-important, coordinate the work throughout the whole building programme so that the services are ready when people move into the town.

Settling the priorities, particularly when money is short, is not easy. Many of the services are discretionary, not obligatory, and endless discussion can go on about whether the new town should have priority over older towns, many of whom need greatly improved facilities. Government money is involved too, either directly, as in the case of trunk roads and hospitals, or through the Exchequer subsidies to local authorities. The total amount available for each service is limited and the priorities often have to be settled in Whitehall rather than locally. The development corporations have no power to insist and many—indeed most—of the complaints and criticism in new towns arise from delay in getting the full range of services that in the cities, where most of the people come from, is taken for granted.

In some things, however, the development corporations can take the initiative. The first jobs to be tackled before any building can start are water supply and drainage. The existing services may be adequate for a year or two but completely new systems are usually needed to cope with the eventual population of the town. Normally this is the job of the authorities in the area but a small district council or water undertaking cannot be expected to finance work on this scale. It is very expensive; and as it has to be done well in advance of any building it can be many years before there is a corresponding increase in the local authority's income from the local rates.

To meet this situation the New Towns Act enables the Minister to give the development corporation special powers.[1] They can then do all the work, borrowing the money from the Ministry and carrying the loan charges and running costs on the development corporation's accounts. When the local authority or statutory water undertaking are ready to take over the responsibility—and this may be ten or fifteen years later— the whole system can be transferred to them at an agreed figure.

In the early days several of the corporations had to bear the cost of bringing water supplies to the town, but in the last twenty years many of the former small companies have been amalgamated into more efficient units, backed by better sources of supply, and these are usually able to supply the new towns without difficulty.

Sewerage and surface water drainage are even more expensive. Most corporations have had to build a new sewerage system and disposal works and although eventually the undertaking is transferred to the local authority at a negotiated price, it is usually round about 'half the written down cost'. This presumably reflects the 50 per cent Government grant normally paid towards the cost of sewerage schemes in rural areas, but in the case of new towns there is no grant. The loss on the transfer has to be borne by the development corporation.

The work itself is usually a straightforward and uncontroversial engineering job dictated mainly by the natural fall of the land towards rivers into which the surface water and purified effluent from the sewage works can be discharged. Only Basildon—a difficult and costly enough town for other reasons—ran into real trouble. The natural drainage of four-fifths of the area was towards the River Crouch; the other one-fifth to the Thames. But when proposals were drawn up for disposal to the Crouch an anguished howl went up. The oyster beds at the mouth of the river would be utterly destroyed.

At first it seemed to the development corporation that there must be a misunderstanding. They explained that there was no danger of river pollution; a very modern sewerage disposal works would be built, and the effluent would be the purest of pure water. But this, it turned out, was the trouble. The Crouch is a saline river, and that is how the oysters like it. To pour in several millions of gallons a day of pure water would freshen it up too much. The oysters would languish and refuse to breed.

Most of Britain's oyster beds are owned by the Crown Commissioners. The Minister of Agriculture, Fisheries and Food has to protect the nation's food supplies and the fishing industry. Oysters, too, are a flourishing export and several Government departments were concerned in those early days after the war with the balance of payments. With such a formidable opposition it was clear that oysters were more important than sewerage for a town of 80,000 people. In the end the Basildon Development Corporation had to arrange the whole of their drainage into the Thames. It involved bringing miners from Wales to drive a tunnel 70 ft deep and the cost went up from about £850,000 to £1¼ million.

The towns to the north-east of London had other troubles. It was known when Harlow and Stevenage were designated that sewerage would be difficult and indeed one of the points made in the Court action against Lewis Silkin was that he had acted almost irresponsibly in designating Stevenage before a solution had been found. The objection did not carry much weight in the Court of Appeal because the problem was clearly capable of solution. It was merely a matter of technical investigation and weighing up the merits of the various possibilities.

The only river available to take the effluent was the River Lee, but this was one of the sources of London's water. Already it was heavily polluted because the sewerage facilities over a very large area had never properly kept up with the growing population and were in pretty poor shape. The consulting engineers recommended a large new disposal works at Rye Meads, near Hoddesdon, which would serve Harlow, Stevenage, Welwyn Garden City, Hatfield, and many of the older towns and villages in the Lee Basin—an expensive operation that would include thirteen miles of trunk sewer from Stevenage. Moreover, it would mean bringing in many local authorities who were unable or unwilling to bear any of the cost. The Hertfordshire County Council turned down the Minister's suggestion that they should promote a Bill in Parliament to make them the sewerage authority for the whole area and finally, after many months of fruitless discussion, the Harlow and Stevenage Development Corporations were given powers jointly to build and operate a new works at Rye Meads. The eventual cost will be about £7 million and although many local authorities were required to connect to the new system and to make appropriate annual payments, there was for a long time a heavy deficit. Over the first eleven years it added up to nearly £½ million but from 1963 onwards there has been a surplus of up to £68,000 a year.

The future of these works is still undecided. They cannot be transferred to the local authority by a simple Ministerial order under the New Towns Act because they serve a much wider area. A special Act of Parliament will eventually be needed. Meanwhile, the Stevenage and Harlow Corporations continue to run the works jointly—and not without some troubles, as when an unauthorized trade effluent upset the chemical process in the digestion tanks. For some weeks, until the source of the effluent was eventually traced to a firm in Welwyn Garden City, lorry loads of crude sludge had to be carted away to the Thames marshes, much to the annoyance of some of the towns through which the lorries had to pass.

The new road system for the town is the third basic need that has to be provided before much building can be started. There are two types of road. The ordinary streets are built and paid for by the corporation and the local authority then adopt them as public roads and become responsible for maintaining them. But new towns need also a 'main' road system to bring traffic into, around, and out of the town. This can be done partly by improving existing main roads and partly by building new ones and, as neither would usually have been necessary but for the new town, it is reasonable for the development corporation to have to pay. On the other hand, most of these roads link up with the main road system of the country and have a traffic value well beyond the needs of the town. They have therefore to be wider and of a higher standard than the town itself would need; roundabouts, bridges, or special junctions may be required; and access and building on the frontage have to be severely limited in the interests of traffic safety. These matters are the responsibility of either the county council as highway authority or the Ministry of Transport who, until 1967, made grants to the county councils of 75 per cent of the cost of Class I roads, 60 per cent for Class II roads, and 50 per cent for Class III roads.

Out of this complicated tangle of interests came a decision that the cost of building main roads in new towns should be shared; but then the question was 'how and in what proportions?' There is nothing in the New Towns Act about it. Numerous highway authorities and development corporations were involved and attempts to get agreement on a uniform policy failed completely. Quite early on, the Stevenage Corporation negotiated an agreement with the Hertfordshire County Council under which, broadly, the development corporation paid the cost appropriate to an ordinary new town road and the Council, with the aid of the standard Exchequer grants, paid the additional cost of building to the higher standards needed for through-traffic purposes. It was hoped that this precedent would be adopted for all the towns but other county councils felt unable to agree and each corporation had to negotiate separately.

As a result widely differing methods were adopted. In the case of Corby the Northampton County Council readily undertook the necessary road works and asked for very small contributions from the development corporation. Essex County Council, on the other hand, took the view that the whole cost of these roads should properly fall on the new town but after many years of negotiation finally agreed to make a 25 per cent contribution—a settlement which the corporation accepted with reluctance.[2] Other counties adopted the formula worked out for Stevenage but with numerous modifications all of which had to be negotiated at length and approved by the Government departments. Some corporations had to bear the whole cost of many of the new roads. Eventually the money has to come from public funds of one sort or another but the quibbling about which pocket it should come from can take up a lot of time. The details are now mainly of historical interest, however, because since 1 April 1967 the system of classifying roads has been dropped and direct grants from the Ministry of Transport are now paid only in respect of work on 'Principal' roads—broadly the old Class I roads.[3] The cost of other road works is covered by the general 'rate support' grant, which deals with all rate-borne expenditure, and this new system will probably make it even more difficult to reach agreement on who should pay. The Ministry have been peculiarly reluctant to lay down a statutory formula or to take powers, as they can for sewerage costs, to settle the argument once and for all; although in the case of Peterborough they promised during the negotiations over designation that the development corporation would meet 85 per cent of the road costs.

Fortunately these arguments did not seriously hold up urgent road-building projects. The development corporation were usually allowed to do the work and leave the finances to be sorted out later. A much greater difficulty arose from the need to establish priorities in the Ministry of Transport's national programme. With so many new roads and road improvements wanted throughout the country, and with money very much restricted, it is very difficult to convince the Ministry that a road needed in a new town is more important than a long overdue improvement to ease the traffic chaos in Wigan or Wanstead or Wolverhampton. Only road works needed to open up land for immediate development are normally given any priority. This has sometimes meant building a road in separate sections, spread over many years and usually at a greater overall cost.

In the same way, because of the limits on capital expenditure, roads designed as dual carriageways were often built in the first instance as single carriageways. Land is reserved—and has to be grassed down and maintained—until the second carriageway is thought to be justified by the volume of traffic; and it then has to compete again in the scramble for priorities. Even after fifteen years or more there are many second carriageways still to be built and a growing apprehension that if they are too long delayed the cost will fall heavily on the local authorities or because of the many other calls for money for improvements they will never be completed to the standards required.

In recent years the position has been eased somewhat by making a separate block allocation of money for new town roads.[4] This avoids having to argue the respective urgency of road works in a new town and improvements in an old area, but it may still mean judging priorities as between one new town and another and the decision must in the end be taken in Whitehall. These new arrangements are, however, a great improvement and could well be extended to other fields such as education, hospitals, and civic buildings; even better would be full recognition that *all* new town expenditure must be looked at as a whole and cannot be subdivided into various categories to which different priority rules apply.

In the early days of a new town the county council have to spend a lot of money. They are bound to provide schools and this is one of the few services for which priority had to be given because of the large number of children. Some very fine schools and technical colleges have been built in the new towns and the important part played by the education authorities is rarely given the recognition it deserves. The Church authorities have also joined in the education programme and there are new Church of England and Catholic schools in most of the towns.

Fire, ambulance, police, library, and welfare services are also the county council's responsibility. Land is reserved and the council make their own arrangements for designing and putting up the buildings. Temporary accommodation is often necessary in the early days, particularly for such services as maternity and child welfare clinics.

Medical services have been rather a disappointment. Some are provided by the local authorities and some by the Department of Health through the Regional Hospital Boards. In the hospital building programme the new towns were given no priority over areas where needs were equally urgent, and despite the very high birth-rate—in some towns it was the highest in the country[5]—it was many years before even maternity facilities could be provided. Some towns, even after twenty years, are still waiting.[6]

Most of the towns reserved land at the outset for health centres. By the National Health Service Act 1946 local authorities were required to provide them and the Reith Committee assumed they would be built in all the new towns.[7] In fact, for many years the only ones built were through the generosity of the Nuffield Provincial Hospitals Trust which financed a diagnostic and health centre at Corby and later built a series of health centres at Harlow at a cost of over a quarter of a million pounds. The Trust also made grants to enable an Industrial Health Service to be established at Harlow. This service, of which Dr Stephen (now Lord) Taylor was for many years the Medical Director, is still in the experimental stage but is providing valuable experience that may one day lead to the acceptance on a wider scale of the need for improved medical care in the industrial sphere.[8]

The success of the Harlow schemes has been one of the factors responsible for the greatly increased interest now being shown in health centres. In the early years, general practitioners —medical and dental—were anxious enough to open practices in these new and growing communities, but for a long time there was no official encouragement for health centres, nor indeed was there much support for them in medical circles. This has always been a 'cottage industry'. Most doctors and dentists at that time preferred to rent or buy a house, which the development corporation could build for them, complete with surgery, and the corporations were powerless to do anything else. They are not dictators. They cannot solve national problems. In the absence of a general policy they had to take the only step open to them to get doctors and dentists into the town. However anxious they may have been to see a modern integrated service, with proper links with the hospital, health, and welfare services—in itself a complicated planning operation—they could do nothing about it so long as the G.P.s were against it, the local authorities were unco-operative, the Executive Councils and Regional Hospital Boards went their own different ways, the Ministry of Health sat on the fence and the Treasury said there was no money in the kitty.

The more forward-looking members of the medical professions now admit that a great opportunity was lost. The Harlow centres demonstrate in a small way what could have been done and it is a sad commentary that in one of the most vital of the social services, and in the context of one of the most advanced health services in the world, it was left to a charitable foundation to find the money and point the way.

The Office of Health Economics, in co-operation with the College of General Practitioners, held a two-day conference in 1966 to discuss a report on this subject prepared by Dr Dilane.[9] It amounted almost to an inquest on what went wrong in the new towns. There are still divided views in the medical profession but there are hopeful signs that the new towns just starting will be able to do better, now that improved financial arrangements have been made to cover rent and rates. The Ministry of Health have reported a 'considerable upsurge of interest in health centres' and expect some three hundred to be built in the next few years.[10] Some of the older new towns are now planning for a medical centre in areas of new development and the newer towns are already achieving a limited success. But many of the local doctors are still as much opposed now as they were in 1950 to any serious change and a building just for doctors and dentists can be little more than a group practice building if it is not linked with other welfare services.

District heating is another service on which progress has been disappointing. The building of a complete new town was expected to give an exceptional opportunity for comprehensive heating arrangements that could serve all the houses, shops, and factories on an economic basis. The Reith Committee's report included a special appendix on the subject[11] and most development corporations made their own investigations and commissioned special reports from experts. The Aycliffe Corporation even promoted a Private Bill in Parliament to give them additional powers for this purpose but their proposals made no progress in the House of Commons and were eventually rejected by the Ministry.[12] They were far too expensive. The rents for houses would have had to be increased substantially and for a town of miners, in those days far from well paid, this was out of the question. The Ministry at least had the grace to make a grant to the Corporation of the £8,700 they had spent on fees in preparing the scheme.

In more recent years there has been the occasional small scheme, such as the 420 houses at Brockles Mead in Harlow and the town centre at Cwmbran, but all the proposals so far examined for comprehensive district heating in new towns have been abandoned. Cost of installation and distribution, cost to the consumer, methods of metering and charging—one or other of these has always been, so far, an insuperable stumbling block. So even in these days of Parker Morris standards, with compulsory heating for at least the main living rooms, every house has to be equipped with its own individual appliance using either solid fuel, oil, gas, or electricity, and installed within the house itself.

Sir Donald Gibson, Controller-General at the Ministry of Public Building & Works, said recently that the cost of domestic heating could be reduced by nearly 50 per cent through the use of district heating. In Britain we are lagging well behind the rest of Europe in this field, despite the keen competition of the oil, coal, gas and electricity industries and the great technical advances that have been made in the years since the Reith Committee reported. 'It seems,' comments Anthony Tucker of *The Guardian*, 'that no man can escape the age in which he lives and adopt the vision which will eventually belong to some future age.'[13] There are hopes that at long last the new city of Milton Keynes will manage to find the key that will open up this new and vital stage in our national progress.

Gas and electricity services present little difficulty. The nationalized undertakings have readily extended their supplies or improved their facilities to meet the growing needs of the town. Postal and telephone services have sometimes lagged behind, particularly where new buildings and new equipment were needed, but in general the Post Office have kept up with, or more often caught up with, demand. Some corporations have succeeded in getting telephone cables placed underground; others tried some years back and decided it was too expensive. But times are changing and it is now fairly normal practice for telephones and other such services to be laid underground in the process of building. The newly appointed Washington Corporation have gone one further by negotiating an agreement with the Post Office for laying during development a twelve core co-axial cable that will give to every house telephone service, all television programmes, including colour, all B.B.C. radio programmes including local radio and still leave spare capacity for other services that may be developed in the years to come.[14] Similar arrangements are being negotiated in Craigavon and Livingstone, and the other new towns just starting can be expected to follow suit if the experiment proves successful.

The early new towns were started when television was in its infancy and before the unsightly crop of masts and aerials began to sprout from every roof-top in the country. Most new town houses are now wired from the start and many of the towns have arranged for the older houses to be similarly connected to a comprehensive relay system installed by one of the commercial companies. This avoids the need for external aerials on the chimneys—if there are any chimneys: new houses with central heating do not need them. Restrictions against individual aerials are not popular with some of the radio and TV dealers but a central distribution point is normal nowadays in new blocks of flats and under most systems the householder can choose his own set. New towns have led the way on this, and the difference in the appearance of an area with the usual battery of aerials and an area without them is so striking that wiring from some central signal point is almost certain to be adopted in future in all large-scale housing development.

Transport services vary somewhat in quality. Buses to the factories and schools at times of peak demand are good but during the rest of the day and during the evening services tend to be infrequent. The relatively low density in the towns and the limited demand result in a mileage/passenger ratio that for most transport companies can be wildly uneconomic, particularly in the early days before the population is large enough to support better services. The New Towns Act contains a special power for the development corporations to run trolley bus services but trolley buses went out of fashion years ago and the powers have never been used. New ideas are now coming along, such as monorails and special lanes for public transport vehicles. In the towns now being designed many changes may eventually be seen.

Train services are not a great problem because, apart from a few commuters, nobody needs them to get to work and industry mostly uses road transport. Most towns were already served by rail at the time of designation and have reserved land for a new station; but getting the stations built is a long job. Harlow and Crawley have managed to persuade British Railways to build new stations but proposals in the other towns are still no more than hopes for the future. At Corby the passenger line has been closed.

The list of 'services' is almost endless. Shop signs, street furniture, traffic and direction signs, car parks, telephone kiosks, seats, bus shelters, pillar-boxes, litter bins, the flower boxes in the town centre, the cutting of grass verges and the tending of trees and shrubs—each one, small though it may be in scale, must be part of the whole. Even outdoor advertising has a place, but there are none of the garish gable ends so familiar in older towns and rarely a hoarding except perhaps temporarily to conceal building work going on. Some towns have put up advertisement pillars on the continental style. They enliven the street scene but instead of advertising somebody's pills, paint, or petrol, they are more often information centres giving notice of what's on in the town.

Most of the new towns hoped to bring some order into the general chaos of street furniture and the hundreds of signs that are found in any busy street. The Hemel Hempstead Development Corporation called a meeting of the nine or ten authorities concerned and drew up a comprehensive plan for co-ordinating bus shelters, telephone kiosks, advertisement stands, pillar-boxes, newsvendors' kiosks, public notice-boards and scavenging bins. But the pattern that ultimately emerged showed little improvement. There were too many separate bodies, concluded A. W. Thomas, Chief Engineer of the development corporation, each of which had to act independently of the other. Special powers were needed to enforce co-operation and co-ordination.[15] Stuart Howgrave-Graham, Chief Architect for the Commission for the New Towns, despite considerable success in regard to shop signs and fascia boards, reached the same conclusion on street furniture, commenting that when the statutory authorities took over the normal British clutter began.[16] Even in the underground services, which have to be laid when the roads and other site works are being carried out and where maximum co-ordination and co-operation are needed, Roy Gazzard comments that even after a quarter of a century of new-town building, they are still being laid in separate trenches.[17]

There is little glamour in the many services needed in building a town but they bring into the job scores of people from the world outside the offices of the development corporation. All, in their various ways, have a part to play in solving the problems that arise in the process of integrating the answers to a thousand and one questions into a consistent and coherent whole.

A new town must be a whole town. It cannot be part-built. If the supporting services are not properly co-ordinated and if divergent policies or priorities are adopted by the other authorities or departments concerned, the town will fail in its purpose. This problem has bedevilled new towns from the start. Even Lord Reith, in his first report as Chairman of the Hemel Hempstead Development Corporation, confessed that he began to doubt whether the object of developing a balanced community could be 'more than an elusive but inspiring concept';[18] and in the development corporation's report ten years later the then chairman, Henry Wells, said: 'Not all the high hopes held in 1947 have been fulfilled. Government policy has prevented many desirable amenities and social attractions from being provided and traffic roads which should have been built remain lines on plans.'[19]

This is one of the lessons of experience that must be taken to heart if the new towns just starting are to achieve their full purpose. The Chairman of Milton Keynes, Lord Campbell of Eskan, made his position clear at a Press conference soon after his appointment, when he said: 'We are not prepared to build a second class city.' If Government placed restrictions on expenditure, he explained, the phasing of the building of the whole town would be slowed, rather than building an unbalanced town without the social and public buildings necessary to complement the housing.[20]

Yet these many services are still only the beginning. With them, people can eat, sleep, and work in reasonable comfort, but there are other things a town must have if the people are to enjoy a full social life and make the most of their leisure hours.

But this is a story in itself.

12. LEISURE

NEW towns are a fruitful field of inquiry for newspaper reporters and a source of constant interest among sociologists. There have probably been more door-step interviews in new towns than anywhere else in the country.

One of the cries so often reported a few years ago was—'There's nowhere to go and nothing to do!' If this is true the new towns have failed in their purpose. But how true is it? By what test can it be judged? Are the leisure facilities too few, or too late or are there perhaps too many of the wrong things and not enough of the right? How is it possible to find out what people want today and what they will want tomorrow or twenty years hence?

Most of the people who move into the new towns have come from the crowded cities. They have left behind an established community and a range of opportunities that was extensive and at the same time limited. Many of them were accustomed to a shortage of open space, a lack of sports clubs and public halls and a long journey to open country. But the bright lights were close at hand, with cinemas, dance halls, football grounds, pubs, and churches round the corner and theatres and restaurants a bus ride away.

No town of fifty or a hundred thousand people, whether old or new, can reproduce this pattern. A much larger population is needed to support extensive commercial entertainment, and in all provincial towns of this size people are thrown much more on their own resources.

For many, therefore, a move to a new town involves a new way of life. It means finding new interests, getting together with friends and neighbours, doing things rather than watching them being done, taking up new sports, learning the joys of the countryside and unleashing talents or interests that life in a city tends to suppress rather than encourage.

Moreover, a new town is not built overnight. Building must keep in step with the growth of population. It is fifteen or twenty years before the full range of facilities can be provided and the early new town dwellers become understandably impatient at the delay. More could have been done in the early years of the first new towns and probably would have been done had not successive financial crises and credit squeezes held up many important projects; but this only reinforces the case for a programme that settles priorities on a logical basis.

The development corporation's role in this, although limited, is an important one. They have to decide at the outset what land to reserve for specific purposes and then, when the time is ripe, negotiate with numerous other bodies concerned— local authorities, churches, brewers, commercial entertainment companies, and the like. The decision on when and what to build does not lie with the corporation: they can encourage but not dictate. They can offer some modest financial help to the local authorities and can let the churches have land at a cheap price; but they cannot help the other organizations and can give no guarantees of commercial success.

Inevitably, this is a long process, and something has to be done in the early years to encourage the beginnings of a social life. A place where people can meet together is essential. It need not be elaborate and costly—indeed if it is too large it defeats its object. In most new towns, therefore, the first step has been to build small community halls in each of the housing neighbourhoods. The development corporations were allowed to build these (provided they recovered the cost from the rents of the houses) on the view that it was a proper part of their housing function by analogy with the Housing Act 1936, which enabled housing authorities to build for social activities. This had been included in the 1936 Act to meet widespread criticism in the thirties that some of the local authorities had failed to provide any such facilities on the large housing estates.

In the early days there was no experience to go on and the development corporations had to work out their own ideas. Money, too, was short and the Ministry would only authorize the most modest of buildings. Some corporations put up small permanent halls which before long were found to be too small for the wide range of functions the people quickly organized.

Farmhouses and other large houses were pressed into service and, although costly to adapt and maintain, for a time made very useful meeting places. Crawley decided to put up temporary timber huts at the start on the view that with the money allowed they could get larger buildings that would serve for a time and the more permanent buildings could be designed in the light of the demand and experience. There was a good deal of criticism of these wooden huts and they certainly looked incongruous in the midst of modern neighbourhood centres; but they served their purpose, though it was fifteen years before a start was made on replacing them with permanent halls.

Some towns decided to build more elaborate community centres. A booklet issued by the Ministry of Education in 1945[1] had been strongly in favour of centres that would cater for all types and all tastes, and the Education Act of the previous year had laid on the local education authorities the responsibility of providing facilities not only for adult education but also for leisure-time activities. Few county councils have done much beyond the usual round of evening classes but some have been willing to play their part in building community centres in the new towns.

These centres are larger and more expensive than a simple meeting hall and because building community centres is the job of a local authority the development corporations were not allowed to build them. The county councils had to be willing to take over responsibility but the corporations and the district councils usually met part of the cost. Frequently the cost of the building was split three ways and the running costs, including the salary of a warden, were met by the county council. But councils vary in their policy. Some were unwilling to spend any money at all on community centres and in some towns a good deal of arguing went on and a lot of time went by before facilities of any sort were provided. Matters were not helped by frequent changes in policy governing the grants which the Ministry of Education could make towards the cost. For some years they were payable, then they were withdrawn; a few months later they were on again and a few years later they were abolished altogether. No local authority can be expected to agree to a forward and worthwhile programme in such a state of uncertainty.

The high percentage of children in the new towns made it particularly important to consider the formation of youth clubs. Youth work has been the cinderella of the education service and many towns are still striving to get better facilities. County councils have to spend a lot on the schools and it needs strong action to overcome the reluctance of some of them to spend more money on youth clubs.

The development corporations can help, as many of them have, by adapting buildings; and where a good-sized house and grounds were available the enthusiasm and hard work of both youth leaders and young people soon turned them into a flourishing and well-equipped club. A notable example of this is 'The Breaks' at Hatfield—a large house and eight acres of land which the young people themselves maintain and to which they have added, largely by their own work, a new hall complete with stage and other equipment generously given by the de Havilland Aircraft Company. Their energetic warden, Bill Salmon, received an award in the Queen's Honours List of 1962 for his outstanding contribution to the youth services of the town.

Many of the churches run youth clubs and bodies such as the Scouts or Guides can usually get land from the development corporation at an almost nominal rent on which to build their own headquarters. One of the most imaginative ventures was at Crawley where amidst the trees of Tilgate Forest twenty-nine semi-derelict Nissen huts—a relic of the war—were made available to the clubs and other organizations in the town. They were repaired, adapted, decorated, and maintained by the clubs themselves and have been a flourishing centre of activity for many years now.

The need for leisure facilities is perhaps less important in the case of school-children because all the schools have generous playing-fields, gymnasia, and other equipment, and the popular Scouts, Guides, and other such bodies give ample scope for those who want to develop wider interests. More difficult is the problem of the teenagers searching for some form of satisfying activity. This is not peculiar to new towns but it is largely from this age-group that is heard the complaint that there is 'nothing to do'. The hundreds of adult clubs do not yet attract them—possibly do not yet welcome or encourage them—and the few that join a youth club find the clubs have little to offer for more than an hour or two a week.

With this problem looming up, the Calouste Gulbenkian Foundation appointed a committee in 1959 to investigate the Needs of Youth in Stevenage. Their report[2] came down firmly in favour of something more extensive and more sophisticated than the typical struggling youth club. 'In this age of breath-taking scientific and technical progress,' they pointed out, 'young people will not be attracted by anything shoddy, inefficient, or inadequate. . . . One cannot hope to hold their interest for long with second-hand billiard tables in a white-washed basement.'

One of the Committee's recommendations was the formation of a Youth Trust to raise money for building a large youth centre in the centre of the town. The Stevenage Development Corporation responded to the idea and the Trust which they sponsored set themselves a target of £100,000. In theory, youth clubs are the responsibility of the local authorities, but the setting up of an independent and non-statutory organization to build and run this centre resulted in contributions from many other sources. The development corporation were authorized by the Minister to give 10s. for every £1 subscribed from other sources, up to a maximum of £35,000, and the local authorities and the Ministry of Education also made a substantial grant. In the final result the Youth Centre was built and equipped on a much more lavish scale than would have been possible if the whole cost had had to be met from public funds. It can take 2,000 young people at a time and has been named 'Bowes-Lyon House' in memory of the late Sir David Bowes-Lyon who was the first Chairman of the Trust.

There is no one answer to the leisure problem. A youth club on the Stevenage lines meets a limited need during the few years of adolescence but youngsters have much wider interests that quickly merge with those of adults. Sports activities are a clear example. The Master Plans for the towns earmarked land on a generous scale for such purposes as parks, open spaces, and playing-fields[3] and the development corporations were able to buy the land and, in some cases, prepare the site before handing it over to the local authority, at a moderate price, to equip and run. Some of the more ambitious schemes such as Gloucester Park at Basildon and the Town Park at Harlow were slow in getting going and will take years to complete. The capital and day-to-day running costs fall mainly on the local authorities and there are limits to what the rates will stand. It just isn't possible to do everything at once.

Some of the larger industrial concerns in the new towns provided sports grounds for their staff. The idea is commendable enough in London but in the new towns it merely adds to the difficulty of creating an integrated community. People must be encouraged to mix rather than keep themselves segregated in the same factory groups as they work with all day long. Many of them indeed would prefer to do so. A survey by the Ministry of Housing revealed a fair body of opinion against sports grounds near the factories. If the money generously provided in this way by many industrial concerns could be pooled with the contributions from other sources, it could be used to much better effect.

In this, as in many other things, Harlow led the way. Refusing to be daunted by the cost and the plea of shortage of money, they decided in 1959 to set up a Harlow Sports Trust. Like the Stevenage Youth Trust it is a charitable body quite separate from the development corporation and the local councils; but it is supported by all the public authorities, the leaders of industry and the professions and, most important, by a very large number of people in the town.

A grant of £21,000 from the Wolfson National Playing Fields Association gave the Trust a flying start. Donations came in from firms and individuals in the town. A Supporters' Club was set up with collectors in almost every road, a 'penny a week' scheme was organized, collected with house-rents from those who volunteered to pay, grants came along from the Ministry of Education, the local authorities, the development corporation and the Building Industry Youth Trust, and the

149

contractors—Wimpeys—agreed to build at cost only. It is now one of the finest sports centres in the country costing, with its later extensions, some £250,000 and further additions are planned. In its thirty acres it includes playing pitches, a floodlit all-weather training area, tennis courts, bowling greens, a pavilion, and a 150 ft × 130 ft sports hall that can be used for twenty-five different sports. A new 18-hole golf course was recently added, landscaped around the winding Canons Brook and an old farmhouse has been adapted and equipped to form a magnificent club house.

The sports centre is open all day until nearly midnight, seven days a week. It is a constant hive of activity, and with its 7,000 membership and over a hundred clubs using it, it is already bursting at the seams. As the development corporation said in their Seventeenth Annual Report, 'a notable feature of Harlow is that there appears to be more players than spectators . . . a healthy reversal of the picture so often found elsewhere.'[4] The team work, the co-operation of the many authorities and voluntary organizations, the success in raising money and in capturing the imagination and support of the people of the town, make this sports centre an outstanding illustration of the enthusiasm that can be stirred into action in new towns in support of worthwhile projects.

The Gosling Stadium[5] at Welwyn Garden City also owes its existence to the far-sighted planning of the development corporation. In the very early days arrangements were made for the building contractors to tip their rubbish into a disused gravel pit on the fringe of the town so as to fashion an arena. Pitches, and cycling and running tracks were then put in at modest cost. Later stands, tennis courts, a pavilion, and a club house were added, a ski-slope was built in 1968 and further additions including squash courts are planned. The development corporation managed the stadium for some years and when it was well established handed it over to a specially formed club.

In some towns sports centres have been built by the local authorities, financed entirely from the rates or with modest contributions from other public authorities. These tend to be delayed because they depend for their timing on loan sanction from the Ministry and on the build-up of rateable value. Telford have ambitious plans for a £375,000 centre, to be paid for by the local authorities with help from the development corporation and the Wolfson Trust. It will include a 6,700 sq ft sports hall, swimming pools, social centres for both youths and adults, and in its twenty-eight acres will cater for athletics, tennis, riding, archery, shooting, and skiing. These many sports centres are making a much-needed addition to Britain's sports facilities and will certainly be extensively used for national and international events. A New Towns Festival of Sport, at which teams from the new towns compete, has now become an annual social function. It is interesting to note that in a pilot survey among youngsters at Basildon to find out what they wanted, a sports centre came second in their choice (a cinema coming first and a jazz club third) and a professional football team came fifteenth and last.[6] Denis Molyneux, Deputy Director of the Sports Council, also comments on the astonishing interest in sport and physical recreation and the latent demand waiting to be tapped when facilities are provided.[7] Private-enterprise organizations are beginning to recognize this. The projected £4 million Aquatel at Basildon is expected to include a 400-bed hotel, with a conference hall, a sports hall, facilities for sailing, fishing, and ice-skating, and an oceanarium complete with performing dolphins.

Successive credit squeezes in the fifties held up the building of new swimming baths for many years. It was not until about 1960 that they were allowed to go ahead and some very fine baths have now been built. But these again are the responsibility of the local authority: the development corporations can help with the design work and can contribute to the cost but they are not allowed to build them. The delay is particularly unfortunate in new towns because, unless there are other places near by, half a generation of youngsters can be deprived of the opportunity of learning to swim.

All these arrangements for the sports, whether indoor or outdoor, are very expensive and the Education Department are at long last supporting the idea that they should be combined with school facilities. Denis Howell, the Minister with special responsibility for sport, said in 1968 that for an extra cost of only £25,000 a school costing £500,000 could provide top rate facilities for the whole community and that a hundred such centres could be built every year.[8] This is a welcome acceptance of a policy that has long been advocated. In some towns separate sports centres were started only after failure to get the school facilities opened for wider public use at week-ends and during the holidays. This suggestion met with little encouragement at that time from the Ministry of Education, local education committees, school governors, headmasters, or caretakers. Admittedly there are problems about supervision and the wearing capacity of turf in some areas, but too often these are just excuses. The real difficulty is that both the design of the schools and the organization for running them are equipped to deal only with children. If wider use is intended, it must be catered for at the outset and this is what Denis Howell now suggests should be done. It is an indication, perhaps, that the Department of Education & Science are beginning to take seriously the responsibility laid down by the Education Act 1944 for providing educational and leisure facilities for adults. Already Glenrothes and Skelmersdale are working out with the education authorities a policy on these lines.

There is no reason why this new approach should be limited to sports facilities. In all the schools there is the usual run of 'evening classes', and clubs can hire rooms for meetings; but this approach to the problem, progressive though it might have been fifty years ago, is quite inadequate today. The late Henry Morris who, when he was Education Officer for Cambridgeshire, was responsible for founding the famous Cambridge Village Colleges, was for some years special adviser to the Minister on the social needs of new towns and constantly urged the need for 'adult wings' to be incorporated in the school design. Only one county council concerned with new towns—Monmouthshire—adopted the principle and on a limited scale, but it has added much, and at little expense, to the social life of Cwmbran. At Hemel Hempstead it was hailed as a major achievement when the plans for the Dacorum College of Further Education were altered to include full stage facilities, thus providing a town theatre at an additional cost of only £5,000, which was paid by the development corporation. Attempts to do the same in other towns failed.

In the teenage field the extended use of school and college equipment could be of particular importance. Those who go on to technical colleges or university are catered for, but many still leave school at 16. Up to that point they have all the facilities provided by a modern school—playing-fields, tennis courts, gymnasia, school clubs and the like—but the day they finish at school these facilities are denied them. No town can really afford to duplicate the expensive school equipment.

Some say the school-leavers wouldn't be interested, that they would dislike 'going back to school'. This has never been tested—though many a grammar school has old boys' clubs which flourish on school premises—and really depends on what the schools and colleges have to offer. In their report on Stevenage the Gulbenkian Committee noted a suggestion put to them

'that the new College of Further Education should provide accommodation for a College Club open to all young people irrespective of whether they were taking formal classes. The facilities of the College would be available to provide richer social, cultural and recreational opportunities than could readily be provided elsewhere. . . . In this way youth work could successfully achieve its rightful position as an integral part of a comprehensive centre of Further Education.'[9]

The Committee were considering only the youth aspect and the colleges, with students mainly in the younger age-groups, were the obvious place for an experiment on these lines. No specially designed buildings or equipment would be needed. The only limitation is the capacity for extended activities at a time when most of the colleges are already too small for the current purely educational demand.

New town youngsters, like new town adults, have their own ideas about what they want to do in their leisure time and not all want to join clubs. But if they do say, as many still do, that 'there's nowhere to go and nothing to do', the education authority must share the blame for not giving them access to the 'somewhere' and the 'something' that already exist in the towns. A little understanding and organization could well revolutionize almost overnight the so-called 'teenage problem'. A little foresight in designing new school and college facilities could quickly change for the better the whole pattern of social, cultural, and sporting activities throughout the country.

If money were unlimited—which it never is—separate buildings would no doubt be preferable. Emrys Williams considered the point in his report in 1963 on the arts in Stevenage[10] and came out against using school premises for adult activities. He recommended the building of a separate Arts Club at a cost of about £250,000 to 'house under one roof and in adequate premises all the groups and societies which are cultivating an appetite for the arts and for all the related creative activities'. This, he said, would weld together the many separate organizations and would 'give their achievements and aspirations a solidarity of purpose which they now lack'. Arts Trusts have now been formed at Stevenage and Harlow to raise money for centres on these lines and other new towns are following suit. The Cwmbran Development Corporation converted a large house near the town centre—Llantarnam Grange—at the modest cost of under £12,000.

Basildon, however, were not content to wait until they could raise the money for a new full-scale centre. The Urban District Council built temporary premises, at a cost of £100,000, which —as Lord Goodman, the Chairman of the Arts Council of Great Britain, pointed out when he opened it in September 1968—was the first to be built in this country since the war for the purpose of serving all the arts in one centre. Within months the Basildon Civic Arts Society were arranging a programme of astonishing variety, including a well-attended production of Molière's *Le Médecin malgré lui*—in French!

Of course nobody, whether teenager or adult, wants to spend all his leisure time in organized activity and it is the lack of commercial entertainment that causes most comment in the early days of a new town. This has been left to the commercial experts and they will not build or take premises until the population is large enough to give adequate support. Harlow partly met this problem by converting a factory into a temporary cinema until a new cinema was built seven years later in the town centre—the first to be built in Britain after the war. But the decline in recent years in cinema attendance is making it virtually impossible to get new ones built now unless, as is happening even in London, they can be incorporated in some other building and kept to a size that makes them economic.

Bowling alleys came suddenly into fashion about 1960 and they have now been built in most of the new towns. How long they will remain popular is unpredictable. Dance halls still attract many people. New lavish ones have been built by commercial firms at Stevenage and Crawley and in some towns there are dance halls and schools of dancing in the upper floors above the town centre shops.

The local authorities also cater for dances, concerts, and other functions in new central public halls. The demand for all-town meeting halls does not arise until a late stage in the building of a town—a hall to take a thousand dancers would be useless to the first hundred families—but some splendid halls have been incorporated in the groups of civic buildings. The £450,000 Pavilion at Hemel Hempstead, for example, is now a flourishing centre for many types of activity and is specially wired for TV shows. The award-winning million pound civic group at Corby, with its 400-seat theatre and other facilities, caters for functions of all types. The new Crawley town hall is widely used for social activity and an extension is to be built, when money is available, to include a theatre and concert hall. In the new towns in the north of England the traditional Working Men's Clubs have put up some very fine buildings, and these have become lively centres of entertainment. Sometimes amateur dramatic organizations take the initiative, as at Crawley, where there is a proposal to convert an historic thirteenth-century rectory barn into a theatre that will serve as a centre for amateur productions. The modest cost of £10,000 is to be raised partly by private subscription and partly by contributions from the public authorities.

One of the ambitions of every new town seems to be to have a theatre for professional productions. Interest in the live theatre is certainly increasing and some of the towns develop a following in the arts, an 'intellectual texture' as one writer puts it, that few older towns of similar size and character can match. But a population of a quarter of a million or more is needed to support a full-time repertory company and some other means will have to be found if these hopes are to be fulfilled. One suggestion which has the support of the Arts Council is the building in a number of new towns of small theatres with identical stage measurements so that the same props, scenery, and other equipment would fit them all. As a joint effort they could support a full-time repertory company if travelling distances were not too great and the theatres would be available at other times for a wider range of other uses, including amateur productions. Plans are in hand for building a theatre on these lines at Glenrothes in Scotland; and the New Midland Theatre Company, directed by Anthony Roye, has already established a circuit covering Corby, Loughborough, and Scunthorpe, based on the new theatre in the Corby Civic Centre. At Harlow the Urban District Council are setting up a £½ million Theatre Trust to build a Playhouse Centre, which, by arrangement with the British Film Institute and with the help of a £10,000 contribution from them, will also become a film centre.

But ventures in new towns are not confined to formal productions and organized activities. The 'Birdcage' at Harlow, started by the Urban District Council in the old Stonecross Hall, with dance floor, bars, and resident band, has been called an 'exciting night spot' and at Corby a discothèque, the 'Crow's Nest', was opened by Tommy Steele on behalf of Youth Ventures Ltd., a body sponsored by the Nuffield Trust. Riding stables, boatyards, water sports areas, golf courses, all find their way into a new town's programme if there is sufficient demand —and money.

The Church organizations have been very active in the new towns and pretty well every denomination and sect is represented. Land is made available by the development corporations at a very moderate price and, because leasehold tenure gives rise to legal difficulties on consecration, freeholds are granted where necessary. The buildings have to be paid for by the appropriate Church authority and this has sometimes led to a sharing of buildings and a welcome sinking of denominational differences. Some of the churches, too, have been designed so that the altar can be screened off and the building used as a church hall. The churches have played an important part in the development of the social life.

Public houses and hotels are now left to the brewers to build. When the new towns were started the intention was to operate a State management system on the lines of the Carlisle scheme but this was abolished by the Conservative Government in 1952[11] and a special licensing committee was set up in each town to decide the number of pubs needed and where they should be built. New hotels have been built in several towns and there is usually one pub in each neighbourhood and one or more in the town centre. Pubs are an important feature of English social life. A survey at Basildon in 1967 reported that all classes of people in the town patronize them and rated the 'frequency of participation' higher than any other activity.[12] One of the new pubs built at Hatfield—'Hilltop'—included a community hall. It was an experiment sponsored by Henry Morris[13] and carried through, but not without some very vocal opposition, with the co-operation of the brewers, McMullens of Hertford and the Guinness Company. The object was to demonstrate that the pub could be much more than a place for eating and drinking and that it could be again—as it once was in the old English villages—a centre for a much wider social life. Whether the high hopes of the sponsors have been realized is open to doubt.

No general account of progress in these many fields can do more than sketch in the highlights and touch on the problems. Some towns are better equipped than others; some have still a long way to go. Throughout the last twenty years shortage of money and arguments about who should pay have bedevilled this important aspect of new towns. But despite these troubles and frustrations the progress is there to be seen and in the older of the new towns there is now little justification for saying that amenities are neglected. That some of them came late cannot be denied; but it is equally true that many, particularly in the commercial field, could not have come earlier.

What has really been lacking, perhaps, is a coherent policy based on a real understanding of the needs of these new communities at the various stages of their development. All development corporations took the social aspects of their work seriously but in the early days few appointed experts to advise them. Indeed, there were few experts available. The Stevenage Corporation even took pride in disbanding their Social Development Department saying, in their Third Annual Report, that 'social development is not a thing apart and must be the direct concern of every one of the corporation's officers'.[14] Nobody would dispute the sentiment. But it still needs the touch of an expert to co-ordinate and guide the thought and action of the development corporation, the local authorities, and the people themselves, who are often looking for a lead and quickly respond when it is given. It needs more than a sociologist or a public relations expert or a statistician. It is a new profession, for which, so far, there has been insufficient recognition and very limited opportunities for training.

There has been an abundance of studies, reports, and surveys, some directed to particular towns, some to the wider problems. Universities, charitable foundations, Ministries, official committees, study groups, and many others have been thinking and writing about these problems for many years and the Arts Council and the recently established Sports Councils can give specialist advice and help. If heed is paid to the lessons of the past the new towns just starting will do better than the old towns for it is now accepted that the social aspects are an essential part of the overall strategy of development. A programme that keeps in step with the growth of population must be carefully drawn up, implemented, and adapted when necessary in the light of experience. The overlapping functions and shelving of responsibilities must somehow be got rid of. The whole financial basis needs urgent re-examination to avoid the constant haggling about money and to enable the programme to be achieved without an excessive burden on the local rates.[15] It must be recognized that special help and encouragement are needed if these new and struggling communities are to develop the richness of life that is essential to their success.

Yet nobody can lay down a blueprint for all corporations to follow. To some extent building for leisure must be guided by local experience and popular demand, but it must look ahead, not backwards. As Gerard Brooke Taylor pointed out in a special report prepared for the Commission for the New Towns,[16] the day of the parish hall is over and the educational emphasis—the measuring of success by the number of approved classes—is disappearing. 'Fashions and needs,' he says, 'are now changing at such a pace that public demand expressed today indicates what was needed yesterday. In the 1950s the public were slow to grasp the changing pattern of teenage behaviour. Commercial experts created the coffee bar as a venture into the unknown. And few people in 1953 would have asked for the bowling alley which later in the decade was to prove such an attraction. It was only a minority of young people who started the beat groups which later made millions and altered the basis of popular dancing and light music.'

A development corporation must attempt the impossible task of forecasting the leisure habits of many years ahead. Needs will vary as the age-groupings change or as new fashions emerge. But buildings are adaptable. The cinema can give place to bingo; the dance hall can house a symphony orchestra; the bowling alley can be re-equipped for other sports. Provided there is the right range of buildings, of the right size and in the right place—and the emphasis in future must be on more central facilities—the people will adapt the use and indeed themselves to the needs and opportunities offered.

For it is people, not buildings, that make a town.

13. PEOPLE

TOWNS are built for people to live in. A truism; but Aristotle thought it worth stating and it should hang over the desk of everybody concerned with the building and administration of new towns. Yet there is much more than desk-work involved. The development corporations and their staff must move about the town, meet people when they arrive, discuss problems with them and keep their ear close to the ground. A conscious effort is needed, a constant testing of consumer reaction, a sustained and fruitful contact with the people of the town and the organizations they set up.

But this comes later. In the early discussions about how the town is to be built, and who should pay for this or that, the development corporation do not know and cannot know much about the people they are planning for. However brilliant the Master Plan, however carefully future needs are calculated and past experience examined, the first step of a corporation must, quite simply, be to take a piece of land, build a few hundred houses and offer them to people from the right areas who manage to get a job in the town. A lot turns on the first few hundred families, the way they think, the way they act.

It is surprising how quickly the process of building a community starts. The very fact that the newcomers are all strangers to each other, paradoxically enough, makes it easier for them to break the ice and get together. They share the inevitable discomforts of a new area where roads are not yet complete, shops have not yet been built, public transport is non-existent, and the nearest 'local' may as yet be a long way from home. The gum-boot days of a new town are for the young and the sturdiest of pioneers.

The first step is usually to form a tenants' association, often for the purpose of urging the development corporation to remedy grievances and press on more quickly with the building programme. This is a move which the development corporations do not find unwelcome. It gives them their first real contact with the people for whom they are building, their first opportunity of finding out the aims and aspirations of the newcomers. And for the tenants it is often their first experience of getting together with their neighbours for organized action.

Their requests and suggestions cannot all be met at once. Many have to wait until the town has grown bigger. But there are other interests in life and the very lack of opportunity, the very lack of the entertainment-round-the-corner, stimulates activity. Horticultural societies are among the first to be formed, led by a few keen gardeners anxious and willing to help those facing for the first time the problem of creating a garden. Numerous other clubs and societies follow rapidly—bridge, chess, table tennis, women's organizations, dancing, drama groups, and a score of others—and these soon lead to the formation of a broadly based community association far more lively, far more effective, and far more comprehensive than is found in any older town or London suburb.

Community organization—not perhaps the most happy of phrases because of its undertones of regimentation and 'doing good'—is an important aspect of new-town development. The report of the Younghusband Committee summed it up as 'primarily aimed at helping people within a local community to identify social needs, to consider the most effective way of meeting them and to set about doing so in so far as their available resources permit.'[1] The staff of the development corporations—themselves usually among the early new town dwellers—play an active part in the build-up of community activity. Officers are appointed who are skilled in housing administration, public relations, and the development of social activities, and their job is to welcome new arrivals, cope with personal problems, help the rapidly developing clubs and societies on such matters as organization and finance, and advise the development corporation on the needs in terms of buildings, sports, and other facilities and the programme for carrying them out. Close contact with the local authorities is particularly important because they must play a major part by building up the welfare, education, and other such services on the scale required. But it isn't all left to official action. In some towns voluntary Councils of Social Service have been formed to act as a co-ordinating body and to sponsor, when necessary, new activities. Help can come, too, from unexpected quarters. At Skelmersdale, for example, it is the senior girls at the County Secondary School who hold coffee mornings to welcome the parents of children who have just moved into the town.[2]

Where a town is being built on a virgin site the early days are likely to be particularly difficult; but where an established community is being expanded the integration of the old and new populations has its problems. Certain essential facilities will already exist but it may be no easy task to persuade the old inhabitants to welcome the newcomers if they had opposed the new town and lost the battle.

Nevertheless, such are the quirks of human nature, it happens. A battle may be lost on a point of principle but the hostility rarely extends to the individuals involved. The late Ernest Stanford in his series of articles on the early days at Crawley[3] commented that many who vigorously opposed the town had since played a prominent part in building up the community and the social and business life. And the Mayor of Hemel Hempstead said in 1957, 'There is a far greater sense of unity between the various communities of the Borough than there ever was before the new town started.'[4]

There are exceptions, of course. There are those who can never reconcile themselves to change. At a meeting in Hemel Hempstead in 1967 one of the older residents is reported as saying, 'I represent Old Hemel Hempstead. . . . The new-towners came down here from dusty smoky London and we absorbed them into our culture. But they don't know the minds of us country people.' This after the town had been established for twenty years and when half the inhabitants had been born there. This attitude is, fortunately, rare; but it's understandable. The old-towners have seen their way of life disrupted and a new one, not of their making, imposed on them. The new-towners, on the other hand, have created the new life for themselves. If they suffer from nostalgia at all, it is for the bright city lights they have left behind.

In the important task of building a community, the quality of leadership that emerges is all-important. Much depends on the personality of the General Manager of the development corporation and of his key staff. They must not seek to run people's lives or tell them what to do; but tact, understanding, a willing ear, a readiness to meet legitimate grievances and to identify themselves both with the hopes of the newcomers and the fears of the old-towners—these are essential if a co-operative, constructive leadership is to emerge and the new community is to get off to a flying start. But the main drive must come from the people—old-towners and new-towners alike. The leaders they select can, by their skill and devotion and by their capacity to influence others, exercise a profound effect on the eventual life of the town. The attitudes of the members and officers of the local council and of the local Press are particularly important. They can make or mar the atmosphere—and it is atmosphere, the feel of the place, the undercurrents, that count for so much.

Harlow is a good illustration of the results achieved by lively leadership. In the early days a few enthusiasts started a musical society which soon attracted a strong following. Very quickly the town became known for its musical interest and as early as 1959 they were able to mount a performance by the London Philharmonic, conducted by Sir Adrian Boult. When, a few years later, Derrick Knight was making the film *The Faces of Harlow* he was particularly struck by the musical talent in the town and soon afterwards the B.B.C. commissioned a special film called *The Pied Piper of Harlow*,[5] devoted entirely to this aspect. The social and cultural achievement of some of the new towns is far removed from the beer and bingo that dominate so much of suburban life today.

Of course, there is beer and bingo too; and it would be idle to pretend that every new-towner throws himself into a welter of community and cultural activity. A much higher percentage actively participates than in most of the older towns but there are still many—the large majority maybe—who are content to stay at home with the family, watch the telly, dig the garden, go out for the occasional ride in the car, make a trip to London or visit the cinema or theatre. There are those, too, who prefer entertainment in their own homes, the evening with friends, the game of cards or the record session. There is room for all tastes.

There is room, too, for all sorts of people and development corporations aim at attracting a wide cross-section. It is not easy to get a house in a new town. To qualify one must usually have a job in the town and as the new industries are predominantly modern and well organized the percentage of highly skilled workers is above the national average.

Sometimes an old-established factory in a crowded area will decide to move lock, stock, and barrel into a new town and any of the existing employees who are willing to move can be allotted a house without difficulty. But many of the industries are new ventures needing new staff. They can only be sure that their new employees will be offered houses if they recruit them through the Industrial Selection Scheme[6] but the recruitment can come from a very wide area—any part of Greater London in the case of the towns near London—and for certain key posts may come from anywhere in the country or even abroad. In some towns the exceptions have amounted to some 20 per cent of the total, which means that the 'overspill' purpose of the new town is being achieved to the tune of 80 per cent.

In addition to taking people from the congested inner London area, the new towns were encouraged to help the outer London authorities, many of whom, because of shortage of land or for other reasons, could not meet the housing needs of their people. At one time each new town was linked with a particular part of London.[6] The towns in Hertfordshire looked primarily to the northern boroughs and urban districts, Crawley to those in the south west, Basildon to those in the east, etc. Among other things, this made possible a closer contact with the local authorities and by arrangement with the Borough Councils coach trips were organized of applicants on the housing lists who were interested in moving to the new town and wanted to see what it had to offer. But the arrangement only lasted a couple of years or so. It was an attractive idea to the London authorities faced with long lists of applicants for houses, but it proved much too narrow a basis for attracting industry and recruiting the right type of skilled workpeople.

There have been complaints that in the new towns catering for London overspill relatively few of the people were on a housing list of a local authority, and this is regarded in some quarters, particularly by the local authorities anxious to reduce their lengthy housing lists, as indicating that the town has failed in its purpose.

There are several answers to this. In the first place, anybody moving to a new town usually vacates a house or flat and thus adds to the number of houses available in the 'exporting' area for those in need. True, the local authority may have no control of a privately owned property, short of buying it themselves, and if it is let or sold to somebody from outside the area there is no population reduction. But at least it has prevented a population increase.

Second, few of the people at the top of a local authority's waiting list have the particular qualifications needed for the highly skilled jobs in a new town factory. Employment must depend on ability, not housing hardship, though more could and should be done through training schemes to give the unskilled a better chance.

Finally, many young people do not bother to put their names on a local authority housing list because they know there is a long waiting period and the 'points' system gives them little chance of a council house. The percentages are thus misleading if used to measure a new town's contribution to the housing problem as a whole. The success of a new town depends far more on its industrial and social prosperity than on housing list statistics. The fact that half a million people have moved away who would otherwise still be crowded into the metropolis speaks for itself.

If the towns are to be successful it is important that they should avoid any resemblance to the large one-class housing estates of the inter-war years and must attract all sorts of people. This takes time. There are many charming houses in the surrounding villages, all within an easy drive, for which a brisk and profitable market soon grew up from some of the more highly paid professional and executive staff in industry or commerce who preferred to live outside the new town. But as the town begins to take shape and the early difficulties and shortages are overcome, demand increases for more expensive houses or for plots on which purchasers can build to their own design. One important factor is the quality of the new town schools which can offer so much more than the average village school.

Most corporations started off with the intention of mixing the various types of houses and avoiding any suggestion of 'class segregation'. Lewis Silkin hoped this would happen. 'I do not want the better off people to go to the right and the less well off to go to the left,' he said when introducing the New Towns Bill. 'I want them to ask each other "Are you going my way?" '[7] But it didn't work out. Harlow, for example, soon found that 'middle-class families . . . like either to be somewhat isolated and to have big gardens or to have a large number of their neighbours drawn from similar income groups'.[8] And other corporations reported much the same experience.

To many this is a matter for regret because it seemed to represent the failure of a philosophy. But this does not necessarily follow, for people still mingle on equal terms in the town's activities. The executive director will readily appear on the stage with the factory worker in the local drama group production. When it comes to playing a violin it is ability that counts rather than job or income level. The women's and sports organizations cover the whole range of people in the town. The children mix on equal terms in the schools.

But when it comes to buying or renting a house—particularly buying—the personal preferences or prejudices take a hand. There are those who are willing to pay for seclusion, those who dislike living near council houses, those who buy not just because it is a better investment but because they regard renting a house as somewhat lowering their social status, those who choose a speculative builder's house—even at a higher price and lower standards—rather than buying or renting from a corporation that draws subsidy like any local authority; though many of the more expensive houses are in fact rented and the tenants may not even realize that their rent is subsidized.

It is no part of the job of the development corporations to change the pattern of British life—indeed, to be successful both financially and socially they must accommodate it. If the towns have, as some put it, developed their 'snob areas'—more so perhaps in the south than in the north—it is because that's the way people want it. The Reith Committee took the idea of a 'balanced community' to mean that 'so long as social classes exist, all must be represented in it.' They recognized that social distinctions and segregation by income groups would probably remain but stressed the importance, nevertheless, of creating a 'socially homogeneous community.'[9] This, most of the new towns can claim to have achieved both in the cross-section of their people, which compares reasonably well with the national average (see Fig. 1), and by the degree of participation of all sections of the community in the social, sporting, and cultural life of the town.

Some people see sinister implications in this social balance. Ruth Glass once suggested that it was a device for securing middle-class control under the guise of leadership, thus avoiding a threat to the established order.[10] This, surely, is naïve. Political power is not really exercised through the local community hall with its bingo, dances, and chess club.

B. J. Heraud has criticized the policy of building houses for owner-occupation on the grounds that, as they are often bought by professional and middle-class families, it does not relieve the overcrowded areas of their overspill population and deprives those in housing need of the chance of moving out. 'It seems to run counter to the social ends inherent in the original new towns idea,' he comments. 'In their desire to recruit at all costs a sizeable middle-class element the development corporations appear to have rejected certain aspects of policy and to have adapted to certain social and political pressures.'[11] And D. L. Foley terms it 'a sort of sidling sideways into policy.'[12]

There are misconceptions here. 'Overspill' is not necessarily synonymous with 'housing need.' If the object is to avoid building one-class housing estates there must be social balance. New towns are not just another housing operation. They are part of a national policy for getting a proper relationship between jobs and houses; and jobs must mean the whole range of employment in modern industry and commerce. A development corporation must reflect the needs, the advantages, and the shortcomings of our current system of society, whether they like it or not.

No town is an island. It is part of the regional economy.

167

Fig. 1: Social structure of new towns

(Comparison with national and regional averages)

Area	Total	Employers and managers, %	Professional workers, %	Intermediate non-manual, %	Junior non-manual, %	Foremen and Supervisory manual, %	Skilled manual, %	Semi-skilled manual, %	Un-skilled manual, %	Personal service and own account, %	Farmers forces, and indefinite, %
Averages:											
England and Wales	14,490,540	10·1	4·6	4·5	12·7	3·6	31·3	14·9	8·1	4·6	5·6
Greater London	2,468,300	12·0	5·6	5·4	18·1	3·3	27·6	12·7	8·0	5·9	1·4
South East Region	5,157,197	12·3	5·9	5·4	15·7	3·3	27·8	12·5	7·2	5·5	4·4
New Towns											
Basildon	19,950	6·0	3·4	4·8	12·4	5·3	33·8	22·3	7·1	4·2	0·7
Bracknell	7,450	9·0	8·7	5·6	13·7	4·3	32·9	15·4	5·2	2·1	3·1
Crawley	19,120	10·0	7·7	6·2	15·4	3·8	33·6	13·4	4·9	4·2	0·8
Harlow	19,740	10·3	6·8	6·2	12·3	4·9	34·9	14·9	4·2	4·8	0·7
Hatfield	7,330	7·6	6·7	4·6	14·7	5·0	37·2	13·8	6·4	3·3	0·7
Hemel Hempstead	19,610	10·1	6·7	5·5	11·6	4·6	34·1	17·1	5·6	4·2	0·5
Stevenage	17,030	8·4	7·5	7·8	14·4	4·0	33·5	16·3	4·6	2·8	0·7
Welwyn Garden City	11,970	11·4	10·9	9·0	14·5	4·2	27·9	14·4	4·3	2·7	0·7
Total, London new towns	122,200	9·1	7·0	6·2	13·5	4·5	33·5	16·3	5·3	3·8	0·8
Aycliffe	4,530	5·7	4·2	4·2	14·6	8·4	37·8	18·5	4·2	1·5	0·9
Corby	13,780	4·4	2·6	3·8	7·6	4·1	42·7	17·7	15·5	1·2	0·4
Cwmbran	10,910	7·3	5·1	5·0	10·0	6·9	30·6	21·7	9·3	3·5	0·6
Peterlee	4,990	5·8	3·0	4·0	9·2	5·4	40·4	20·6	8·2	1·0	2·4

Source: Census, 1966: Socio-economic groups of economically active males (age 15 and over).
Note: Classification is by area of *residence*, not place of work. Retired people are excluded.

While a new town is being built controls are necessary to establish the basis of employment and secure the right balance of houses; but the controls cannot go on for ever. People must be free to move in or out, to change their jobs, to choose where they will live and the house they want or can afford. Given a proper distribution of employment throughout the country and enough houses in relation to jobs—and we are slowly making progress towards both goals—the new towns must eventually take their place as any normal town in the economic life of the area. This indeed should be the object of all planned development. The treatment of housing and housing need as a thing apart, unrelated to planning and economic policy, was for years a serious defect at both local and national level.

Development corporations keep careful records of the people who move into and out of the town—where they came from, what they do, the age and size of their family, why they came and why they leave. These records have only been kept on a systematic basis since 1966, and it will be some time before long-term trends can be judged; but some of the tables have been published,[13] and their main value will be in planning future growth and working out the programmes for houses, schools, and employment. They will also repay close study of the social conclusions to be drawn from them. The 1966 figures certainly bear out the fact that the movement away from the established new towns, particularly those near London, at 3 or 4 per cent is well below the national average of movement of about 10 per cent revealed by the 1966 sample census; and of the many reasons given, such as purchase of a house, change of job, emigration, domestic troubles, etc., less than one in a hundred gave dislike of the new town as their reason for moving.

Balance in a town is not just a question of social structure. The age of the population is an important factor and over this the corporations have little control. Inevitably, new towns are young people's towns, and will remain so for many years. With their modern industries they offer particularly attractive opportunities to young couples in the overcrowded cities living with in-laws or paying high rents for a couple of rooms. The table at Fig. 2, which gives the age structure of eight towns as revealed by the 1966 sample census, shows how similar is the age grouping, particularly in the 'overspill' towns, and how much it differs from the national pattern. After some fifteen years of development the main group of adults is in the thirty to forty-four age band, with an almost negligible percentage over sixty, and the high birth-rate is reflected in the numbers under the age of fourteen.

The lack of 'old people' is often criticized. The new towns, it is said, do not make sufficient arrangements for parents to move at the same time as their children. This is another misconception. The parents for the most part are not 'old' at all. They are generally middle-aged, in secure jobs, and living in a house they bought twenty or thirty years earlier. They have no desire to change their job and move away from the circle of friends and other interests they have built up over the years. Where a whole factory or office organization moves to a town the employees moving with it usually cover a wider age range but this is the exception rather than the rule.

With fifteen or twenty years gone by, however, many of the parents are around retiring age and some are anxious to make the change. All development corporations encourage this, but it must be admitted that in many towns the process started too late. Because of the pressing needs of expanding industry a small quota only of the suitable dwellings could in fact be allotted to parents and a waiting list of several hundred applicants built up. But in the long run, when the population structure becomes more normal, there should be enough suitable dwellings of this type to meet all needs. Though the number may be relatively small so far, the elderly are not inactive. Harlow commented in 1961 that 'in a town known for its youthfulness it is surprising to find that some of the most flourishing groups are the old people's clubs.'[14]

At the other end of the scale are the children. For almost all the young couples moving into a new town with a new job and a new house, the next priority was a new baby. The high birth-rate resulted in pressures first on the primary schools, later on the secondary schools and technical colleges and then on the recreational facilities and employment market.

Fig. 2: Age structures: new town populations at 1966 sample census

(Percentages)

Age groups (years)	Bracknell	Crawley	Harlow	Hemel Hempstead	Corby	Aycliffe	Peterlee	Skelmersdale	England & Wales
0–4	10·3	10·1	12·9	9·5	13·5	12·9	15·1	11·8	8·5
5–9	11·4	11·3	12·6	10·2	11·2	11·3	13·7	8·2	7·6
10–14	9·2	10·6	10·2	9·4	9·2	9·1	8·6	5·7	6·9
15–19	8·2	8·4	7·3	8·2	8·0	6·4	6·8	8·4	7·8
20–24	5·9	4·7	6·0	5·7	7·2	6·1	8·6	5·6	6·7
25–29	6·9	5·6	7·2	5·5	7·9	8·2	9·3	8·4	6·0
30–34	7·8	7·9	8·6	7·2	7·0	8·0	8·4	6·8	5·9
35–39	9·0	9·1	9·0	8·9	7·1	9·3	7·2	5·1	6·2
40–44	7·3	9·3	7·7	8·2	6·4	8·6	6·5	6·4	6·7
45–49	6·5	6·8	6·0	6·5	6·3	5·6	3·7	7·4	6·3
50–54	5·4	5·0	4·0	6·1	4·9	3·5	3·1	6·1	6·6
55–59	3·7	3·6	2·9	4·3	4·5	2·9	2·1	6·0	6·5
60–64	2·9	2·6	1·6	3·2	3·1	3·0	2·3	3·9	5·7
65–69	2·0	1·8	1·5	2·6	1·8	1·8	2·1	4·1	4·6
70–74	1·6	1·2	1·2	2·3	0·9	2·0	1·1	2·4	3·4
75+	1·9	2·0	1·3	2·2	1·0	1·3	1·3	3·7	4·6
All Ages %	100·0	100·0	100·0	100·0	100·0	100·0	100·0	100·0	100·0
No.	23,710	62,680	67,920	64,130	43,850	15,850	18,330	12,040	

Note: Percentage figures have been rounded and do not therefore always add to 100 per cent.

Some of those moving into the new towns already had children of school age and it is worth recalling two conversations to illustrate the effect of the change of environment. Listen first to a teacher describing his early days at an old, tough, and overcrowded school in London. 'I soon acquired the technique,' he said. 'You walk into a classroom, where the noise is unbelievable, and clout the first three children you see. Then, and only then, do you get some sort of order. You can't teach them much, but if you manage to keep them quiet you're a success.'

Now listen to a headmaster in a new town school with many children from similar areas. 'When I first came here, soon after the town started,' he said, 'there were less than two hundred children in this school, all from the overcrowded parts of London, and it was as much as I could do to keep any control. Now, I have nearly a thousand children but I can get silence in a second.' The children were well dressed, well behaved, and the scholastic record impressive. It was one of the many excellent new schools, fully equipped and surrounded by spacious playing-fields, and the children had built their own school swimming pool. The school building itself was well looked after—there wasn't a mark on the walls.

'The change in the children,' went on the headmaster, 'is unbelievable. I put it down entirely to the change in environment. They live in new homes, of which they, no less than their parents, are very houseproud; they have the country on their door-step, open spaces and sports facilities, a school of which they are justly proud, and a general atmosphere in the town so different from the parts of London they came from.'

These children are the lucky ones, the few among the thousands still spending their most impressionable years in the slums or near slums and in the antiquated school buildings of last century. A large slice of our post-war capital investment on education has gone, necessarily, into the building of new town schools and technical colleges, and to some extent this has been at the expense of the modernization programme elsewhere. The pity of it is that an equal priority could not be given to all areas. It is an investment that should yield larger and quicker social dividends than any other field of public expenditure.

There are problem children in new towns as elsewhere, but the available delinquency figures show an encouraging reduction on those in most areas.[15] Outbreaks of vandalism occur but the general experience is that they are not prolonged and the children soon learn to appreciate and respect the carefully planned and well maintained landscaping of the towns. There is one school where two headmistresses are said to have resigned through the activities of a group of young thugs, but the fact that it is singled out for mention as something exceptional in the 200,000 school places in the new towns only serves to emphasize the success in character training and in scholastic and sports achievements.

The rapidly growing groups of teenagers are neither insulated nor immune from the influences of the outside world. Lurid Press accounts of drug-taking may give the impression that the new towns are hotbeds of vice, but in fact even at Welwyn Garden City—one of the towns particularly in the news at the trial in 1968 of Dr Petro—the figures of drug addiction are lower than in the largest towns near by. Crawley, too, hit the headlines when the doctors in the area made a concentrated effort to spot any youngsters taking drugs. When, inevitably, the Press and TV cameras came along Dr Rathod, the consulting psychiatrist at Graylingwell Hospital, Chichester, explained that 'a great deal more was being done in Crawley by way of research than in most places.'[16]

When it was rumoured that a 'Samaritans' service was to be set up in Bracknell one paper headlined the story: 'The heartbreak of a new town's lonely wives.' 'Startling figures,' it said, 'reveal that there are about twenty-five known suicide bids in Bracknell each year.'[17] The Samaritans say the report is quite incorrect, but this sort of news travels quickly and gathers much in the process, for a month or two later Sir Frederic Osborn reported a letter from the architectural critic of the *Washington Post* saying: 'I heard a very famous and presumably very intelligent American architect tell an influential gathering that the British new towns were simply horrible, because the suicide rate in them was higher than anywhere else.'[18]

'Why,' asks Sir Frederic, 'do they say such things?' Why indeed; but more important, what are the facts? Attempted suicide is no longer a crime since the Suicide Act 1961 and no current figures are available; but official figures show that, compared with the national suicide rate, the rate in new town areas is very much below the national average.[19]

This is not complacency. The truth must be brought out into the open. Whether it be drug-taking, suicide, road accidents, or any other of the many calamities that surround us, if it happens in a new town and results from new town conditions it should be nailed down, investigated, and the cause eliminated wherever possible. Unfortunately, the garbled and exaggerated statements that appear from time to time usually go unchallenged and the true facts never get equal publicity.

There are some unhappy people in new towns as elsewhere. Unhappiness can have many causes that are nothing to do with living in a town. A feeling of loneliness is common, however, where people have had to pull up their roots and move to a new place and in a newly established community there are many such people together. It happens in some of the local authority housing estates, and it happens no less in the select areas of suburbia. But a few cases in a new town led somebody to invent the phrase 'new-town blues'. It caught on, as an easy and vivid catchphrase, to such an extent that the reputation of new towns began to suffer through the popular misconception that it was a widespread malady peculiar to new towns. The difficulty is that there are no statistics by which these assertions can be proved or disproved. In their Report for 1960 the Ministry of Housing & Local Government commented, 'The malady known as "new town blues" has been greatly exaggerated in some press articles, but it undoubtedly exists. Social workers and doctors have long recognised it as one of the difficulties in building up a new community and it is one which perhaps only time will overcome.'[20] But sometimes a new-town resident is moved to protest, as for example, the lady who wrote to a national women's journal saying 'New town blues? Never! . . . The only blues I know are those of the doors and magnificent swimming pool'; and former County Councillor Maureen Davis-Poynter, at a conference and 'leisure and pleasure' exhibition which she organized in Crawley in 1964, stressed the lively social life in the town and added that reports of a lot of lonely women crying their eyes out were just not true.[21]

The most extensive investigation into this question was that made by Drs Taylor and Chave into the medical record of Harlow. 'Our survey,' they wrote, 'has shown that the creation of a new town with full social and economic planning results in an improvement in general health, both subjective and objective. About nine-tenths of the new population are satisfied with their environment and the one-tenth who are dissatisfied are for the most part constitutionally dissatisfied—that is to say, they would be dissatisfied wherever they were. Full satisfaction with environment is a product of time.' Neurosis, they concluded, is not greater in new-town areas than elsewhere. 'We have found no evidence of . . . new town blues,' they reported. 'Some people had indeed shown loneliness, boredom, discontent with environment and worries, particularly over money. It is easy enough for enterprising enquirers to find such people and to attribute these symptoms to the new town. But a similar group of similar size can be found in any community, new or old, if it is sought.'[22]

Nevertheless, even though the numbers may be small, it is a problem that must be taken seriously. It may amount to little more than the occasional newly-wed, bored with the housework, desperately missing her mother and too shy to speak to her neighbours; or it may reflect a serious fault in the social organization of the town, the employment opportunities for married women or even in the physical layout of the housing areas.

Some say the 'garden city' conception, with its well-spaced houses and sizeable gardens, causes loneliness; people—particularly the housewives—aren't near enough to each other to break the ice and get friendly; it creates a sense of isolation. They would cure this through higher densities. Others plead for a better grouping of houses—the more intimate close instead of long terrace rows. In his researches into the pre-war L.C.C. estate at Dagenham, Peter Willmott found that the 'banjos' or short cul-de-sacs, with their clear physical identity, were a help in creating sociability; but if the contact was too close, as in the case of houses with a shared porch, tension and friction was inevitable.[23] People vary so much that there is no one cause and no one solution. Many find living in high-density development, with perhaps noisy neighbours or children, much more disturbing than isolation.

This is a field of sociological research to which too little attention has been paid. Loneliness in new towns is certainly not widespread and most development corporations take the view that it can best be met by personal contact and encouragement. In many towns 'welcome' parties are still held, even after twenty years, so that newcomers can be brought together. The friendly eye of the housing officer or rent collector can often spot difficulties and an effort can be made to draw people into the life going on around them. It may not always succeed. Some do miss the bustle of city life, the chatting on the doorstep, the pub or cinema round the corner, with family and friends close at hand. The husband's job in the town usually makes it impossible to move away and only time and maturity can provide an eventual cure. To some, joining in community activities is no answer. Others want to do so but are too shy to take the plunge. The very fact that so many seem to be living a full and contented life can make matters worse: the highest suicide rate in New York is said to be on New Year's Eve when the lonely see so many others enjoying themselves.

In grappling with this problem many of the social studies place particular emphasis on the break-up of the 'three generation pattern'. The Duke of Edinburgh stressed this in an interview in February 1967, when he said:

'The difference between a new industrial town and an old town is that an old town is organic, it's grown up, everybody is related to everybody else, they are all inter-married, they are all uncles and aunts, they've all known each other's families for generations. . . . In a new town . . . there are no mothers-in-law, there are no uncles and no aunts, no grandmothers, there are no maiden aunts. You've created a totally different human society. . . . I think the philosophy of the construction of these new towns is slightly wrong. . . . Somehow or other the deep emotional attachment to a system isn't allowed to come out. . . . How do you contend with young people, old people, the relationship between people in their off-duty periods and things of that kind? There's no easy answer but you've got to damn well go and find out.'[24]

Sociologists have been probing this problem for years. In their penetrating analysis of Bethnal Green and the social effects of slum clearance Michael Young and Peter Willmott placed great stress on the close family ties in London's congested East End and the need to protect and preserve these important relationships.[25]

In terms of slum clearance, when a whole area is being demolished and the people are all being rehoused not far away, this can be done up to a point. The atmosphere of the old 'street' can never be fully recaptured in a new housing estate and often the younger members of the family will have moved away long before the demolition gangs finally take possession; but those who are rehoused will still be with people of their own kind or with friends and neighbours they have known for years, and the building up of a new life in new surroundings will be the easier for it.

New towns are a completely different operation from slum clearance and the ordinary rehousing process. People come from many different areas and however eagerly the younger members of a family may welcome the chance of a new house and a new job in a new town, their parents usually have no desire whatever to move. Occasionally members of the same family have followed each other one by one until, as the Hemel Hempstead Development Corporation put it 'whole clans have re-established themselves in new surroundings'.[26] At Harlow, 45 per cent of families now have relatives living in the town.[27] But this is not the whole answer. New towns must look beyond the family circle for a solution. It is very doubtful, in any case, whether the pattern in London's East End is at all typical of other parts of London and elsewhere from which most of the new town people have come. Peter Willmott says as much in his study of Dagenham.

Thus it can only lead to faulty conclusions to argue from the premise that the one social unit that matters is the close-knit family huddle to be found in the near-slums, with grandma, mother, and young Sally and her four children all living in the same street or more likely in the same house. To do so is to ignore realities. Sally and her husband are usually only too glad to escape with their children from the poor housing and crowded living. They may miss the willing babysitters and the help ready to hand, but few would go back and few parents would wish them to. Indeed the social, cultural, and economic success of the new towns may be due in no small measure to the fact that they are young towns with young people who have escaped from a three-generation pattern that had become a tyranny and a brake on personal enterprise.

However close the family ties, the truth is that the old town 'street' is not just a composition of separate self-contained family units. It is the whole street and all the people, with the chair outside the front door giving a ready view of all that is happening, the small general shop in a converted front room acting as a social focus for the women and the pub on the corner for the men. There are scores of these Coronation Streets falling rapidly into decay, yet the cohesion remains long after children have flown or grandparents have died. It is still 'our street'; but more and more only for the poor and the ageing.

The real test of a new town is whether people are able to recreate, in a modern setting and in modern conditions, a way of life that replaces this in a satisfying way. It is no answer just to build new Coronation Streets or juggle about with densities. The old communities are seizing up functionally. A technological society demands mobility and a break up of kin groups. A whole new physical framework has to be drawn up that meets the needs of life both for today and tomorrow and within which a social content can develop. It will be different; it will go through many phases as age-groupings change, as leisure interests extend, and as the social and economic pattern of society develops.

How can we be sure the new towns can provide the answer? Is it perhaps all too clinical? Do the architects and planners, as Arthur Ling has suggested,[28] spend too much time reading papers to each other and too little time talking to the people whose needs they serve? Lord Silkin said recently, 'I would have liked to have had a new town completely or almost completely unplanned, let it grow and develop as an experiment and see what would happen. So that your shops were intermingled with housing and your offices and your industry and your public buildings.'[29] He was joking, of course; or was he? Has he not pinpointed the need to rethink our current philosophies, check them against the natural expressions of community growth, see where the roots go down, examine the social contacts and content that emerge and then go on from there to new plans with greater knowledge of what really turns a collection of individuals into a living and thriving community? Jane Jacobs coined the right phrase for it—planning for vitality —in her devastating analysis of American experience;[30] Christopher Alexander, in a thoughtful and detailed analysis, sums it up as the 'design of culture';[31] and from Japan comes the term 'the metabolism of urban society[32] to describe the incessant rhythmic flow of city life. All over the world the search is going on to find the elusive key, the right physical framework for a truly flourishing community.

One of the most provoking studies of recent years is Christopher Alexander's prize-winning essay 'A City is not a Tree.'[33] He tears to pieces the 'neighbourhood' conception, almost every plan prepared for town or city in the last thirty years, including Professor Abercrombie's analysis of the London structure, the separation of vehicles and pedestrians, playgrounds for children, the exclusion of industry from residential areas, in fact every conception that denies the 'overlap' inherent in the life of any community or fails to analyse fully the interrelationships inherent in the way people live. In mathematical terms a town is a lattice, not a tree. 'We are trading the humanity and richness of a living city for a conceptual simplicity which benefits only designers, planners, administrators, and developers,' he asserts; but he cannot, as yet, say what should be put in its place. 'To have structure, you must have the right overlap, and this for us is almost certainly different from the old overlap which we observe in historic cities. As the relationship between functions changes, so the systems which need overlap in order to receive these relationships must also change. The recreation of old kinds of overlap will be inappropriate, and chaotic instead of structural.'

All progress is a matter of trial and error. Each new phase builds on the experience of the last. Planning for people does not go by the book; there is no standard philosophy, no blue-print, no fixed ideas to which everybody must conform. We are in the middle of a revolution in planning thought that has been slow to mature and get a sense of direction because needs themselves have been changing so rapidly.

We concentrate for a time on housing layout, swinging away from the high slum densities to the ten-to-the-acre garden city idea and back again to the patio houses to recover the lost social huddle.

We provide large gardens and people want them smaller. We provide small gardens and they say they are too cramped. We earmark land for allotments and they remain unused. We take the land for garages and they prefer front-door parking.

We design Radburn layouts to keep the traffic away; but the children play in the garage courts and a writer to the local paper says 'they're ruddy hell; I know—I'm a milkman!'[34]

We carefully work out traffic flows, garage needs, parking spaces on the basis of current experience and twenty years later the calculations are hopelessly wrong because more people have bought cars than we ever thought possible.

We plan a series of separate neighbourhoods equipped for all local needs near to people's homes and then find they travel around quite willingly and prefer the attractions of a town centre.

We experiment with multi-deck central shopping centres, equipped with escalators and all modern conveniences for the greater glory of supermarket shopping, and find that people long for the old 'shop round the corner'.

The brewers build a bright new pub for a population of so many thousand, all carefully calculated to give just the right amount of drinking space per person, and then find people would really prefer three or four smaller, quieter, and more intimate pubs much nearer home. Some people, that is. Two teenage girls had only one fault to find with Hemel Hempstead: the pubs didn't have juke boxes.

Is there such a thing as 'people'? A town is a collection of individuals, each with his own ideas and desires which as often as not conflict with those of his neighbour. Is it possible to plan for them all? Should majority vote or the influence of pressure groups settle these important issues? Many of the issues are determined by factors of cost or profit. Should people fit the economics or economics fit the people? No society has yet found a complete answer to such questions but the benevolent despotism of the new town development corporation may well have got nearer than most in the difficult task of holding the balance.

Twenty years is too short a time by which to judge results. In these days of technological advance there can never be perfection and certainly no perfection that will last for sixty years. Already yesterday's new towns are out of date and those we are building today will be out of date before the turn of the century. And yet the story is one of progress. The new Master Plans of recent years have made great strides forward. The needs of growing communities are beginning to be better understood. The predictions of the future can now draw on experience in a way that was not possible in the early fifties. But it is still only a framework within which people must work out their own way of life. Already they are confounding the planners and creating for themselves the 'overlap' for which Dr Alexander is searching.

But the point made by the Duke of Edinburgh must still be met. Can a town function without mothers-in-law, uncles, and maiden-aunts? The answer is that they are now there. The first children who moved into the new towns are already grown-up, marrying, and having children of their own. There are few grandmothers yet, but time will soon remedy that. A new community is not just an old community transferred ready-made to a new place: it has to create itself, it has to learn to grow, it has to have time. To the first of the newcomers it was a challenge to lay the foundations of a new life in strange surroundings. But to their children it is neither new nor strange; their roots are already there, it is home, the place they were born in—it is their town.

14. MONEY

ALTHOUGH it is generally supposed that the new towns are 'paid for by the Government' this is far from true. In a sense the Government do not pay for anything—any more than a building society 'pays' for a house being bought through a mortgage arrangement. All the capital needed by a development corporation is borrowed from the Government and has to be repaid with interest over sixty years. The money for the repayments comes mainly from the rents of the houses, shops, and factories so that in a sense the people who live, work, or do business in the town actually pay for it.

The Government carry the risk, of course. If there is an overall loss on any town it falls on the taxpayer but when a town makes a profit the Treasury can claim it.[1] The Government also pay annual subsidies on houses built for letting which come out of general taxation and are not as such repayable; and to help a new corporation get on its feet they used to make a small contribution towards the deficiency in the first three years.

The cost of building a new town comes from many sources other than the Government. The local authority services have to be met by the responsible authority and are paid for out of the local rates. Some of these services, such as schools and roads, are themselves subsidized by the Government, not only in new towns, of course, but as part of a general system of Exchequer support for local services of national importance. The development corporations can also contribute to the cost falling on the local authorities and special financial arrangements can be made for water and sewerage services; but any capital monies provided in this way by the development corporation are again borrowed from the Government and have to be paid back over sixty years.

The statutory undertakers responsible for gas, electricity, telephones, transport services, etc. usually meet the cost of supplying these services, making the usual connection charges, but the development corporations may have to pay for any special arrangements such as placing cables underground.

Finally, some of the building in a new town is financed by private capital. There is no fixed rule about this. It varies with the economic climate and the wishes of the organizations concerned. Many of the industrial and commercial firms and the larger retail organizations have built their own factories, offices, or shops; and the money for churches, public houses, commercial entertainment buildings, etc. has to be found by those who wish to build. In some towns a good deal of building in the town centre has been financed by the estate development companies and insurance organizations who build shops, offices, etc. as a commercial investment. Part of the £8 million town centre at Runcorn, for example, is to be built in partnership with the Duke of Westminster's family estate company.[2]

Because so many sources of finance are involved, it is not possible to answer the question, so often asked, 'What does a new town cost?' The amount of private investment is not usually revealed, and the cost of services such as electricity and gas is not calculated separately. The amount of direct Exchequer investment is, of course, known and the annual accounts of the development corporations show the state of their own finances. But the division between public and private capital varies with each town and the cost of services can vary enormously according to local conditions. Astragal in the *Architects' Journal*, however, says that a 'tame quantity surveyor' has given the following breakdown of new town costs— housing 48 per cent, industry 12 per cent, education 4 per cent, shopping 2 per cent, administrative and commercial 2 per cent, hospital and health 3 per cent, social and recreation 1 per cent, services 20 per cent, roads 7 per cent, miscellaneous 1 per cent.[3] These percentages are borne out very broadly by unofficial estimates made by the Ministry of Housing & Local Government; and as housing costs for a given population can be calculated with reasonable accuracy, they give a rough-and-ready means of estimating the total cost of a complete town. There are no official figures of the cost falling on the local authorities, but it is certainly substantial. Jasper More said in

Parliament that at Telford the cost of county council services alone was estimated at £100,000 for each thousand houses[4]— i.e. about £1½ million for a population of 50,000. It seems a somewhat low estimate, and in any case to arrive at the total cost to the local authorities there must be added as much again to cover the services provided by the district council.

The first estimates in 1946 put the cost of a town for 50,000 people at £19 million of which it was thought £15 million would be borne by the development corporation and £4 million by the local authorities;[5] but this was very quickly recognized to be a serious underestimate. By 1948 a total of £25 million of public money was thought to be nearer the mark.[6]

Since then, building costs have more than trebled, land is more expensive to buy and salaries and other overheads have gone up. By 1969 the figure was probably in the region of £2,500 per person—or £125 million for a town for 50,000 people. Under the programme ahead the towns already designated will be building for another 1½ million people over the next twenty years or so, giving a cost, at 1969 prices, of about £3,500 million, in addition to the £750 million already spent. But it will not all be public money. Private finance will account for a good deal.

The really important question, however, is whether the new towns programme has placed an additional burden on the economy as a whole—greater, that is, than if the needs of the country had been met in the traditional way of letting towns expand according to the dictates of the land market. No serious attempt has been made to evaluate the new towns in these terms. Indeed it is an impossible exercise because there are so many unknown factors.

The houses, for example, have been built to meet the needs of an expanding population. If they had not been built in new towns they would have been built elsewhere. The industries that found their opportunity in the industrial estates of the new towns would have competed for space in some congested and expensive industrial zone. Schools and shops would still have been needed to meet the needs of the growing population. And with continued uncontrolled expansion of the older towns and cities the traffic congestion at the centre would have become worse and even more expensive to solve. Indeed, much of the cost we are having to incur today to prevent the older towns and cities seizing up completely might well have been avoided if new towns had been established in the twenties instead of the fifties and the sprawl of the inter-war years had been kept in check.

Calculating the cost of what might have been is a pointless exercise, even if the data were available; but it is not unreasonable to assert that the new towns, rather than costing the taxpayer money, have in fact resulted in a net saving to the nation. True, money has had to be spent on some new roads that might not otherwise have been necessary. New schools have been built for children who, for a time, could have swollen still further the already overcrowded classes in the older towns and cities. Money has been spent on building new shops that might not all have been necessary if the older communities had just been allowed to expand.

But any such so-called 'savings' would have been purely temporary. The stock of social equipment that has to be provided is a direct reflection of the number and distribution of the population. The cost of the new schools needed in a new town where they can be brought fully into use as soon as they are built, is probably much lower in the long run than the cost of providing schools in dozens of new suburbs sprawling out into the countryside at an unpredictable rate.

The new towns have, however, altered the incidence of expenditure among the local authorities. Facilities that might otherwise have been the responsibility of the local authorities in London, for example, had to be provided in the Home Counties. At one time, Hertfordshire County Council, with four new towns and two large L.C.C. housing estates in their area, predicted that it would be impossible for them to face the additional cost. In the event, their fears proved unfounded. The housing estates, with no industrial and commercial development, remained a liability but within a few years the rateable value per head of population in the new towns was higher than the average for the county as a whole. (See Fig. 3.)

More important perhaps from the economic point of view is

the fact that the new towns have changed the balance of investment as between the private and the public sectors. Almost all the houses were built by the development corporations with public money, whereas in the inter-war years private enterprise met most of the housing demand through the speculative building of houses for sale. Some change in the balance was in any case inevitable in post-war conditions, and by their control of the overall national programme the Government restricted the total public investment in housing to levels which the economy could sustain. For the future, it is expected that many more of the houses in new towns will be built by private enterprise.

A sizeable amount of Government money has also been invested in industrial and commercial development in new towns which might otherwise have come from the private sector. Here, the Government are faced with a dilemma. This is the main source of a development corporation's profit and the more private capital is encouraged, the smaller the annual surplus. Indeed, unless development corporations are able to take reasonable advantage of the investment opportunities and new values they create they are unlikely to cover their overheads at all and some of the towns will appear—on paper—to be financially unprofitable ventures.

Some development corporations aimed at financing as much as possible of the commercial and industrial development—and, in general, those that did so are now showing very favourable financial results. Others considered it important to persuade some industrial and commercial concerns to provide their own capital for building, on the view that it gave them a 'stake in the town'—a sense of permanence they would not have in a rented factory or shop.

This argument is probably not as valid as it sounds. The sense of permanence is created far more by the conduct of a satisfactory business and a stable employment roll than by owning a factory building. Many firms owe their success to the fact that by taking a rented factory they had greater resources available for plant and equipment and were thus able to set up a more efficient unit. The gain to the national economy cannot be measured solely by the profits made by the development

FIG. 3: Growth of rateable value

(Comparison of the rateable value per head of population in four new towns with the rateable value per head of the county)

	Crawley[1]			West Sussex			Hemel Hempstead			Hatfield[3]			Welwyn Garden City			Hertfordshire		
	£	s.	d.	£	s.	d.	£	s.	d.	£	s.	d.	£	s.	d.	£	s.	d.
1948-9							6	4	7	7	8	11	8	7	6	7	18	10
1949-50							6	2	2	7	12	0	8	12	0	7	17	11
1950-1							6	3	8	7	16	6	8	13	10	7	19	9
1951-2							6	8	5	7	17	2	8	16	0	8	0	5
1952-3							6	15	10	7	17	6	8	18	9	8	1	4
1953-4							7	5	9	8	4	3	9	9	8	8	2	10
1954-5							7	1	10	8	7	7	9	8	6	8	5	2
1955-6							7	2	9	8	15	5	10	3	11	8	8	5
1956-7[2]	18	4	0	18	13	0	15	1	4	14	3	2	15	1	9	14	13	2
1957-8	16	0	0	17	15	0	14	6	0	13	9	9	13	13	7	13	17	11
1958-9	15	15	0	17	16	0	14	2	1	13	0	8	15	4	11	14	1	2
1959-60	18	0	0	19	4	0	17	15	4	17	0	11	23	4	10	16	16	3
1960-1	19	4	0	19	16	0	18	3	5	16	15	10	22	8	7	16	16	3
1961-2	19	10	0	20	3	0	17	1	7	17	17	5	22	8	0	16	15	6
1962-3	20	6	0	20	5	0	17	3	4	17	13	0	23	1	3	16	19	2
1963-4[2]	56	17	0	52	12	0	53	2	7	59	10	8	77	11	11	54	4	6
1964-5	56	15	0	53	3	0	55	5	6	60	9	0	75	18	4	55	5	7
1965-6	56	2	0	53	12	0	56	3	9	60	5	11	55	2	7	55	10	4
1966-7	56	5	0	54	14	0	57	16	5	61	3	11	77	16	10	56	8	7
1967-8	57	14	0	56	5	0	62	17	1	63	2	1	78	15	0	59	1	4
1968-9	61	18	0	58	3	0	65	6	5	65	16	0	80	9	11	60	17	10

[1] Crawley Urban District Council was created on 1 April 1956.
[2] Rating revaluations from 1956 and 1963 account for the increases in those years.
[3] The new town area is about one-half of the Hatfield Rural District Council area.

corporations on their land and building transactions. The new industrial ventures were part of the post-war re-equipment of our system of production and many of them now have a large export trade that is far more important than the rack rent or ground rent they pay.

Nevertheless, this question of the balance of private and public investment in our orthodox economy has become increasingly important and in every successive financial crisis of the fifties and sixties the Government placed severe limitations on investment by the public sector. At the same time social needs made it essential to launch a programme of further towns. In an effort to meet these needs without straining the economy too much, the new towns have been told that in future at least half the houses are to be built for sale, many of them by private enterprise, and severe limitations will be placed on the amount of public capital available for shops, factories, and other buildings which can readily be financed from private sources.

To meet this new situation the new-town organizations are searching for ways of raising capital that will meet the restrictions on public expenditure but at the same time retain the important controls over planning, design, shopping balance, and industrial intake. The corporations are forbidden by law to borrow money from any source other than the Government, but there is a considerable amount of institutional money seeking long-term investment outlets, such as pension funds, insurance monies, and the like, which can be made available for building on relatively advantageous terms. The arrangements usually involve sharing future increases in value, thus giving the investor a very necessary hedge against inflation. Sometimes an agreement is made under which the corporation grants a ground-lease and takes a lease back of the building when it is finished. The investor has a guaranteed return on his money increasing possibly as rack rents rise during the term of the lease, and the development corporation have full control of lettings and the rents to be charged. This principle can also be applied to property already built and paid for by the development corporations, the lease-and-lease-back providing capital for new building, but at the sacrifice of some of the surplus they expected to make on their original investment.

From a long-term financial point of view, bringing in private capital in this way is a disadvantage. Profits will accrue much more slowly. Increases in property values, whether resulting from prosperity or from inflation, will go wholly or partly into private hands instead of being available to help in the development of the town and the image of the new towns as a prudent and profitable Government investment will perhaps suffer. But if that is the price of keeping the economy on an even keel and at the same time organizing development to meet the national needs, it must be faced. The social and economic dividends which the new towns yield are far more important and far more rewarding than the financial picture in the balance sheet.

The amount of public money spent by development corporations is subject to a very thorough control by Parliament but the money is not all voted at once. The cost of building a town is spread over some twenty years or more and Parliament only provides enough for a few years ahead. Thus the first New Towns Act in 1946 authorized expenditure up to £50 million and by 1969 this had been increased by successive Acts to a figure of £1,100 million.[7] Of that, about £720 million had already been spent and as Kenneth Robinson explained to the House of Commons the £300 million authorized by the 1969 Act was only enough to last for about three years.[8] The total liability for the towns already designated, however, was estimated at £2,090 million,[9] and this arrangement means that Ministers have to go back to Parliament from time to time and give an account of their stewardship. Between the 1946 Act and the 1969 Act there were seven Acts authorizing more money[10] and on all these occasions both Houses of Parliament took full advantage of the opportunity to mount interesting and, on occasions, critical debates. Even though some of the Bills before the House were no more than one-clause money bills, the Speaker has always allowed a very wide latitude to bring up any new town point.

In some ways it is an odd situation. The Minister can start a new town without even telling Parliament and by doing so virtually commits the Government to expenditure over the following twenty years or so well beyond the amount authorized. In the early days this rather worried the Public Accounts Committee because twelve new towns had been started and, as Sir Thomas Sheepshanks, then Permanent Secretary to the Ministry, explained, if Parliament refused to vote the money to complete them they would have to be abandoned and some of the money spent would be wasted.[11] The Committee accepted the situation but suggested that the Minister ought perhaps to tell Parliament before designating any more towns.[12] The Treasury agreed that the annual accounts of the towns ought to show the total potential Exchequer commitments, and this is now always done; but they felt it would hardly be proper to ask the Minister to adopt the Committee's suggestion.[13] In the event the then Minister, Harold Macmillan, promised Parliament that he would consult them before making any more designation orders,[14] but in fact he did not designate any more towns and the practice was not adopted by later Ministers. In a debate on the 1966 Bill, however, the Government indicated their intention of announcing any future schemes to the House of Commons, and in any case designation orders, other than minor extensions, can now be the subject of an annulment resolution if the local planning authority maintain an objection.[15]

Parliament has, of course, many other methods of control. The capital expenditure by development corporations is included in the annual parliamentary votes of the Minister concerned and may thus become a topic for discussion in the supply debates when the expenditure of Departments comes before the House of Commons.

Full details of all expenditure are also given in the annual accounts of the development corporations. Each corporation has to send to the Minister an annual report, together with the audited accounts. The audits are carried out by private firms of auditors appointed by the Minister and they are instructed to report direct to the Minister if they find any expenditure which has not been authorized or is of an extravagant or wasteful nature judged by normal commercial practice and prudence.[16] The accounts are sent by the Minister to the Comptroller and Auditor-General, with a full account of the monies

that have been advanced to the new towns and of the payments
the Minister has received from them; and the Reports and
Accounts are then laid before Parliament with the Comptroller
and Auditor-General's report.

Sometimes the Comptroller and Auditor-General comments
on particular items and the Public Accounts Committee usually
investigate any matters he raises; but they can also ask any
questions they like on the accounts, and the Permanent Secretary of the appropriate Department and the Chairman of the
development corporation can be called upon to explain or
justify any item of expenditure. On several occasions the Committee have spent a long time examining witnesses. In the years
1949–52, they went very thoroughly into the whole question
of Parliamentary and Departmental control, the method of
financing new towns, the system of auditing and the Board of
Trade's industrial policy. They even took up such detailed
points as district heating, the cost of tree planting, charges for
the use of Government cars, salaries of corporation members,
the frequency of their visits to the town, land prices, and
numerous other questions. In later years they again took up
the method and form of auditing, and held a lengthy inquest
into overspending on some industrialized building contracts at
Basildon and Livingston and the scope for recovering liqui-
dated damages. Every minute detail of a corporation's activities
can come under close scrutiny.

This very detailed parliamentary control inevitably means that
Ministers must in turn keep a very close control over the
development corporations. Each year the corporations have to
submit a budget with estimates of the amount they expect to
spend and receive on capital and revenue accounts, split up
under a score of different heads—expenditure on land, site
works, building of roads, sewers, houses, shops, factories, contributions to local authorities, salaries, furniture and other
equipment, receipts from rents, subsidies, and interest.

The total of the estimated capital expenditure of all the
development corporations then has to be brought together and
considered by the Government as part of the overall national
budget of public expenditure. In most years, the total demand

from all sources far exceeds the amount available and some items have to be cut out of the programme. A limit is placed on the total amount that can be spent on new towns and the Ministers then set for each corporation a ceiling on their expenditure in the forthcoming financial year.

It is usually about the end of March—or even later—before this stage is reached and it is clearly not possible to control new town spending on such a hand-to-mouth basis. Most building contracts are a year or two in preparation and a couple of years or more in execution, so that much, if not most, of the capital expenditure in the year ahead is already the subject of contracts long before the budget approval comes along. To ease the process there is a good deal of forward thinking outside the formal budget submissions. Broad five-year programmes are prepared which, each year, are 'rolled on' for another year. These enable the calls on public investment to be examined, and priorities to be established, on a wider and long-term view.

Budget approval does not, however, mean that the corporations are free to spend the money. Each building proposal has to be submitted in detail for the Minister's approval and before he agrees to advance the necessary money—and the corporations cannot borrow from any other source[17]—he must satisfy himself and the Treasury that the development is 'likely to secure for the corporation a return which is reasonable, having regard to all the circumstances, when compared with the cost of carrying out the proposals.'[18]

The phrase is very elastic and enables financial policy to be varied according to the nature of the development and the needs of the time. In some circumstances even a deficit is a 'reasonable return'. For factories or shops the Minister can specify a minimum yield or a minimum profit above borrowing rate. For houses he is usually satisfied if the rents are sufficient to cover cost. So many factors affect the decision, and circumstances differ so much from town to town, that any fixed formula can be little more than a working guide.

The Minister's examination of a proposal is not confined to the financial aspects. He also goes into the planning merits, in consultation with the local planning authority and his approval carries with it a planning permission.[19] This control can also be used to implement policy objectives such as the use of industrialized building methods, tender and contract procedure or standards of house-building. It was used, for example, to fulfil Harold Macmillan's policy of 'people's houses'; it is used in conjunction with the approval for subsidy to ensure the minimum standards of the Parker Morris report and compliance with the housing cost 'yardstick'.[20] It is also a means of controlling the general level of rents charged by a corporation to their tenants.

The need for this close control by Ministers has frequently been questioned. What is the point, it is asked, of appointing capable people as members of a development corporation, with a highly skilled managerial and professional staff, if every single thing they do is pored over and pulled to pieces in Whitehall? Apart from the delay and frustration involved, does it not make for too much uniformity, stifle new ideas for fear of upsetting the Ministry or Treasury and drive away from new town work the very people with imagination that it is particularly important to recruit?

There is a lot in this argument; but reconciling Parliamentary control of public expenditure with a proper measure of independence for public corporations seems a well-nigh insoluble problem. As long ago as 1950, the Public Accounts Committee asked Lord Reith for his views. He suggested investigation by a royal commission[21] but nothing ever came of it. In 1957, Dame Evelyn (now Baroness) Sharp, when she was Permanent Secretary of the Ministry of Housing & Local Government, said in evidence to the Public Accounts Committee that she thought the control—the 'harrowing control' she called it—on all spending by development corporations was perhaps too close a control.[22] Corporations have been hoping ever since for some relaxation; but in fact, in their 1968 Report the Harlow Development Corporation commented that the degree of meticulous central control had increased steadily, particularly over the last few years.[23]

On the other hand, it is argued, how can the Minister's approval carry a planning permission unless the proposal for development is closely examined by his own advisers; how can he agree to pay subsidy on houses without satisfying himself they are up to modern standards; and how can he satisfy the financial duty laid on him by Parliament unless he knows the cost and return of each project? Few development corporations would give up the arrangement for getting planning approval from the Minister if it meant submitting every proposal to the local planning committee. There may be frustrating moments but they recognize that there is in Whitehall a breadth of view, a knowledge of modern architecture and engineering and a wide experience of housing problems and estate management that are not always found in the district councils to whom most planning functions are delegated—or even in the planning departments of some county councils.

But the financial controls could perhaps be operated more loosely, within the framework of the corporation's budget and a general policy directive; and with the greatly extended programme of new towns some means of reducing the volume of detailed work in Whitehall may have to be found. Indeed, if the Minister could be sure that a reliable team of corporation members is in control, advised by professional staff and consultants of suitable calibre, little harm would be likely to result, and much good, if he were able to say to them: 'Here's £100 million; go away and build a new town!' This perhaps is expecting too much, but the report of the Fulton Committee[24] which recommended hiving off detailed scrutiny of this sort from Government departments may at least point the way.

Whatever the financial results of a proposal and whatever the purpose for which the capital is needed—whether it be a building that will last a century or a lorry that will last five years—the development corporations borrow from the Ministry on the same terms. All advances are at the rate of interest in force at the time the money is borrowed and are repayable over sixty years by equal half-yearly[25] instalments of capital and interest. The early payments contain a high element of interest and a small element of capital, and the balance between the two gradually changes as the years go on; but the capital element means a relatively small addition to the simple interest rate. Thus, for advances made when the interest rate was 3 per cent the payment for each year per £100 is £3 12s 0d; with an interest rate of 9 per cent, the annual payment per £100 is £9 1s 0d.

Interest rates are fixed by the Minister (on instructions from the Treasury) and have risen steadily throughout the period of new town building. In twenty years there have been no less than 68 changes—43 of them upwards—and as shown in the graph at Fig. 4, they have risen from 3 per cent at the outset to nearly 10 per cent in 1969. No statutory basis is laid down, and originally the rate was the same as that charged by the Public Works Loan Board for long-term advances to local authorities. In September 1957, however, it was changed to the rate at which the Government are able to borrow in the market on a long-term basis,[26] and for some years this was more favourable to the development corporations. In theory, therefore, the Treasury finance new towns at no more than the cost they have to incur. This may not be strictly true because development corporations are repaying capital throughout the period, and this is available for relending at, of course, the full interest rates then in force. Moreover, much of the Treasury's borrowing is redeemed within the sixty-year period and borrowing then may cost marginally more or less than the interest rate payable by the development corporation. Technically, the money is issued to the Minister by the Treasury out of the National Loans Fund. This consists largely of money borrowed by the Government, such as Government Stock, National Savings, etc., but there is a daily balancing with the Consolidated Fund, which is fed mainly from taxation and as no specific sums are earmarked for particular purposes it is not possible to say how much of the money used for building new towns is borrowed money and how much of it comes from taxation and other sources.[27]

It is on the industrial and commercial success of a town that a development corporation has mainly to rely for any profit. It takes time for values to build up—particularly shop values, which are so dependent on the rate of population increase; but once the shopping and industrial areas are firmly established, values can rise remarkably quickly. Even then the corporation may not be able to collect this increase until leases fall due for

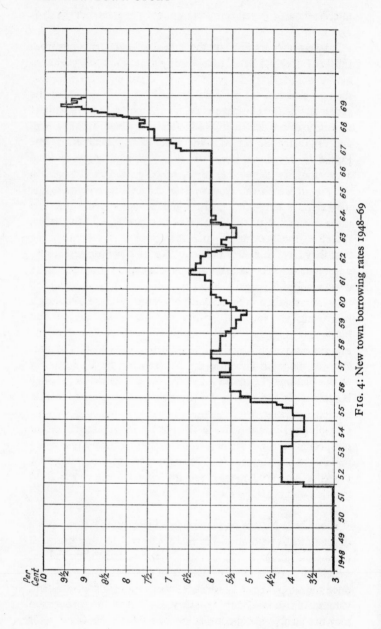

FIG. 4: New town borrowing rates 1948–69

renewal or rents can be recalculated under a review clause. Leases vary in their terms, but for industrial and commercial buildings leases of up to twenty-one years are usual, with reviews at the seventh and fourteenth year. In the case of ground leases the period is much longer, and until recently it was normal estate practice to have a fixed ground rent with no provision for review. In the new towns, with their rapidly rising land-values, this was soon seen to be unsatisfactory and the development corporations pioneered a new practice, now widely adopted, of rising ground rents or a review at various times during the lease.

When fixing the terms of a lease of a factory or shop the development corporation aim to get a rent that shows a return on capital of at least 3 or 4 per cent above their own borrowing rate. The corporation carry the risk that the lessee may go out of business and leave them with an empty building on their hands. Unless market rents enable a margin of this order to be obtained the corporation ought not to be building, if the transaction is judged solely by commercial prudence; but frequently there are other considerations of a social nature, such as the need to attract employment. This applies particularly to the new towns in the areas of high unemployment scheduled by the Board of Trade for special help.

About half the capital investment in a new town (and some 70 per cent of a development corporation's investment) goes into building houses, and on this the corporations are not expected to show either a profit or a loss. Rents have to be fixed at a level that is sufficient, with the aid of the Government subsidy and grant, to balance the outgoings. This policy had to be modified in Scotland, where there is a long tradition of low rents, and special grants are paid from the Exchequer in respect of interest on the accumulated deficiency in the General Revenue Account; but even in England some of the newer towns are finding it difficult to achieve balance at present though they aim to do so eventually.

The outgoings cover much more than the bare cost of building. Land purchase, professional fees, administration overheads and a proportion of the cost incurred in laying out main roads, providing a sewerage system and other such items have to be added. In normal commercial practice interest charges during the period of construction would also be capitalized but the Government have always insisted that they must be charged against revenue. Many corporations think it to be unrealistic accounting and most of them have mentioned the point in their annual reports. The Hemel Hempstead Corporation pointed out at the end of fifteen years that the amount of interest during construction charged to revenue amounted to £489,000 and in East Kilbride's twenty-one years it adds up to over £1½ million.[28] This is no more than a technical accounting point, but it makes all the difference to the financial picture, and if capitalization were permitted many of the towns still showing a deficit would be in surplus on their General Revenue Account.

Rents must also cover the cost of repairs and maintenance and a fixed sum per dwelling is usually set aside each year for this purpose. At one time a sum of £10 a house was enough but rising costs have now forced this up to £20–£25 and it may have to go up further. When the houses are new the amount should be more than is needed in the year so that a balance can be built up against the day when major repairs or renewals have to be carried out. This spreads the cost evenly and equitably among all tenants over the years and avoids fluctuations of rent in periods of unexpected or unusually heavy repairs. Not all the new towns, however, have yet managed to achieve this result. The Accounts show that the Commission for the New Towns have over £1 million to the credit of the maintenance and repairs fund for their four towns, with current repairs expenditure running at some £860,000 a year. Harlow have £524,000 in credit, against expenditure for the year of £518,000. At the other end of the scale are Basildon, with 16,000 dwellings and a nil balance, and Peterlee with a deficiency of £115,000.

The rents of dwellings vary, of course, according to the size and type of house or flat; but there are also substantial differences as between one town and another, due mainly to the fact that the houses were built at different times. For a house that cost, say, £1,300 in 1950, when the interest rate was 3 per cent, the loan charges would be £47 a year. A similar house built in 1969 would cost about three times as much—say £3,900. If interest rates were still 3 per cent the loan charges would be £141 a year; but with an interest rate of 9 per cent the loan charges become £353 a year. The threefold increase in building costs itself trebles the loan charges, and that is about in line with changes in the value of money and increases in wage levels throughout the country; but with the interest rate also trebled, loan charges are seven and a half times the earlier level.

In the ordinary way this would mean rents much too high for the average family, but in the older new towns the position has been alleviated by the device of 'pooling'. Under this system, the loan charges and other expenditure on all the corporation's rented houses are added together and the rents are fixed at a level sufficient in total to cover the outgoings. Thus, similar rents are charged for similar properties, irrespective of the historic cost of building them. In a town with a large number of houses built in a period of rising costs, pooling can have a dramatic effect on rents. The older houses show a substantial profit and the new houses can be let at a loss. This is not a subsidy: rather it is a measure of justice as between tenants. The principle is demonstrated in Fig. 5.

The other factor that helps to keep rents to a reasonable level is the annual subsidy and grant paid by the Ministry on all houses built for letting.[29] The subsidy is the same as that paid to local authorities. In 1949, when the first new town houses were built, it was £16 10s 0d a year, payable for sixty years, but each new Housing Act changed the amount and for houses built between 1961 and 1967 it was £28. For houses built after 1967 a flat-rate payment was replaced by a formula that relates subsidy to the difference between the actual average loan charges and the loan charges that would have been incurred if the interest rate had been 4 per cent.[30] By contrast with the former figure of £28, the subsidy under this new formula, assuming a house costing £4,000 and an interest factor of 9 per cent, will be £185 a year.

This new basis represents a tremendous advance in housing policy. Unpredictable fluctuations in interest rates have, in the past, caused so much uncertainty that rent levels could never

FIG. 5: The theory of rent pooling

(Take a 'pool' of seven identical houses built at different times, different costs, and different interest rates)

Year	Cost	Interest	Total annual interest £	Rent charged in year						
				1 £	2 £	3 £	4 £	5 £	6 £	7 £
I	£1,500	3% = £45	45	45	62·5	83·3̇	107·5	135	165·83̇	200
2	£2,000 (average 2 × £1,750)	4% = £80 (average 3·57%)	125	—	62·5	83·3̇	107·5	135	165·83̇	200
3	£2,500 (average 3 × £2,000)	5% = £125 (average 4·15%)	250	—	—	83·3̇	107·5	135	165·83̇	200
4	£3,000 (average 4 × £2,250)	6% = £180 (average 4·7%)	430	—	—	—	107·5	135	165·83̇	200
5	£3,500 (average 5 × £2,500)	7% = £245 (average 5·4%)	675	—	—	—	—	135	165·83̇	200
6	£4,000 (average 6 × £2,750)	8% = £320 (average 6·03%)	995	—	—	—	—	—	165·83̇	200
7	£4,500 (average 7 × £3,000)	9% = £405 (average 6·6%)	1,400	—	—	—	—	—	—	200
			Totals	£45	£125	£250	£430	£675	£995	£1,400

Thus, at each point, to keep the pool in exact balance the appropriate rent needed per house to cover loan charges is the *Average Annual Charge × Average Cost of Houses*. The figures are merely given to illustrate the principle. Actual loan charges over 60 years are, of course, slightly more than the flat interest rate, and the rent must cover numerous other items.

be fixed with any confidence that they would prove right. Programmes of building have been disrupted and even suspended in the hope that interest rates would fall. Now that housing finances can be geared to a 4 per cent borrowing rate and the Government have guaranteed to meet the loan charges above that figure, continuity of programmes and reasonable stability of rents are assured.

Certain other subsidies are also paid to local authorities such as the 'expensive site subsidy' where the cost of the land exceeds £4,000 an acre,[31] and the additional subsidies for blocks of flats of four storeys or more.[32] These arise mainly in the larger towns and cities but they are also paid to development corporations in appropriate cases. All subsidies are normally payable for sixty years but the Minister has power to reduce or withdraw them, subject to getting Parliamentary approval,[33] and a subsidy is automatically stopped when a rented house is sold or let for a term of more than seven years.

In addition to the standard subsidies, the Government pay a grant for a period of years in respect of rented houses built by a development corporation.[34] Originally this was equivalent to the contribution which local authorities were required to make out of the local rates in respect of their own houses but when this ceased in 1956 to be a statutory obligation on local authorities the special grants to development corporations were continued, with the object of encouraging the building of houses and the movement of people away from the overcrowded urban areas. For the first ten years, half the amount of this grant in respect of a new town house is recovered by the Government from the local authorities in whose area the tenant formerly lived, on the theory that the grant of a tenancy in a new town has relieved the 'exporting' authority from part of their housing obligations.

These grants are entirely at the discretion of the Minister. No period of payment is specified and they can be withdrawn or reduced at any time. The grants started in 1940 at £5 10s 0d per house per annum and were increased by stages to £12 a year. But in 1967 the Minister decided that the time had come to reduce grants for the English towns that no longer needed the extra help and to increase the payments to the newer towns that were finding it necessary to charge very high rents in order to meet their costs. Under these new arrangements, all new grants will cease after ten years and the older ones will be phased out by 1977, but the amount has now been increased for the newer development corporations to encourage them to increase the pace of house-building in the early years. For houses built during the first four years, a grant of £30 a year is now paid; for those built in the next four years it is reduced to £24; the following four years, £18, and £12 thereafter. The amount recovered from the exporting authorities is now fixed at £12 a year for ten years.

Each development corporation operates a separate housing pool and rent levels vary considerably from town to town. The rents in 1969 for a typical three-bedroomed house ranged from about 30s to nearly £6, but all new towns operate rent rebate schemes under which rents can be reduced for tenants with small incomes.

It is difficult to say how long it will be possible to defend these differences in rent levels. Eventually it may be desirable to regard the whole of the new town housing as one financial pool. This problem, however, is not confined to the new towns. The rents of local authority houses throughout the country show an even greater divergence[35] and with the heavy programme of building ahead and the forthcoming changes in local government structure, widespread changes of policy may have to be considered. The volume of publicly provided housing is now so extensive and reasonable equality of rents such an important factor in the mobility of labour, as well as in equity, that nothing short of central financing through some national body could fully solve the problem.

Special difficulties and misunderstandings can arise when the rents of the houses built by the development corporation become higher or lower than the rents of comparable local authority houses in the same area. Within these small geographical limits, contributions can now be made by either body to keep the rent levels about even and the two housing revenue accounts in balance. The Commission for the New Towns have paid substantial amounts to the Hemel Hempstead Borough Council and the Crawley Urban District Council.[36]

As a result of these various methods of pooling, rents in the older new towns are a good deal below the full economic rent and much lower than the cost of mortgage repayments on purchase. Even those tenants who are particularly anxious to become owner-occupiers have to think twice before they decide to buy and as Barry Cullingworth has already pointed out[37] not many can afford to do so. Most people buy with a mortgage through a Building Society or Insurance Company and the interest qualifies for tax relief which, for people paying tax at the full standard rate, is equivalent to an annual subsidy of 41 per cent of the interest. The higher the income, of course, the greater the tax relief: for a person with an unearned income of £10,000 a year it is over 97 per cent. For purchasers with low incomes who do not secure the full tax relief the 'option mortgage' scheme gives a broadly equivalent subsidy; but as their income is usually too low to qualify for a full mortgage on the present cost of a new house it does not help much in new towns, where there are very few older or cheaper houses available.

Even people with reasonably average incomes find difficulty in raising a mortgage, particularly in the south of England where costs are higher than elsewhere. Many Building Societies will not normally advance money unless the applicant has an income at least four times the amount of the repayments. Some will take account of a wife's earnings, others will not. Government statistics[38] show that fewer than 20 per cent of the people of Britain have incomes, inclusive of bonus and overtime, sufficient to support even a 90 per cent mortgage for buying, at present values and present interest rates, a three-bedroom house built to Parker Morris standards. And many of the 20 per cent are already owner-occupiers, so that the scope for sales is very limited.

The development corporations were at one time allowed to offer 100 per cent mortgages for all but the most expensive houses at an interest rate $\frac{1}{4}$ per cent higher than the interest they were paying to the Treasury. For several years they were thus able to offer better terms than the Building Societies. This arrangement was brought to an end in 1966 when the Ministry raised the interest rate on mortgages to the Building Society's level and told the corporations they could only be 'lenders of last resort'; and with the severe increase in borrowing rates in subsequent years development corporations were required to charge well above the building society rates. To the would-be purchaser it must seem that every possible obstacle is being put in his way.

Certainly the aim of 50 per cent owner-occupation is not in sight of achievement without radical financial changes. When the new subsidy was fixed in 1967, interest rates were around 6 per cent and a purchaser could, in effect, buy at about 4 per cent. When interest rates went up this was no longer true. An extension of the principle of the option mortgage scheme, with more generous grants to help purchasers with incomes of up to, say, £30 a week, would be one way of encouraging more owner-occupation. Better still would be a general scheme for financing house-purchase at a fixed rate—say 4 per cent—in place of tax relief. Several continental countries appear to have arrangements of this sort.

Outside their main field of building houses, factories, and offices development corporations have a number of other financial obligations, running into many millions of pounds, that yield no direct financial return. Some £25 million have been spent on main sewerage and considerable contributions have been made to building main roads. The services are eventually handed over to the appropriate authority at much below cost, leaving a liability in the corporation's balance sheet that is not represented by any tangible assets. When a surplus becomes available from other transactions it can be used to write off these deficiencies but it is usually many years before this becomes possible. Corporations can also contribute to the cost of other local authority projects, but apart from roads and sewers, they have hitherto been called upon to pay very little towards ordinary routine services. When the designation of Peterborough was being negotiated the Ministry promised that, if and when the cost of schools went above £300,000, the corporation would meet half the excess—the first time help with the education services has been thought necessary—but in the main contributions have been confined to recreational, social, or other amenity services, most of which are the responsibility of the district councils whose resources are generally lower than those of the county councils.

Financial help is not limited, however, to local authority activities. The contribution which the development corporations and the Commission for the New Towns can make towards the cost of amenities in a new town is a quite general one.[39] The word 'amenities' is not defined in the Act and there appears to be only one recorded judicial interpretation where, in a somewhat different context, the Courts adopted the meaning 'pleasant circumstances or features, advantages'.[40] In its application to new towns the word can be interpreted to cover anything that makes the town a pleasant place to live in. In addition to helping with the cost of swimming baths and meeting halls, car parks, sculpture, town seats and such like, contributions can be made to clubs and societies, an arts festival, town pageant, or the many other functions that help to make a worthwhile social life in the towns.

All monetary contributions have to be approved by the Minister with the consent of the Treasury and the extent and method of such payments have never been properly settled. The swimming bath, sports facilities, community halls, open spaces, parks, etc. are mostly needed in the early years and are mainly the responsibility of the district council. In the older towns which grew slowly over the centuries, these facilities were provided over a long period, as and when demand became pressing and money was available. In a new town the process has to be telescoped into a much shorter period and, ideally, ought to be started before rateable value has built up to the point at which the local authority can comfortably carry the capital and running costs.

The development corporation's power to contribute towards the cost thus becomes a powerful instrument for seeing that these facilities are provided at the time they are needed by the growing population. Very full co-operation between the corporation and the local authority is needed as Government spokesmen have made it clear that the development corporation is not to be regarded as a 'milch cow or universal fairy godmother' and that contributions will not be authorized unless the local authorities are pulling their weight. In one debate Robert Mellish recalled an occasion when a local authority discussed the need for an open space costing £50,000 and then solemnly resolved to bear £100 themselves and to ask the development corporation to contribute the balance![41]

Many reasonably generous contributions have been authorized over the years—usually a percentage of capital cost—but there has never been a systematic and consistent policy. Following widespread complaints at the lack of sufficient amenities and the unfavourable publicity that followed the stories about 'new town blues', the Ministry agreed in 1961 to allow development corporations to make contributions out of revenue towards the cost of minor amenities, up to a maximum of £2,000 a year in each town; and for contributions to major items they adopted a figure of £4 a head of new population as giving, they suggested, a reasonable overall total for these items. The local authorities have for some years been pressing for £10 a head as a more realistic figure; and in the towns where the development corporations are making a surplus they urge that this should be used for the benefit of the people in the town. The Minister promised in 1966 to consider increasing the amount[42] but felt unable to do so during a time of financial stringency when public expenditure had to be severely restricted. The reason given is hardly convincing, because the Government have complete control over the level of expenditure by granting or withholding loan sanction and, where a project is allowed to go ahead, sharing the cost makes no difference to the total amount.

The effect of new town building on the local rates has worried the local authorities from the start and in reply to representations on this point they were given an assurance in 1946 that the local rates would not rise because of the new towns.[43] Ministers have been equally firm that amenity contributions in a new town should be on the basis of need, not the profit available. Henry Brooke emphasized this when he said, 'Neither I nor the Government will stand for the proposition that amenity expenditure among the new towns should be distributed strictly according to the profitability of the town concerned. That would be wholly wrong.'[44]

He did not, however, say what would be 'wholly right'. It is particularly important to establish first the object of these contributions and then to work out a basis for calculating and making payments that achieve the desired result. The starting-off point must surely be to relieve the ratepayers from an excessive burden. But what is excessive? And which ratepayers?

Take as an example a swimming pool that, because of the large number of young people, ought to be provided early on in the process of building the town. It may cost £250,000, with a loan sanction period of thirty years and the interest, repayments, and net running costs showing an annual deficit of perhaps £30,000. If at the time the pool is built the product of a 1d rate in the town is, say, £2,000, the burden on the rates in the first year would be of the order of 1s 3d in the pound. Rateable value in new towns builds up quickly, however. Ten years later, a 1d rate may be yielding £5,000, involving a rate burden for the swimming pool of only 6d in the pound and in the latter part of a thirty years' loan period the rate burden may be negligible.

The figures may not be quite so dramatic as this because many local authorities receive a general 'rate support grant' from the Exchequer. But this in itself would not be sufficient to encourage the local authority to build the swimming pool at the time it is wanted. It is in the early years that help from the development corporation is particularly needed, and a capital contribution does not do this. It helps to a very limited extent in the early years and goes on helping a little throughout the whole loan period. But it is the ratepayers in the early years who need help, not those who will be living in the town twenty years hence, by which time it is reasonable to assume that the rates will readily support the annual cost.

A much more helpful method of contribution therefore is to pay part of the loan charges, on a decreasing scale, over a period of, say, eight to ten years. As the graph at Fig. 6 shows, the total amount paid by the development corporation may well be the same as a capital contribution but the relief to rates is dramatically different. It is this relief to rates in the early years that is absolutely crucial if the local authorities in the new

H

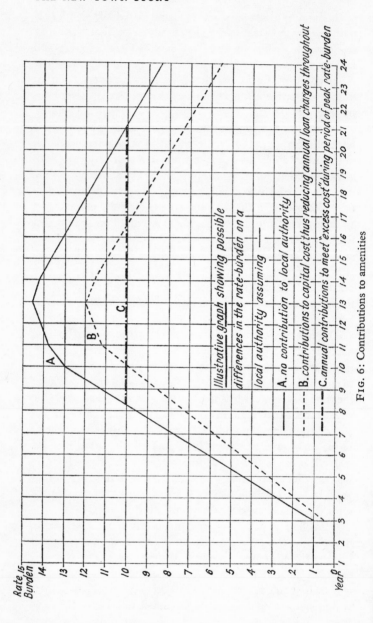

FIG. 6: Contributions to amenities

towns are to be encouraged to provide these important amenities when they are wanted. In the first new towns they were much too late because the Government failed to allow development corporations to give the right amount of help at the right time. But both the method and the amount of help are still the subject of argument. Some local authorities prefer to have a capital sum in their pockets rather than promises for the future; Ministries dislike complications to an already complicated general rate-support system of grant; and the Treasury abhor open-ended commitments. After twenty years of new town building there is still no agreed policy or formula and, even more disturbing, there is still insufficient recognition of the importance of the problem. When the Rouse brothers started to build Columbia, a private enterprise new town in Maryland, U.S.A., they built first of all the swimming pools, golf course, lakes, and community buildings and other amenities. Only then did they seriously start building houses to sell, and the town became an immediate success. We could well take at least half a leaf out of their book.

The swimming bath illustration demonstrates the principle in a simple way; but there are many other facilities needed in a town to match the growing population and the cost is cumulative. A comprehensive programme is an essential part of the process of building a town and it should not be allowed to remain a paper programme for lack of the right financial formula. So far as money can help, there must be no new town blues.

A brief summary of the new town balance sheets as at March 1969 and of the General Revenue Accounts for the year 1968–9 is given in Part III of the Appendix, but close study of the full accounts over the years is necessary to get a full appreciation of the position. The financial framework laid down some twenty years ago has stood the test of time although on some aspects clarification and uniformity of practice are desirable and the treatment of new towns in the national public expenditure allocations is still a cause of delay. But nobody can dispute the fact that the towns are proving a financial success.

It is essential to take a long view of the finances—indeed, one of the justifications of the system is that a public corporation can do this whereas a private firm has to look for quick profits to satisfy its shareholders. A town is bound to show a deficit in its early years before it becomes fully revenue producing. The first dozen towns were fortunate in being able to make a start while interest rates and land prices were low. The towns more recently established will have to face much more intense financial problems and if the interest rate remains, as it seems likely to do, at its present high level, it will be many more years before they begin to show a surplus on their operations.

It is also important to take a comprehensive view. New towns have a social objective as well as an economic one, and even if a town shows a loss in the accounts it may yet be the cheapest way of doing an essential job. The task of buying and demolishing the shacks at Basildon, for example, has so far cost the corporation over £4 million, yet by the time the town is finished and values have matured this load of debt will probably be wiped out. The £7 million Middle Lee Regional Drainage Scheme is being financed largely by the corporations of Stevenage and Harlow and though it serves a very large area of Hertfordshire it is still carried on the accounts of the new towns. The £500,000 water supply system at Crawley serves much of north-west Sussex but the quarter of a million pounds revenue loss to the corporation when it was handed over to the newly formed North West Sussex Water Board has now been written off by the Commission for the New Towns out of the surplus from other sources.

It is necessary, too, to consider the new towns as a single national investment. Some of those near London started showing profits on general revenue account after only eight to ten years. Others have not yet reached that stage and the towns recently started may show a deficit for even longer. Taking the British new towns as a whole, there is still a loss on general revenue and ancillary accounts of £6 million a year, on capital advances of £660 million; but with forty to fifty years of the loan repayments still to run, the expenditure bids fair to become one of the best investments ever made of the taxpayers' money. The eventual surplus could well be used to finance further new towns and thus limit the need to borrow from the Ministry.

Capital appreciation must not be overlooked. Values grow quickly in new towns, particularly of industrial and commercial properties. Revaluing the assets would be a massive task and would not justify the work and cost involved but the Commission for the New Towns have made a broad estimate and reported in 1968 that the assets in their four towns were worth at least £175 million, compared with their book value of £100 million.[45] It must be remembered, too, that very little industrial and commercial land in new towns has been disposed of freehold. When the reversions fall in about the middle of next century the physical basis for redevelopment will already be there without the costly business of buying the land all over again.

But long before next century the new towns will already have proved to be, as Sir Henry Wells has predicted, the 'gold mines of the future'.[46]

15. COMMISSION

IN 1961 the Government created a new body called the Commission for the New Towns to take over and manage the property of the towns as and when each was completed. They said it was an interim arrangement. There has been controversy for twenty years about what happens to a town when it has been built and the battle of ideas still rages.

The people, of course, go on living and working in the town. The local authorities carry on, as they have throughout the period of building, with the usual tasks of local administration. But when the development corporation responsible for the planning and building have finished their job, a town must gradually cease to be a 'new town' with special privileges and special financial arrangements and must stand on its own feet, no longer insulated from the outside world.

Yet it is not quite so simple as that. It is easy to start a new town but much more difficult to stop it. Its very success generates fresh demands as industry expands and children grow up, marry, and have families of their own. With nearly half the inhabitants under the age of twenty, over three-quarters under forty-five, and less than 4 per cent over sixty,[1] new births will exceed deaths and removals by a substantial margin and it will be many years before the age-grouping becomes normal.

In order to leave room for this 'natural expansion' the period of rapid growth has to stop a good deal short of the ultimate population for which the town is planned. The precise point will vary according to the age structure in the particular town but in general it has been found necessary to leave about a 25 per cent margin. Thus a town planned for 100,000 will have to stop taking in new people from outside when the population has reached 75,000–80,000; and it is calculated that the ultimate population will then be reached in another twenty years or so, by which time the age structure will be getting more in line with the national average.

It is not possible to exclude new immigrants altogether during this second stage. If an industrial company needs a highly skilled worker who is not available from within the town, clearly the post must be filled from outside; but by and large employers must at this stage look for their labour force primarily to the people in or around the town including, in particular, the growing number of school-leavers.

For many years, therefore, the town will continue to grow and more houses will be needed, more factories and offices to provide employment and more shops to meet the needs of the expanding population. This is a very important stage in the building of the town. The planning and development must be carried out with the same care and skill as the earlier development and to a carefully calculated programme that meets the special needs of the people. The towns represent too large a public investment and have made too great an impact on world opinion to let them be spoiled in this final stage of their growth.

The pace of development is, however, expected to be slower and the full organization of a development corporation is no longer appropriate. Government loans may still be needed to finance further building but the emphasis turns more towards management and less towards new construction.

It is just about this time, too, that some of the towns will begin to overcome the inevitable earlier losses and may be showing a modest revenue surplus; but there may still be substantial capital charges outstanding for roads, sewers, etc., and it will be many years before values become stable. The assets consist mainly of land and buildings that will eventually be worth several thousand million pounds—by far the largest single property undertaking in the country—and a highly skilled and co-ordinated system of estate management will be needed to look after them.

As with many other new town problems, the full implications could not be seen at the outset. The Reith Committee in 1945 were well aware of the importance of ultimate ownership but decided that correct solutions must wait upon experience. They would probably have made a tentative recommendation but for the fact that this was the one question on which there were divided opinions on the committee. They accordingly did no more than draw attention to it and indicate the various arguments and solutions.[2] In their view there were three possibilities—transfer of the assets to the local authorities, transfer to a national body, or continued ownership by the development corporation, with a modified constitution, as a permanent local landowner and estate manager.

Some members of the Reith Committee—rumour has it that it was one member only but there is no recorded evidence of this—favoured transfer to the local authorities; but a 'large majority' thought that it would be unwise to combine in a single body the functions of landowner of practically a whole town and the functions of the local authority. The Committee accordingly contented themselves with an analysis of the problem and added: 'The matter will be unlikely to need decision for some twenty years, and the issue may be determined in the meantime by national land policy.'

The Committee's optimistic reference to a solution through a 'national land policy' is intriguing. It must be remembered that they wrote their report in 1945 at a time when the report of the Uthwatt Committee[3] was under discussion, when the Coalition Government's White Paper on the Control of Land Use[4] had already been published and debated, but before the Labour Government had produced a Bill to give effect to their own conclusions. It was well known, however, that some form of central organization was likely to be set up to take over all development rights in land on the lines of the Uthwatt Committee's recommendations and that this body would need to have the power to buy and own land.

Also in mind at that time, perhaps, was the even more forthright suggestion in Chapter X of the Uthwatt Committee's report that the reversion to *all* land some 80–99 years hence should immediately be vested in the State, thus providing eventually a permanent, though long-term, solution to the compensation and betterment problem. It was not a unanimous recommendation: one member thought it would create too much uncertainty and another member objected on the grounds that it involved land nationalization; but the other two members put the idea forward for consideration, adding: 'They hold it to be the task of this generation to take stock of the possible needs and views of succeeding generations with respect to national planning. They wish to start time running in favour of succeeding generations.' Ministers were considering this suggestion at the time the Reith Committee were sitting but it was strong meat even for the first post-war Labour Government and, like many such recommendations in committee reports, is now buried in the dust of history. As always, future generations were left to seek their own salvation.

The Central Land Board was, however, set up in 1948 to collect increases in land-values resulting from planning permissions and was also given limited powers to buy and own land. This could well have fitted in with the Reith Committee's hope that there would be some landowning organization resulting from a national land policy that could eventually take over the nationally-owned assets in the new towns. The Central Land Board has long since been abolished[5] but a new national land body has now been set up in the form of the Land Commission[6] which also has power to buy and develop land and this may have a substantial bearing on future policy regarding the new town assets.

Back in 1946, however, when the first New Towns Bill was before Parliament, none of the major decisions on land reform had been taken. The Government had to take a decision about future ownership and in the event they decided in favour of the eventual transfer to a local authority. The New Towns Act 1946 accordingly gave the Minister power to wind up a development corporation when he was 'satisfied that the purposes for which it was established have been substantially achieved and is further satisfied, with the concurrence of the Treasury, that the circumstances are not such as to render it expedient on financial grounds to defer the disposal of the undertaking.'[7] Subject to those ifs and buts the Minister was able, with the consent of the Treasury, to make an Order providing for the 'transfer of the undertaking or any part of the undertaking of the corporation to such local authority (being an authority within whose area the new town is situated) as may be specified in the order or, in so far as the undertaking consists of a statutory undertaking, to such statutory undertakers as may be specified.' The financial and other terms, too, were left vague. They were to be determined by the Minister, with the consent of the Treasury, at the time of any particular transfer.

In 1946 these arrangements for ultimate ownership had the support of all parties in Parliament. In fact the only amendment of importance on this point came from the Conservatives who seemed to fear that financial considerations might *stop* the transfer to local authorities, and they accordingly sought to reduce the Treasury's power to say No![8] But they were also concerned that the development corporations, which, as W. S. Morrison said, were 'something of a novelty in the body politic', should not stay for too long. 'Like the grain of sand in the oyster,' he went on, 'they may become encrusted with some precious material that will make them of great value; on the other hand, they may develop into an irritant.'[9]

By the late fifties, when the first new towns were nearing their population target, the then Conservative Government came to the conclusion that it was premature to consider any transfer to the local authorities. Henry Brooke was Minister at the time and he and the Parliamentary Secretary, J. R. Bevins, gave the reasons to the House of Commons in the long debates on the New Towns Bill of 1959.[10] Many of the local authorities, they said, were newly formed urban district councils, with no experience of large-scale property management. For a local authority to own almost all the properties in their area was, in any case, undesirable on social grounds and outside the proper functions of elected authorities. 'Estate management should be stable,' said Mr Bevins, 'and it is unwise to mix it with politics.'

It was a bad moment, too, they thought, to consider financial terms. By then some £200 million of Government money had been spent on new towns but there was an accumulated revenue deficiency of £4½ million and an annual loss running at about £1 million. Long-term prospects were bright but no local authority should be asked or indeed would be willing to carry such a deficit. Taking Crawley as an example, Henry Brooke said that it would mean increasing the loan debt of the Urban District Council from £1½ million to £35 million and would put about 2s 9d on the rates.

Moreover, he pointed out, the new towns were a taxpayers'

investment which Parliament had a responsibility to protect and the assets ought to continue as assets of the nation at any rate until the taxpayer had got his money back. A period of consolidation, of settling down, was needed during which values would mature and stabilize. Some of the towns might soon be making a profit but others would still show a loss. He was anxious that the new towns should be good places to live in, with adequate help towards amenities, but it would be impossible to achieve that if each of them had to be taken as a separate financial entity. The strong must help the weak. One of the greatest merits of the single Commission, added Lord Waldegrave, the Government spokesman in the House of Lords, was that financially all the new towns could be treated as a whole.

For all these reasons the Government decided to appoint a new body called the Commission for the New Towns, to which would be transferred the property owned by the development corporations when they had finished the major work of building for new immigrants. The Act applies only to England and Wales and the Minister stressed that it was an interim arrangement. The whole question could be looked at again in ten to twenty years' time but he was quite frank in saying that he did not know what the ultimate solution might be. The circumstances years ahead would dictate the final decisions and he steadily resisted all attempts to extract a firm promise about the length of the 'interim stage'.

Henry Brooke admitted, however, that he was uneasy about housing. He did not like the idea of a central management remote from the towns dealing with such essentially local questions as allocation of tenancies, keeping property in repair and coping with the many personal problems that inevitably arise in dealing with thousands of tenants. To meet this situation the Bill required the Commission for the New Towns to set up a local committee in each town and to delegate to this committee the job of managing the Commission's houses. This would be obligatory. Other matters could also be delegated if the Commission wished.

The Bill had a rough passage, with some forthright and colourful speaking from the Opposition.

'This is a scandalous Bill. It plumbs the depths of doctrinaire reaction,' was Gilbert Mitchison's opening shot from the Labour front bench.

'Bureaucratic bumbledon in Whitehall,' was Hugh Dalton's description of the proposed New Towns Commission.

'It's nationalizing the new towns in perpetuity,' complained Gilbert Mitchison again '. . . destroying democratic institutions and nationalizing a great deal of property under the harshest bureaucratic autocracy that the Tory party or anybody else has ever succeeded in inventing.'

'This Measure destroys democracy,' asserted Emmanuel Shinwell, the Father of the House of Commons.

A foreign observer might have been forgiven for thinking the party labels had got switched! Here was a Conservative Government insisting on State ownership of land and buildings worth hundreds of millions, and the Labour Opposition, pledged for over half a century to the nationalization of land, protesting that a national landowning body, controlled by a Minister fully answerable to Parliament, was a dictatorship!

The key probably lies in the political undertones at which one can only guess. Certainly the Conservative leaders were adopting a policy that was quite different from the one they had supported eleven years earlier. Henry Brooke's arguments had a good deal of support in other quarters and he was not deterred by the fact that they led to a conclusion so out of line with traditional Conservative thinking. But it is always good Parliamentary sport to twist the tail of Government speakers by quoting from earlier speeches to demonstrate their inconsistency; and on this the Opposition pulled no punches.

But there was much more to it than that. The Labour Opposition were highly suspicious of the Government's motives. At about that time Labour were advocating the transfer of all privately rented houses to the local authorities[11] to help wipe out the increasing exploitation of the housing shortage that was eventually revealed in the Rachman scandals. This new move they no doubt saw as a threat to their policy. They feared, too, that the proposed Commission was intended by the Conservative Government to be in the main a 'disposals board' for selling off to private owners these valuable publicly-owned assets.

Despite many assurances by Henry Brooke and others that there was no such hidden motive and that under the Bill as drafted wholesale disposal by the Commission would be illegal, this lurking fear runs through the debates, right up to the last stage in the House of Lords.

On the main issue, however, the Labour spokesmen were certainly sincere in their view that, as Gilbert Mitchison put it, 'the right people to own and manage new towns are the local authorities'; though Emmanuel Shinwell, speaking for himself, was prepared to concede that it might be necessary to hive off housing and leave the factories either to be managed by the Minister or even leased or sold outright to the factory owners. At that time, as was clear from the debates, the Opposition were largely voicing the strongly-held views of some of the local authorities in new town areas. These views were not necessarily representative of local authority opinion generally, and had little support in other circles. Following a Conference in 1958 the Executive Committee of the Labour Party had set up a special sub-committee on the subject, but the sub-committee did not report until after the Bill was nearly through Parliament. Their conclusions were published in July 1959[12] and were adopted by the National Executive.

This document made some interesting concessions compared with the forthright assertions made in Parliament a few months earlier. Briefly the committee agreed that the ordinary small local authority could not immediately take over the assets and the programme of development in the second phase of natural expansion. Special Exchequer subsidies and finance would still be required, the administrative resources of the authority would have to be built up, staffs would need to be enlarged and more civic buildings constructed to accommodate them. They recognized that the management of commercial and industrial properties called for specialized knowledge and experience for which independent professional advisers might need to be used.

The Labour Party committee proposed therefore that the development corporation should remain in being, with their membership broadened to include local authority members, until the amount of new building dropped to a level which the authority could handle. Then the property should be transferred piecemeal, neighbourhood by neighbourhood, so that the development corporation's organization could run down and that of the local authority could build up. Transfer should be on the basis not of market value but a simple transfer of actual assets and liabilities, the local authority, in effect, just going on paying to the Minister the outstanding loan charges for the remainder of the sixty-year period.

This policy statement was too late to influence the debates as the Act was by then through Parliament. The Minister did not set up the Commission for the New Towns until 1 October 1961, however, and they were given six months to get themselves organized. On 1 April 1962, the assets of the Crawley and Hemel Hempstead Development Corporations were transferred to them by Ministerial order; and on 1 April 1966, the assets of the Welwyn Garden City and Hatfield Development Corporations were also transferred to them by the new Labour Government pending a review of policy and Parliamentary time for new legislation.

Thus the Commission own the assets in four of the new towns and their job is to 'take over, hold, manage and turn the property to account, and to maintain and enhance the value and the return obtained from it having regard to the purpose for which the town was developed and to the convenience and welfare of persons residing, working or carrying on business there.'[13] The Commission members are appointed by the Minister and, as in the case of development corporations, membership disqualifies from membership of the House of Commons.[14] The number of members is limited by the Act to fifteen, but so far, with only four towns transferred, membership has not exceeded eight, including the Chairman and Deputy Chairman. At the time the 1959 Act was under discussion it was confidently expected that by about 1968 all the first round of new towns would be substantially complete and that the Commission would own the assets in a dozen towns. It has not worked out in this way because the strong pressure for more housing has resulted in expanded programmes for all the other towns in England and Wales. These will take the development corporations some eight to ten years to complete and by then new legislation is likely to be in force.

What form this legislation will take is not yet certain but it is clear that the Government and the Labour Party are having second thoughts. Ministerial statements have been very guarded, particularly on the question of industrial and commercial property. Richard Crossman, when he was Minister of Housing & Local Government, commented that 'these questions have been far too little considered by the planners and the politicians';[15] and Prime Minister Harold Wilson said that 'the industrial and commercial assets raise special problems which are very complex and difficult'.[16] The Labour Party itself is also changing its view. A resolution to the 1968 Party Conference advocated the transfer to local authorities of houses and neighbourhood shops but for the industrial and commercial Properties, including town centre shops, transfer to a new central Government agency—a New Towns Industrial Corporation—was suggested.

To provide further guidance on housing the Minister commissioned Professor Cullingworth of Birmingham University to study the present pattern of house-ownership and management and the advantages and disadvantages of the various possible forms for the future. His 200-page report[17] (with full reports of the surveys to follow) was based on a study in depth in four towns and a mass of evidence taken from the local authorities, the local authority associations, the development corporations, and the Commission for the New Towns. He analyses in great detail the pattern of housing administration in the towns, the pros and cons of transfer to the local authorities, the effect on rents and other financial aspects, the extent of the demand for owner-occupation, the ability of tenants to buy at current prices and possible means of helping them. The text is supported by a mass of valuable statistical evidence. He was not asked to make recommendations. The data he provides must now be the subject of examination and political decision; but among other things, his report has highlighted the complexity of the problem even on the subject of housing, to which his terms of reference were confined.

Meanwhile, despite the threat of summary abolition, the Commission for the New Towns are carrying on with the job of managing property in the four towns so far under their control. It consists of 34,000 rented houses of all types, over 4,000 houses on long lease, 16,000 garages, 9 million sq ft of factory space, over 1 million sq ft of shopping space, $1\frac{1}{4}$ million sq ft of office space and 1 million sq ft of service industry. Much of it is rack rented, some of it is on ground lease. In all they own about 10,000 acres of land, of which some 2,000 acres are held in reserve for future building, and a miscellaneous collection of other property, such as community buildings, car parks, etc. They are also the ground landlords of about 27 public houses and numerous commercial entertainment buildings, most of which are on 99-year leases. This property stands in the books at some £100 million, representing cost less depreciation; but the Commission recently estimated the value in 1968 to be at least £175 million. Their gross income from all sources for the financial year ended 31 March 1969, was over £8 million, of which over half was from rented housing and the rest mainly from the rents or ground rents of shops, offices, and factories.[18]

The Commission's role is not confined to management. Although Henry Brooke forecast in 1959 that the Commission would not need to build many houses, they are in fact building a high proportion of the additional houses needed to meet the needs of industrial and natural expansion. Some are to let, some to sell and in general they build slightly more expensive houses than the local authorities, who are also playing a major part in the programme. The Commission are also selling land for private enterprise house-building.

Most of the land held in reserve for more shops, offices, and factories is also owned by the Commission and it is their job to organize this building to meet the needs of these still-growing communities. The Minister has also placed on the Commission the responsibility for rebuilding Old Hatfield—a £2 million job. In the four towns they have a £23 million programme ahead of them, to be carried out in the next four or five years, that will need all the co-ordinated efficiency and finance of a new town organization to carry it through. And when that programme is completed a great deal of building will still be needed as the second and third generations grow up and the towns advance to full maturity.

It is clear from their annual reports that the Commission are very conscious of the suggestions in Parliament that they would be a 'remote bureaucracy' and have been at some pains to dispel this feeling. Delegation to a local level, they explained in their 1965 Report, is the basic principle of their organization. The Commission, with a total headquarters staff of only thirty, maintain general control over policy, finance, and capital investment but the execution of policy and detailed management are the responsibility of a manager in each town. He and his staff—and in the four towns there is a total staff of over 1,000—are in touch with all activities in the town, with the local authorities and with the local Press and are well informed on local needs and local opinion. Much of the work is highly specialized, particularly in the field of estate management, needing the expertise of the commercial world and continuing contact with the practice and experience of new towns elsewhere. The Commission are just as much a part of the new town movement as a newly-appointed development corporation.

For the purpose of housing management, where local knowledge is particularly important, the Commission have appointed a local committee in each town, the members of which live in or have detailed knowledge of the town. Several of them are members of the local council and the chairman of each local committee is a member of the Commission itself, thus ensuring a complete interchange of views from the various towns and direct and continuous contact between the central body and the local organizations.

It is true that the members are selected, not elected. The members of the Commission are appointed by the Minister and the members of the local committee are appointed by the Commission after consultation with the local authority and with the Minister's approval. In this way the views and suggestions of the elected body are taken fully into account and at the same time the Minister's responsibility to Parliament is preserved. The Commission's view is that 'these arrangements have ensured informed and sympathetic management, sensitive to public opinion without being unduly influenced by local or political pressures or the varying fortunes of the political parties at local elections.'[19]

On the whole, the Commission got into its stride quickly and successfully. In the early days there was a feeling that some of the local authorities did not want the system to work lest it should prove too successful; but the Commission made it clear that so long as the present Act remained in force they had a duty to make it work and relationships with the local authorities soon became cordial and co-operative. As soon as it becomes possible, a single housing waiting list is set up in each town covering both local authority and Commission houses with comparable rent levels, a common rent rebate scheme and where necessary a joint committee of members. The power to make financial contributions from one housing revenue account to the other[20] has helped this forward so that despite divided ownership there can now be a completely unified housing administration that embraces both the local authority housing responsibility and the somewhat wider new town role. As a spokesman for the Commission has put it, 'These joint arrangements have made the transfer of houses to the local authority much easier. It could be done by the stroke of a Parliamentary pen. On the other hand, it has made it much less necessary.'[21]

To the people in the towns, the question of ultimate ownership does not seem a burning issue, though many of those in Commission houses say they have no wish to become council tenants! As the Cullingworth surveys indicate, owner-occupation interests them far more. But there are too many unknowns for a clear line of policy yet to be seen. The whole local government system is certain to be reorganized in the light of the Redcliffe–Maud report[22] and nobody can yet say what the effect will be on the present housing authorities.

The Commission's housing role is very much wider at present than that of the local authorities in the towns because they have to look beyond purely domestic needs. They have a responsibility to industrialists and others who often need to recruit key workers from outside the town and they have a responsibility to parents of tenants who sometimes wish to move into the town to be near their children. If the local authority were to take over all the houses these special needs would have to be safeguarded and their role would have to be extended well beyond that of a normal housing authority; but as they are answerable only to the local electorate and, quite naturally, have a distinct bias towards the interests of the existing residents, there must be some doubt about whether the wider policy could be effectively administered.

Some people fear that ownership by the local authority of so large a proportion of the rented housing in the town would mean that rents—always a politically explosive issue—and the allocation of tenancies would become particularly important issues at elections. In a situation where most of the electors and many of the local councillors would be tenants of the authority and where most of the councillors would be employed by the industrial or commercial concerns that would be looking to the council to satisfy the housing requirements of their workpeople, problems could arise on a scale not usually encountered in a normal local authority housing administration.

The future ownership of the industrial and commercial property in the new towns raises very different issues. These are the main source of profit from which to meet the costs of roads, sewers, and other services that yield no direct return and the financial success of some of the earlier towns is such that many of these debts have already been discharged. In the years to come they will show a very handsome profit which many say ought to be used to help the less successful towns or to help with the cost of new building or rebuilding elsewhere.

Certainly there would seem to be no real case for handing these profits to the local authorities to be used for the relief of rates. New towns have many privileges denied to most other towns but this is a source of help that could hardly be given to a few local authorities whose areas happened to be selected for development under the new town machinery. Indeed, these resources are potentially so valuable that an authority owning all the houses, shops, and factories might eventually be able to run all the services for the town out of the profits without needing to levy a rate. The whole local government system would be in turmoil!

Nor, it is argued, is there any case for handing over to the various local authorities even the management of these industrial and commercial assets that will eventually be worth several hundred million pounds. It is a highly skilled branch of estate management, outside the normal experience of local authorities and quite inappropriate for control by elected councillors. If the taxpayers' investment is to be fully safeguarded some form of expert co-ordinated management must be preserved.

These are the sort of problems that the Government must now grapple with. Widely differing opinions are held and they do not necessarily divide along political party lines. Much has changed since the debates of 1958 and there will be more changes before these problems are settled. Local government will be reorganized, the Land Commission will have got into its stride as a national land purchasing and development agency, and the new regional planning machinery will have pointed the way to a more positive, more co-ordinated and more constructive approach to the future needs of the country. More new towns, new cities or major expansion of existing communities have already been started that may eventually involve capital assets of some £3,000 million, and there will be more to come.

It is in this wider context that the question of the new town assets must now be examined. A new, cool, and objective look is needed, unbedevilled by preconceived ideas, pressure groups, or political lobbying. The future well-being of too many people is at stake for decisions to be lightly taken or for the argument to degenerate into a battle for the spoils.

Yet however long the argument goes on and whatever the final answer, it concerns only the bricks and mortar, the money, and the profits. The first fifteen towns are nearly built; already a million people have found a new life; a score of thriving communities have been created. These are the real assets and they will always lie with the people. For you cannot put a price on human happiness and a child's rosy cheeks.

16. ACHIEVEMENT

THE new towns are a success—of this there is no doubt. They are not perfection. Lack of experience and economic squeezes and freezes have left their mark. With ideas rapidly changing, some of the development of twenty years ago is already becoming out of date; but this is inevitable. Indeed, it is an encouraging sign that the revolution in thought that was first able to find expression in the new towns is still in progress.

The statistics for Britain are impressive. Fifteen towns almost built: a dozen more started. Nearly 175,000 new houses; hundreds of new industries in 35,000,000 sq ft of modern factory space; 350 new schools with 150,000 school places; 4,000,000 sq ft of office space, 100 new pubs, scores of churches and public buildings, several thousand acres of park, playing-field, and open space, and a host of minor achievements too numerous to catalogue. A detailed summary is given in Part II of the Appendix.

But a new town does not exist in a vacuum. It can be studied as an individual project, it can be pronounced a success or failure according to a critic's view of the planning, design, rate of building or social content. But in the national context the achievement of the new towns must be judged by the collective contribution they have made to the problems of overcrowding, the progress they have brought in the science of 'building for living', and the lessons they point for the future.

Too few and too late may well be the verdict of history on the first twenty years of work under the New Towns Act. Even in 1969, with twenty-seven towns designated in Britain, the total contribution to the national house-building programme is no more than 12,000 houses a year out of an annual total for Britain of over 400,000. Of the 7 million houses built since the war less than 200,000 were in new towns. Yet people still live in overcrowded conditions, in slums or near slums, or lack adequate bathroom and toilet facilities.

This is the measure of our national failure. The very success

227

of the new towns in providing homes for less than a million people in well-planned surroundings only serves to emphasize the contrast. The imagination and enthusiasm that inspired the new town organizations have not been matched by an equal fervour in dealing with the rest of our housing and planning problems.

The new towns were a symbol, an expression of the determination that in 1946 placed Britain in the van of European thought and progress. Since then we have fallen behind. Disillusionment, apathy, reaction or inaction replaced the vigour and understanding of the forties. Almost all other European countries, many of them much more shattered by wartime devastation, have gone ahead at greater speed and with greater effect.[1] Lewis Mumford, with his broad international perspective, has described the abrupt termination of the new towns programme in 1952 as 'a failure of the British political imagination, not a failure of the new towns themselves and still less a failure of the premises on which they were built.'[2]

Lewis Silkin told the House of Commons in 1946 that he thought about twenty new towns would be needed in the first stage. He and Hugh Dalton who succeeded him as Minister in 1950 had every intention of continuing the programme and were investigating proposals to deal with overspill from Manchester and Liverpool. The problems of Leeds, Portsmouth, and Plymouth were mentioned; several towns were in mind for the Clyde valley and some for eastern Scotland. When Harold Macmillan became Minister of Housing in the new Conservative Government of 1952 he said he intended to assist and further the work of the new towns by every means in his power[3] and both he and successive Conservative Ministers certainly gave full support to the towns already being built; but nothing more was heard of the new proposals and Baroness Sharp, in her book about the Ministry of which she was for many years Permanent Secretary, reveals that she had to 'fight for the life of an apparently puny and much too demanding child'.[4] It was not until November 1957 that the Government officially admitted that there were to be no more new towns[5]—a belated admission because, with the single exception of Cumbernauld in Scotland, there had been no new designations for seven years.

The Government at that time were in fact relying heavily on the Town Development Act 1952, which left it to local authorities to get together on overspill schemes and reach agreements on finance. Many of these schemes are little more than small housing estates added to an existing town. They are thus quite different in concept from the new towns and even the few larger schemes that were started in the 1950s are, in the opinion of many, well below the standard of achievement in the new towns.

The former London County Council—one of the few local authorities in Britain with the capacity for undertaking development on the scale needed—prepared a plan for a new town of 100,000 people at Hook in Hampshire.[6] Their proposals, which drew heavily on the experience of the Government new towns, and the Cumbernauld plan in particular, made quite a stir at the time; but there was strong local opposition and the Government turned down the project. The Greater London Council are now building a new town for 60,000 Londoners on the Erith marshes, to be called Thamesmead. The plan is an imaginative one and may well match the achievement of the Government new towns; but there is a fear that it may produce, in terms of social structure, another Dagenham. This is one of the dangers of leaving development on this scale to the local authorities. Their preoccupation with housing lists, which after all is one of their main duties, and the need to use their financial resources to achieve the maximum housing benefit over the limited field of those who happen to be on the 'housing lists', are almost bound to give a very different result from the broader new town conception. The housing problem is not divisible in this way. It is an integral part of the whole programme of planned development. Our national stock of houses must match the whole range of national need in terms of numbers, types, and distribution and must cater for the many millions who will need houses but whose names will never appear on a council list.

Developments under these other powers are outside the scope of this book but they are relevant to an assessment of post-war achievement simply because they arose from the Government's refusal at the time to continue using the New

Towns Act. Honourable mention must also be made of the Northumberland County Council who, having failed in the early sixties to get Government support for two small new towns at Killingworth and Cramlington, set about finding the money themselves to build them under planning powers.

It was over eleven years before another new town was designated in England. The Liverpool 'overspill' discussions had dragged on for years and, although in 1955 the Lancashire County Council had suggested Skelmersdale in their development plan as a suitable new town site, the Ministry were pressing them to use the Town Development Act instead. No progress whatever was being made. But by 1961 the new towns—still regarded by some as socialist madness—were not only showing signs of becoming highly profitable ventures but with the Cumbernauld plan hitting the world headlines were being recognized abroad as one of the most successful ideas Britain had produced. At the same time the plight of the homeless and the Rachman scandals had put the Government's housing record and policy under heavy fire and the growing traffic congestion in towns, which later led to the Buchanan Report,[7] had revealed the lack of any sense of urgency in dealing with this pressing problem. With a sudden switch in policy in 1961, the Conservative Government decided in favour of more new towns. Skelmersdale and Runcorn were designated to take Liverpool overspill, Dawley and Redditch to take Birmingham overspill, and a new town was proposed at Washington to help with the problems of Tyneside. At the same time a planning study was started into the problems of the south-east and all the existing new town corporations were asked to consider whether their towns could be expanded. Most of them have now prepared revised plans for larger populations.[8]

The years of complacency were over. This new impetus was already having its effect when the Labour Government came to power at the 1964 elections. The Washington proposal was quickly confirmed and Regional Economic Councils were set up to make a thorough study of planning and economic problems. Within the next few years the Government decided to build a new town for 250,000 Londoners in north Buckinghamshire (Milton Keynes); to use the machinery of the New Towns Act to increase the size of Peterborough and Northampton, each by 70,000 people; to double the size of Dawley (now renamed Telford) by including the adjoining areas of Wellington and Oakengates; to designate another new town at Irvine in Scotland; to build a small new town at Newtown in Wales with the possibility, if it is a success, of extending it to Caersws, as recommended by the consultants; and at long last, after nearly twenty years of discussion and search for a suitable site, to build at Warrington for Manchester's overspill.

When the New Towns Act for Northern Ireland came into force in 1965 the Government quickly accepted it as a powerful instrument of regional and economic policy, going well beyond the simple task of relieving overcrowding in the big cities. Already development is well ahead at Craigavon; the plans for the twin towns of Antrim and Ballymena are taking shape; and the whole of the Londonderry County Borough and Rural District Council areas are now under the control of a new town development commission.

In addition to these firm decisions several other investigations were set on foot, some of which are bound to lead to further new towns in due course. To meet the long-neglected problem of Central Lancashire a new city for half a million people is proposed in the Preston–Leyland–Chorley area, to act as a growth point in Lancashire's economic revival. Following two studies by consultants a draft Designation Order was made covering 41,000 acres and a local inquiry has been held into the 650 objections.[9]

The Government also commissioned a report on the possible expansion of Ashford, a historic market town in Kent that is likely to play an important part in the development of the South-East when the Channel tunnel comes into operation in about 1975. Consultants reported that it would be feasible to increase the population by 150,000, resulting in a new city of 240,000 by about 1991; but they clearly had doubts about the precise impact of the Channel tunnel and about the wisdom of such extensive and rapid growth in the area.[10] The Kent County Council shared these doubts,[11] and the Minister decided not to adopt the proposal, for the time being.

The expansion of Ipswich was first suggested many years

ago, and was the subject of several reports by consultants[12] before the Minister made a draft Designation Order in 1968. The intention was that the town should be expanded under the New Towns Act by 70,000 people from London, in partnership with the local authorities, as is being done at Northampton and Peterborough. At the local inquiry the agricultural objections were strongly pressed and doubts were thrown on the need for the expansion by the recently published reports of the Greater London Council, which suggested that the overspill problem was rather less than had hitherto been thought. The Minister decided not to confirm the Order—the first time that a project has been entirely abandoned after reaching the stage of draft designation. The East Anglia Consultative Committee have now put forward a proposal for a new town at Breckland, a bleak stretch of Norfolk heathland,[13] and this is no doubt being closely examined.

In Wales there is a proposal to build a new town at Llantrisant, by the foot of the Rhondda valley, where coal mining is rapidly declining and new centres of industrial growth may soon be desperately needed. The new Royal Mint is already being built at Llantrisant, and the consultants' Report,[14] which the Government are now studying, has recommended a new £381 million town to be built over thirty years for up to 140,000 people.

On the wider regional scale, several major investigations have been launched. The large area on the south coast embracing the cities of Southampton and Portsmouth is likely to be one of the key expansion areas in the years to come, acting as a 'counter-magnet' to London, and a planning study in 1966[15] suggested the lines of expansion for another half-million people. With two such important cities closely concerned in the development, the Minister decided that the next stage should be the preparation of a Master Plan by the authorities themselves, through a committee chaired by a senior official of the Ministry, and that it would not be appropriate to set up a new town development corporation for the purpose. A decision on the appropriate method or agency for implementing the plan will no doubt come later.

A report on the Humberside area[16] suggests various methods for dealing with a possible influx of up to 750,000 people by the end of the century. A new bridge over the Humber has already been authorized, and a decision on the rest is not needed just yet. Some new town development—possibly a new city at Limber and a major town in the North Cave area—seems almost certain to be required in the 1980s.

The Tees-side area of County Durham and Yorkshire has also been the subject of an extensive report[17] which envisages a population increase of some 220,000 within a generation. New villages and towns are proposed at Levenside, Nunthorpe, Martin, Hemlington, Wolviston, and between Marsk and Redcar; but it will be some time yet before any decision is taken about whether, if at all, the new town machinery is appropriate.

Studies of Tayside, where, with the completion of the Forth and Tay road bridges, the population could increase by 150,000, may well lead to the creation of one or more new towns; and the examination of Severnside will involve close analysis of the effect of the new Severn Bridge and the extensive motorway network on the economy of the whole south-west region.[18] The possibility of catering for overspill from Merseyside in north-east Wales, with a Dee Estuary crossing, is also being examined.

All this adds up to a massive programme, both existing and potential, that matches the needs of the time. Planning strategy has undergone both a quantitative and qualitative change in the last few years. New towns are no longer merely satellites for dealing with overspill: they are essential elements in the economic development of the country, providing a focus for industrial growth and counter-attractions to the present over-large conurbations for the purpose of securing a more satisfactory distribution of people, jobs, and traffic. They will make heavy demands on Exchequer investment and even heavier demands on our technical and professional resources. But one thing is certain: new towns have come to stay.

So the major tasks are ahead of us. The new plans now emerging are imaginative, and there is every indication that they will more than match the achievements of the past. Much will depend on the economic situation and on whether shortage of capital and other restrictions will limit their scope and depress standards. Perhaps the most significant advance in thought was the decision to use the new-town powers to ensure the planned expansion of sizeable existing towns where the inclusion in the designated area of the built-up areas makes it possible to tackle the difficult and expensive problem of urban renewal.

In a few of the new areas building has already started, but it will be some years yet before they can be judged on the ground. For the present a judgement of current achievements must depend mainly on the 'first round' of new towns, the 'Mark I' towns, and on Cumbernauld, the first of the 'Mark II'. Despite the small part they have so far been allowed to play in Britain's post-war programme, these towns have already been hailed as one of the achievements of the century. Architects, engineers, planners, sociologists, and historians from all parts of the world come to study the new towns. Foreign governments look to Britain for advice on how it is done. Sightseers flock to see them. A visit to a new town is becoming as popular with foreign visitors as seeing our ancient cathedral towns or the rebuilt Coventry. Only the British people seem to be quite unaware of the significance of this new chapter in the history of our time. Richard McDougall, former General Manager of the Stevenage Development Corporation, tells of a twenty-year-old English girl who worked for a while as secretary to a famous architect and town planner in Sydney, Australia. 'How lucky you are to live only twelve miles from Stevenage new town,' he told her. 'I didn't dare to tell him,' she said, 'that I've never seen the blooming place.'[19]

Abroad, however, many countries have now followed Britain's lead, adopting the principle and adapting the method to their own circumstances. Sir Frederick Osborn lists some sixty countries in which development has been planned for communities, as distinct from suburban growth,[20] and most of them owe much of their inspiration to British new-town experience. The export of ideas in this field has greatly added to British prestige, and several of our leading planning consultants are engaged by governments or development organizations in many overseas countries to advise on new-town projects. Indeed there are some who think that the reputation the British have acquired of having invented the new towns is somewhat overdone. One American commentator complained that

> 'the term "new town" seems to have acquired a European overtone. . . . Even among some architects and planners the impression has spread that New Town is not exactly a hundred per cent American. Such chauvinists ignore their own history for nothing could be less foreign or more a characteristically American "mix" of Anglo-Saxon tradition, Puritan sentiment, capitalistic enterprise, and pioneer communism than the New Town that was established in 1638 at Sudbury (Massachusetts).[21]

All assessments are, in a sense, comparative. It is no use comparing the new towns with the terraces of Bath that were built for a bygone age; or with the once-sleepy market towns of Britain that grew over hundreds of years and contain within a single street a score of different architectural styles that give them a special visual and nostalgic charm. The new towns are built in today's idiom and for today's needs. The building standards are reasonably good and, though there are few architectural gems, some of the houses and flats and some of the public buildings will certainly rank among the best examples of current achievement.

Of course, there are plenty of comparable examples outside the new towns. There are many excellent local authority housing schemes and numerous town centre redevelopments that are themselves valuable examples of comprehensive treatment. Private enterprise in recent years can also show some houses of good modern design and layout, though they are mostly in the higher price ranges. At least one builder engaged a firm of architects with wide experience of new towns to design a garden village as a self-contained community, with shops, school, church, and other community facilities.[22]

There are, too, the vast office developments in London and other cities during the late fifties and sixties, some very good, some incredibly bad. The difference between all these and the new towns lies in the scale and social content. Housing schemes in or on the fringe of towns usually have a more limited objective—often too limited; and there is little human or social interest in the city shopping centres and office blocks, unless it be in the system that made possible the millions of pounds in profit that Oliver Marriott has already analysed with remarkable effect.[23]

In their historical perspective the right comparison to draw is with the building of the thirties, for it was the glaring defects of the inter-war years—the one-class housing estates, the aimless spread of suburbia, the frustration of ribbon development —that the new towns were planned to avoid. But the main reason for the interest and acclamation given to the new towns lies in the fact that they are about the only examples in Britain— and probably the first in the world—of truly comprehensive development, aiming to produce a complete pattern of living for a full cross-section of people and in which the driving force is the social content and not the financial gain. Taken as a whole they have set a standard a good deal higher than in most comparable fields elsewhere, not merely in planning and design but in social content.

This is why they have aroused so much interest among sociologists and other investigators. The new towns are a framework for a million human stories, too many by far to be sorted out individually. A talk with a dozen, a hundred, a thousand people gives a wide variety of response. Some will criticize, some will grumble; some will recall with nostalgia their early life in London or Glasgow; others will count it among their blessings that they escaped. Almost all will say it was a wonderful thing for the children.

But this is no basis for a serious judgement. Much more independent social research is necessary to build up a greater knowledge and a greater understanding on which the developments of the future can be based. Hitherto the main interest has been necessarily confined to the early stages when the towns were getting established. This is important, but it tends to distort the assessment by concentrating on temporary difficulties or shortcomings, most of which can hardly be avoided at the outset. Now that the first fifteen towns are nearing completion and the growing pains are over, it is time to begin to examine them on a wider basis. Sociological study must be a continuous process but the true test, the really important verdict, will be in another ten or twenty years when the towns are no longer 'new', when they have become normal towns with a normal age and family pattern and when the long-term influence of environment can be more fully judged.

Even to see all the new towns is now a vast undertaking. Already they extend over hundreds of acres, with an immense variety of architecture, layout, and landscaping. For any visitor aiming to get a general impression it is difficult to know what to look for and where to find it. Without some guidance he may do little more than stroll around the shopping centre and never see the many other features that make up the town as a whole. Even the small touches are not to be missed.

There's 'Joyride', the symbolic Belsky bronze of mother and child in the famous Stevenage town centre.

There are the water gardens at Hemel Hempstead, with their nesting swans, and 'Rock-n-Roll', the exquisite sculpture by Hubert Yencesse of two young figures dancing over the water.

There's the flash of inspiration that led the Crawley Development Corporation to rescue a rusting Victorian bandstand from the old Gatwick racecourse and plant it, painted and gilded, in the middle of the shopping centre. And near by—a bit of playful nonsense—a clock tower that plays *Genevieve* on bells to mark Crawley's historic association with the annual London to Brighton old crocks' race. Not everybody approves.

Basildon is noted most for its massive achievement in converting a rural slum of shacks and railway coaches into a flourishing town with a spacious town centre and the ambitious Gloucester Park. But tucked away just off the town square, is 'Little Chelsea'—a gem of design and layout that seeks to recreate the close-knit urban huddle and pattern of living so sought after in London.

Welwyn Garden City is particularly proud of the Digswell Arts Centre where sixteen top-line artists and students of all types live and work in an old Georgian mansion that was rescued from demolition on the inspiration of Henry Morris.

237

Here some of the stained glass for Coventry Cathedral was being made when it was officially opened by the late Lady Mountbatten.

Harlow, a town full of charm and surprises, is most noted for its achievements in health, music, and sport, and for its modern sculpture. The new Sports Centre is a hive of day-long activity. Most afternoons you can find a roomful of small children being minded while the mothers play badminton or indulge in some other form of strenuous relaxation.

Look, too, in Harlow for the controversial housing development at Bishopsfield—nicknamed the Kasbah by the irreverent, but a striking example of current style—and the four other versions in recent schemes of how to cope with the motor car.

Bracknell is only just growing up after being told to double its size. The new town centre, now beginning to take shape, will be widely acclaimed in a few years' time. Much of the attraction of the town lies in its charming houses and the careful preservation of the many trees that give to the town an immediate maturity that usually takes a generation to establish.

Now and then the architects seem to have jumped a generation. Take the new town churches. They startle anybody over forty who likes a church to look like a church, but they are a vivid demonstration of the step forward of twentieth-century church architecture and the influence on design of the Second Industrial Revolution.

Sometimes you can't move in the shopping centres for prams. It was Harold Macmillan who said he had never before seen so many happy healthy children. But the toddlers of those days are growing up now. Look in any evening at the new £120,000 Youth Centre at Stevenage. You can't hear yourself speak; but it's an education in teenage activity.

Take note in Cumbernauld of the careful layout of the houses giving privacy and views across the valley, and the inlaid granite setts of the walkways pointing the path to the town centre. And, after seeing the impressive arcaded town centre at East Kilbride and the new Inland Revenue computer building close by, stop off overnight and enjoy the cabaret in the new hotel. Or come down south on a Friday to Welwyn Garden City where you can pay tribute at the memorials to Ebenezer

Howard and Louis de Soissons and enjoy an *haute cuisine* dinner-dance at the Homestead Court Hotel.

And don't just dismiss the industrial districts as bound to be uninteresting and pass them by. Some of the towns contain excellent examples of industrial architecture, and the care and attention given to landscaping makes them a striking contrast to the general run of industrial areas in Britain.

These are but a few of the smaller touches to be sought out by any visitor. It is the attention to detail and the unity of purpose that have helped to turn what could have been just a dreary succession of housing estates into interesting places to live in. Even the street names are often the result of hours of study of local history, old maps, and ancient field records and have preserved for posterity some of the colour of our farming heritage. Sometimes they commemorate famous figures in local history—or even infamous ones. Seymour Road, one of the new roads at Broadfield in Crawley, is to be named after Admiral Lord Seymour, who in 1548 put forward a plan to 'buylde a towne' on land he owned in the area. He was executed for treason shortly afterwards.

These are the 'old' new towns, almost finished and beginning to mature. Now the eyes of the world will be on the 'new' new towns and cities at a dozen or more places throughout Britain. They have much to learn from the old, but they will be no mere replicas. So much has changed: car ownership, television, supermarkets, leisure habits, and rising pay packets have led to important changes in planning thought and practice. The new towns of the seventies will mean a new revolution and a new miracle.

One day, perhaps, the history of each town will be written. Indeed, each development corporation or local authority ought seriously to consider this while events are fresh in people's minds. Arrangements are being made for the permanent preservation of important official records in either the Public Record Office or the County Archives[24] but without the human stories behind them much of the colour of contemporary life will be lost and posterity will be the loser.

In a book directed primarily to examining the general philosophy of new towns and the way they are built, it is not possible to give much of the history of each town or to study in detail their individual achievements. Nor is it necessary to do so because Sir Frederic Osborn and Arnold Whittick have already covered that ground elsewhere.[25] Details, necessarily brief, are given in Part I of the Appendix of the size and object of each town, and this demonstrates the changes in policy and approach over the years. For full study of a particular town the Master Plans should be read; and for those needing less detailed information the publicity literature issued by the various corporations gives a very full background.

But new towns cannot be appreciated by just reading books and pamphlets. To those who are interested in human affairs and in the physical fabric that is the background to living; to those who take pride in this nation's achievements in the field of social advance; to those who are concerned to improve the conditions in which many millions of their fellow-countrymen still live; to those who want to judge for themselves whether in the new towns can be seen an encouraging glimpse of the future; to all these, the best advice that can be given is: 'Go and see'.

The miracle of today may be the commonplace of tomorrow.

17. FUTURE

THE experimental stage is over. We must now as a nation take stock and decide on the organization needed to cope with the massive building and rebuilding programme ahead.

In terms of population growth the Registrar-General and Government Actuary have made the following predictions:[1]

	millions			
	1970	1980	1990	2000
England and Wales	49·3	53·1	57·8	64·1
Scotland	5·2	5·3	5·5	6·0
Northern Ireland	1·5	1·6	1·8	2·0
Totals	56·0	60·0	65·1	72·1

All such estimates contain a margin of error but for the present it is reasonable to assume that between 1970 and the turn of the century we will need up to five million more houses for about sixteen million more people.

But this is only half the problem. More difficult is the vast question of urban renewal. Our present stock of houses in Great Britain is about eighteen million of which some two million are condemned as unfit and another four to five million are lacking in essential facilities. Almost all these were built last century and a former Minister of Housing accepted, as a rough-and-ready rule, that a hundred years is about the limit of the life of a house.[2] This would still leave a large number that are already obsolete but at a minimum we must aim at replacing over six million houses by the year 2000. As most of these older houses are in congested areas where more open space and other facilities are badly needed, only about four million can be built in the areas cleared by demolition and the other two million must go elsewhere.

In the next thirty years, therefore, to cope with population expansion and the minimum of urban renewal we need a total programme of some seven million dwellings to be built in areas of new development and four million to be built in the older areas of our towns and cities. This means an average of about 350,000 a year which is well within the country's economic capacity. The current rate of building, public and private, is over 400,000 dwellings a year which represents 38 per cent of the current output of the construction industry[3] and about 3 per cent of our gross national product. Of all expenditure in the public sector, housing accounts for about 7 per cent. New methods, new materials, and increasing industrialization should improve efficiency in the years to come and there will be ample capacity in the building industry for the many other things that must be included in any comprehensive programme such as shops, roads, schools, hospitals, factories, offices, public buildings, sports facilities, parks, and open spaces. There is plenty of scope in such a programme for private investment and owner-occupation.

This programme has been described as equal to building another sixty Nottinghams or a new town for 60,000 every month for thirty years. As a graphic means of stressing the size of the problem this is useful, and on the face of it the statistics do indeed point to a further large programme of new towns. But it is not quite so simple as that. What governs housing need is not the total population but the number of new households and this is a reflection of the changing pattern of birth-rates since about 1890. By the early 1970s, because of the number of births around the end of last century, we can expect a peak death roll. At the same time there will be a reduced marriage rate because of the lower number of births that followed the bulge of the immediate post-war period. Statistically we already have more dwellings in Britain than households but many people are living in shared or sub-standard accommodation and in many areas there is an acute local housing shortage.

Nevertheless the temporary slump in new household formations during the seventies will make possible—indeed necessary—an early start on urban renewal. The building industry is geared up to an output of nearly 400,000 houses a year, and if the rebuilding of obsolete areas is not brought in as part of the national programme the industry will start to run down in the early or mid-1970s, with widespread redundancy and unemployment. Once that happens it may not be easy to build it up again.

Given acceptance of a programme of this order, the first important question is where to build the new houses to fit in with the economic pattern of the future. Housing must be related to jobs and a very far-sighted examination of our industrial economy is needed. For we are an ageing country. Although in another fifteen years or so we will still have an expanding population, the actual labour force will no longer be increasing and the national capacity for industrial expansion may therefore be limited. Technical changes, automation, and national, European, and world economics will have effects not yet predictable; but it would be unsafe, on present data, to assume that many more new areas of industrial growth, such as in the present new towns, will be either necessary or possible. From the aspect of physical planning, therefore, many of the new houses will have to be built for the purpose of meeting the labour needs of the existing industrial and commercial centres.

This means a fundamental change of approach to the whole process by which development throughout the country is controlled or directed. No longer can the programme be dictated mainly by the accident of whether a builder happens to be able to buy some land, by the decision of a district council on whether to grant or withhold a planning permission or by the outcome of thousands of separate planning appeals. It must be a much more sophisticated process, in which growth areas, small or large, are carefully selected on the basis of regional needs and possibilities. Employment, services, and communications must exercise a decisive influence on the size and location of the area selected and the development must then be planned and carried out on a comprehensive scale and to a co-ordinated programme.

There are several possible ways of doing this but they all depend on a willingness to use effectively the powers that Parliament has provided. In the twenty years or more since national planning of our land resources was adopted as Government policy and Lewis Silkin set up the machinery by which this was to be achieved, much good has been done and much harm has been prevented; but apart from the new towns there is very little that can be called a positive planning achievement. The powers were there, but somewhere along the road the imagination that inspired them got lost. The development plans of the 1947 Act became hedged around with a mass of detail, regulations, long-drawn-out inquiries and indecision. Instead of fulfilling their main function of laying down a broad programme of development they became little more than an inadequate background for dealing with hundreds of thousands of planning applications and thousands of appeals to the Minister.

Now, following the report of the Planning Advisory Group,[4] the development plans are to be consigned to the vaults to join the pre-war planning schemes as historic monuments to what went wrong in the years when planning was an unpopular word. Under the Town & Country Planning Act 1968, the local authorities will draw up 'structure plans', 'local plans', and 'action plans'; and to guide them they will have the benefit of the studies of the Regional Economic Councils which are made against a background of national need and capacity and in which local and central government meet round the table. At long last the Minister may perhaps be able to fulfil his basic statutory function.[5]

But it will need more than a change of name. The Government's White Paper suggests that the failure of the local authorities to make use of the power to designate areas for comprehensive development was partly due to the complication of the designation procedures.[6] But this was the least of their difficulties. Basically the cause lay in a combination of local political unwillingness, lack of Government support and failure to tackle the financial aspects. The new and simplified powers of the 1968 Act, welcome though they are, will not by themselves solve these problems.

The agency for carrying out the programme of future development is thus crucial. There are now six alternatives to choose from. First, there is the ordinary planning application by private builders on land they are able to buy. Much of the small-scale building in the outer rings of existing towns and cities will undoubtedly continue to be carried out in this way but it is not a satisfactory method for dealing with larger-scale development that needs planning as a whole.

Second, there is development by local authorities under the powers of the Housing Acts, which accounts for nearly half the current housing programme. Although some of the larger authorities have built some excellent housing estates under these powers they are limited in scope; and the smaller authorities, in whose areas much of the development needed in future may lie, could not cope either organizationally or financially with large-scale comprehensive projects.

Third, there are the powers of the Town Development Act 1952 which depend on agreements between two or more housing authorities. These were intended to facilitate overspill development on a substantial scale and at minimum cost to the Exchequer; but they have never proved very satisfactory and, apart from some schemes for overspill from the London and Birmingham areas, have been little used.

Fourth, the Town & Country Planning Act enables local authorities to buy land for comprehensive development, but they are unlikely to use the power unless the Government finance or subsidize the operation on a much more generous scale than hitherto.

Fifth, the Land Commission have similar powers to buy land for development. They have not yet used them on a substantial scale but in suitable circumstances they could readily use these powers to create an appropriate unit for comprehensive planning and development by other bodies, whether public or private.

Finally, there is the New Towns Act under which the Minister takes the initiative by designating areas for development, setting up the organization, and providing some of the money. So far, this is the only power that has been extensively and successfully used for large-scale comprehensive development involving a mixture of public and private finance and giving opportunities for the old, the migrant, the business girls, the bachelors, and the many others who rarely manage to get their names on a local authority housing list.

All these powers will still be needed, in greater or lesser degree. There is merit in overlapping powers in that the most

245

suitable agency can be selected for the particular project. But there is a danger, too, in that endless argument can go on—as has happened in the past—about which power to use and who is to pay. Meanwhile, nothing gets done. On the face of it, the new town procedure, supported by Government money, offers the most hope for carrying out successfully the sort of plans envisaged in current thinking on the scale that will be needed. Already Peterborough and Northampton have pointed the way. Major new developments will emerge from the studies at Southampton/Portsmouth, Severnside, Humberside, Tees-side and Tayside, and the need for many smaller expansions of towns is likely to be demonstrated by the studies of the south-east and other regions.

Within this changing situation the new town powers and procedures may need modifying if they are to prove an effective instrument for widespread development of this sort. If the forthcoming changes in local government structure include the setting up of some form of regional authority it may be that regional development agencies will emerge, either as self-contained organizations or as part of some national development body. That is looking rather far into the future but even the present new town arrangements could be improved and strengthened financially if the separate development corporations were in some way linked together in a national framework.

When introducing their new planning proposals the Government stressed that 'people must be able to participate fully in the planning process'. One of the difficulties about planning large-scale development in rural areas is that the people who will eventually be living there cannot be consulted. Only the local authorities and landowners in and around the area have a voice and if their views had been decisive in the case of the early new towns, hardly a single one of them would have got off the ground. There is a lesson to be learned here which the new Planning Act has not thoroughly digested and which the Skeffington Committee failed to tackle in their report on public participation in planning.[7]

The other part of the problem is urban renewal. Important though the areas of new development may be, no examination of future needs can afford to ignore the more difficult, more intractable but much more important question of how to get our old towns and cities rebuilt on modern lines. For twenty years we have been so busy overcoming the housing shortage and clearing isolated pockets of slums that the systematic rebuilding of the decaying urban areas has been sadly neglected.

The powers in the Town & Country Planning Act enabled urban land to be bought for comprehensive redevelopment but no local authority has been able to face the financial implications of using the powers on a really effective scale. From now on much of our building effort must be turned in that direction but there is, as yet, little recognition of the need for a new and forthright approach. Here, too, the new town experience has much to offer and may provide the only effective key to progress.

The problem hardly needs stating: it is better seen. Take a short stroll from any railway terminus in London or any other big city. Within minutes, almost, you are in shabbiness verging on squalor. The city centres are being rebuilt with massive new office blocks and modern shops. That is where the money lies. Property and investment companies have poured millions into these projects and in some of the more fashionable areas blocks of flats have been built by private enterprise to let or sell at prices far beyond the purse of ordinary people. But even on the very fringes of these new and expensive developments are the crowded areas of little houses built over a century ago. These, the twilight areas of our cities, have been near-slums for a generation but despite the programme of post-war building most of them remain.

There are some, of course, that still retain an old-world dignity. The one-time luxury dwellings of the Kensington squares will go down in history as architectural achievements of the nineteenth century. They are not perhaps in the same category as the crescents and terraces of Regent's Park or Bath but structurally they will last for years if properly maintained. The problem is to adapt them to the needs of modern living before they disintegrate from neglect. It is a costly business. Many are now converted into hotels, flats, or single-room lettings—and in the fashionable areas even the stables and coachmen's mews fetch enormous prices as converted cottages. It is to be hoped that for a long time yet there will be enough people able and willing to pay for the privilege of the spacious living which they offer, even though it be no more than a Kensington bed-sit. But many of these once dignified areas have already degenerated to a point beyond recall.

Houses of this quality and calibre are however the exception, only to be found in a few select parts. For the rest, the inner ring of all our towns and cities consists largely of mean and squalid houses, many of which lack the basic necessities and are long past the time when money could usefully be spent to recondition them. Paddington, Islington, Bethnal Green, Hoxton, Stepney, Bermondsey, Southwark, Lambeth, Battersea: to those who know London the mere mention of these places is enough to make the point. This is a belt of land some five miles wide, much of it within easy walking distance of the City or West End and, whether valued in social or commercial terms, some of the most valuable land in town. And the same pattern is repeated in varying degrees in all our towns and cities throughout Britain.

Further out from the centre are the later houses of the Victorian era, nowhere near slums yet, too well-built to tumble down, and now mostly housing two or more families but costly to convert properly into separate dwellings. These are the twilight areas of tomorrow. Most towns and cities have an 'age and condition' survey which readily shows the ring after ring of obsolete houses spreading out from the centre like a spider's web.

Everybody knows, and officialdom admits, that these areas must be dealt with within the present generation. Few would deny that complete replanning and rebuilding is the only answer. But the political, administrative, and financial implications of a really effective programme have yet to be faced. Unless the whole problem of urban renewal is tackled quickly and comprehensively—and new slums are forming more quickly than they are being demolished—the situation will get completely out of hand. Already it is past the eleventh hour.

Professor Buchanan has pinpointed the traffic crisis and solutions are being sought in bigger and better motor roads, traffic boxes, more fly-overs, more Los Angeles. But this is not enough. The Malthusian pessimists who bemoan the seize-up of the cities, and whose thinking is dominated by the state of Hyde Park Corner at 5 p.m. on a Thursday, must be met with a wider vision and a determination to provide the framework within which vision can become reality.

Local authorities are doing what they can to deal with the worst of the slums and the traffic jams within their financial capacity and the limits of spending laid down by the Government. But it is pitifully small, haphazard, and piecemeal. Good though any particular project may be if looked at in isolation, piecemeal action is, in the long-term, the worst possible solution. Small slum areas are bought here and there and re-developed as isolated schemes, within a century-old road framework, with little regard to the surrounding areas and usually unrelated to any overall long-term strategy. Many authorities would do more if they could, but they cannot do it alone.

One example of a piecemeal traffic improvement is the new Elephant and Castle in London, just south of the Thames. As a traffic improvement it is impressive; but to help meet the cost office blocks and shops were included, all with underpasses, overpasses, split levels, and pedestrian segregation to ensure free traffic flow and safety. It is set in an area of semi-slum and decaying houses, many of whose occupants have no wish to carry a shopping basket through the tunnels and up the stairs to the brand-new supermarkets. They have little enough money to spend when they get there and in any case prefer the cosiness of the old shops in the Walworth Road near by. Yet this is a key position, within a mile or two of the heart of London, and in the centre of one of London's oldest communities stretching south from the Thames with thousands of houses long past their useful life. A team of planners, architects, engineers, and landscapers, such as is found in any new town, could readily have replanned the area as a whole, with a new traffic system, open spaces, and modern dwellings. And the last place they would have put the new shopping centre would have been in the middle of the fifteen lanes of a major traffic intersection.

The cost of rebuilding such an area on a comprehensive scale would be no greater than a new town—less in fact because these areas are already well provided with water, a sewerage system and other services—and the whole programme could easily be carried out in some twenty years. The cost of the land, under present law, would however be crippling. In some way or other that aspect of the finances of redevelopment must be tackled.

One can go round all the inner London areas and find the same story—communities that are collapsing into decay through want of a comprehensive and imaginative policy. This inner core must be completely transformed within an overall strategy for the main traffic routes and if this were done the pressing traffic and transport problems would be greatly eased. For three generations now, London workers have been leap-frogging outwards to escape from the poor living conditions. Now there is pressure on the green belt, and commuting from the areas beyond, right down to the coast. The transport system is in danger of breaking down and vast sums are spent on road and rail improvements to meet the pressure of the daily rush hours from the million and a quarter workers who travel into London each day to their jobs. These are some of the people who must eventually be attracted back to the rebuilt inner suburbs where many could be within walking distance of their work and better able to enjoy and support the myriad cultural and entertainment facilities which London provides, instead of spending two or three hours a day travelling back and forth from suburbia.

It is a quarter of a century since Hugh Molson from the Conservative benches in the House of Commons described London as 'like a rotten pear that is going bad from the middle' and appealed to the Minister not to overlook what was happening;[8] and a year or two earlier Lord Latham, then leader of the London County Council, had written, in the foreword to the Abercrombie Plan,[9] 'There are giants in the path of city planning. There are conflicting interests, private rights, an outworn and different scale of values, and lack of vision. . . . A new London cannot be built out of mere wishing. . . . The fate of London in the post-war years will be one of the signs by which posterity will judge us.'

London, of course, is the supreme example that demonstrates

the need for a new approach, new machinery, new financial solutions. But in greater or lesser degree the same problem must be tackled in every city and every town in Britain that grew up from the industrial revolution onward. Figures about Bradford were recently given in Parliament. In this city of 300,000 people in the north of England 28,800 houses have no inside toilet facilities, over 20,000 have no bath, and 13,000 have no hot-water system.[10] And it is reasonable to assume that in design, room size, and structural condition, they are mostly incapable of satisfactory modernization. The same story could be told of a hundred other places.

In some areas temporary improvements are possible but if they are to be worth while they need to include large-scale work on the environment as well. The Deeplish Study[11] shows that it can be done—at a cost. The Minister of Housing, in his foreword to that study, says about the run-down areas that surround the centres of our industrial cities, 'The city planner, ambitious for wholesale redevelopment, easily writes them off as the slums of tomorrow and decrees a clean sweep. Yet on closer examination these twilight areas are often found to contain hundreds of family houses of marked character and community feeling.' True enough. It is the planner's dilemma and the planner's challenge—to create anew, in a better setting and a modern idiom, and despite the financial difficulties, both character and community life. It cannot be done through piecemeal slum clearance efforts. It can be done only if, from the start, redevelopment is planned as a complete and comprehensive operation, in which social content and community structure are essential ingredients.

The finances of the Deeplish Study are illuminating. Even on the conservative estimates given—and there can be many costly unforeseen factors in an operation of this sort—the rent of the three-bedroom houses in the improved Deeplish would be about 61s a week, and they would still have a limited life. If, instead, new houses were built at Deeplish to full Parker Morris standards, the rents would be 73s a week. For houses built on a new site (thus avoiding expensive purchase and demolition) the rents would be 57s 6d. The figures may be a little out of date now but the comparison remains valid.

251

Of course it is true that some areas are worth preservation, costly though it may be; and often the chances of early re-development are so remote that modernization is the right policy. But it is a temporary expedient. Before the end of this century these improved houses must also come into the field of comprehensive development. This is not a policy of destruction: there is much beauty in our towns, and more should be done to preserve the best of our heritage. But it must not become an excuse for failure to tackle obsolescence with vigour and foresight. The problem is the rebuilding of Britain—no less.

In terms of professional skill, it can be done. The number of university places for planning students is being increased with the hope of doubling the number of qualified planners by 1974[12] and more need to be attracted to the professions; but already the younger recruits have shown their eagerness and ability to contribute to this century's achievements. Given the tools they will do the job; but they cannot operate effectively without a suitable organizational and financial framework. That, only the Government and Parliament can provide.

The problem is surprisingly simple, once the magnitude of the job is accepted and the main points are allowed to stand out clearly from the mass of statistics, reports, and surveys that deluge in from all sides. They can be set out under four heads— People, Land, Money, and Machinery.

The human problem is the most important and the most difficult to solve. People resent being turned out of their homes, even though it be a condemned slum, and few of those living in the shabby areas so badly in need of redevelopment can afford the rent of a new dwelling. Yet no scheme of redevelopment is worth while unless the people displaced or uprooted are treated with imagination and even generosity. Some will be able to move into the new dwellings being built in the area but it will not be possible to re-accommodate everybody. New roads, open spaces, schools, public and community buildings will be needed and, as a rough rule-of-thumb guide, not more than two-thirds of the population displaced by urban rebuilding can be rehoused within the area. A greater variety of houses or flats will also be needed to attract into the area a wider cross-section of people than those who live there now.

Timing can play an important part in minimizing disturbance of people, particularly in an operation that may take twenty years to complete; but some houses will have to be provided elsewhere for those willing and able to move away. Most of these will have to be in the new or expanding towns or in extensions of the suburban fringe. This is why it is so important that the building programmes in the areas of new development and the programmes of redevelopment in the old towns should march in step. Up to now they have not done so.

On the land question there is only one answer. As with extensive war damage and new town development, it is essential to bring a whole area into public ownership so that it can be replanned and redeveloped as a whole. This does not mean the exclusion of private enterprise. Many agencies will have to participate in the programme and in these near-central areas there is certain to be much more scope for private enterprise than under a policy of inaction or piecemeal slum clearance. Indeed, without a comprehensive programme for purchase and disposal private enterprise will find little scope at all.

Some method of purchase by a centrally-financed organization is essential, but this is not the whole solution. The crux of the problem is not merely the capital cost of buying but the annual loss that for many years is almost inevitable on any plan that reduces density and provides more roads, open spaces, and cultural and recreational facilities. In the early post-war years the central Government helped quite generously with the cost of rebuilding the war-damaged areas, underwriting for a period up to 90 per cent of the annual loss, but successive governments have consistently refused to make adequate arrangements for dealing with blight and decay. The financial problems are, if anything, even more difficult than in the case of war damage, because the scale is immeasurably greater. The grant under the Planning Acts is now replaced by that under the Local Government Act 1966, and can amount to up to 50 per cent of the annual loss incurred by local authorities on schemes of comprehensive development, leaving the balance to be met from local rates. This takes no account of the fact that the burden falls unevenly. Some of the inner housing areas—and this applies particularly to the London Boroughs—need virtually complete rebuilding. But it also ignores the fact that, in the long term, as the new towns are demonstrating, the deficits of the early years can easily be overcome by later surpluses if the redevelopment schemes are truly comprehensive, covering all forms of land use.

Local authorities naturally regard it as their job to plan and organize the rebuilding of their areas, and few would deny the logic of their claim. The powers of the Town & Country Planning Acts were based on the assumption that they could and would do so; but experience in the last twenty years leads regrettably to the conclusion that, in general, they are ill equipped for such extensive operations. Apart from the heavy initial cost of buying land, the financial structure of local government is not suited to long-term projects of this sort, and even the Greater London Council, with all its vast resources, could not tackle the problem on the scale needed. The same is probably true of most other big cities, and it is quite certain that the scores of smaller northern towns can only be rebuilt with outside help. And rebuilt they must be. As the Hunt Committee[13] have pointed out, the modernization and renewal of our industrial equipment cannot be separated from the physical and social setting, the 'total environment'.

Again, therefore, machinery is crucial. Sir Henry Wells has expressed the hope that the Land Commission may eventually be able to help by using the Land Fund to buy areas of this sort and make land in them available at a price appropriate to the new use proposed.[14] Whether this will be possible, and whether the Land Fund will have sufficient resources, remains to be seen. However it is done, considerable financial help will be needed; and land is only part of the problem.

Twenty years ago Lord Reith's Committee emphasized that for the building of new towns an organization was needed that could concentrate wholly on the task and with very different financial arrangements from those of the local authorities. This is even more true for rebuilding old towns. If the new-town arrangements could be adopted or adapted for dealing with urban renewal it would be a virtual guarantee of success.

A dozen new-town corporations in England have built a dozen towns in twenty years. A dozen such bodies appointed to tackle the various inner areas of London could achieve a similar result. A few score throughout the country could transform all our towns and cities by the turn of the century. They would have to work in particularly close harmony with the local authorities, but it is not a question of putting in an alien body to usurp the powers of the authority. Rather it is working out with the local authority a form of agency that will have the skill, the organization and the money to get on with the job.

This is not to suggest that rebuilding the decaying city areas is no more than building a series of new towns. Far from it. A city with its many parts is an integrated whole. The parts themselves may have their special emphasis, character, and tradition with a supporting range of interrelated uses and functions that give them social and economic purpose. But they do not exist in isolation.

The new towns have the difficult enough task of creating a history and building up a tradition. Rebuilding old towns presents the even more difficult task of retaining history and recapturing centuries of tradition within a structural framework suited to modern life. It needs a new philosophy and a new understanding that as yet are only beginning to peep through the mass of technical and social analysis. Indeed, many in the planning profession still need convincing that something more is needed than a policy of jumble, with its ill-assorted mixture of *ad hoc* planning permissions, road widenings, motor-boxes, and spasmodic slum clearance.

Nor is it an idle dream to suggest that at long last we can rebuild our towns to a proper plan. In twenty-five years we have moved a long way: from the simple ideas of Ebenezer Howard to a new city for half-a-million people. Progress will not stop there. From the experience of the past will emerge new forms, new ideas, new solutions through which the generation now growing up will be equipped to tackle the problems that lie ahead.

The technical skill is there. The construction workers are there. The money is there to the extent that priorities allow. What percentage of our national production capacity can be afforded for this task depends on major political decisions affecting the balance of payments, exports, defence policy and the many other claims on national resources, but, as the figures on page 242 show, it can be done within a programme that does no more than maintain the present level of building. The right question to ask is not how much we can afford on rebuilding but how much we can afford not to afford.

* * *

The new towns chapter in our history as we know it today is closing. It was the easy part of the job. Now, with the experience of twenty years behind us, we can see more clearly the road we must travel to take us on to the turn of the century. We must have the same vision, the same determination, and the same social understanding that inspired the new towns of the past and we must tackle with the same devotion the more difficult tasks ahead. It is our old towns that must be the new towns of the future.

APPENDIX

PART I of this Appendix contains details, necessarily brief, of all the new towns in order of designation in each part of the United Kingdom. It illustrates the scope of the new town programme, and the changes in both policy and planning thought over the years.

Details are also given of the main publications concerned solely or primarily with the town. Some of them, particularly the earlier ones, are out of print now but can usually be obtained through libraries. The lists do not include general publicity literature which can be obtained free of charge on application to the Information Officer in each town. A few of the towns also have stocks of colour slides and photographs which they are willing to lend to approved applicants.

PART II contains a statistical summary of progress in the main building operations as at 1 October 1969.

PART III analyses the accounts for the financial year ended 31 March 1969. The capital account shows the total amount of Exchequer money advanced since designation, the main items of capital expenditure and the accumulated surplus or deficiency. The analysis of Revenue shows the revenue position for the financial year ended 31 March 1969. As the accounts for each corporation occupy some ten pages, these one-line summaries omit much of the detail. The student wishing to examine the finances in depth should refer to the full accounts, which are published each year with the annual reports.

Note: 1 acre = 0·405 hectares
     1 mile = 1·609 kilometres
     D.C. = Development Corporation
     N.T.C. = Commission for the New Towns

PART I: THE TOWNS

I ENGLAND

II SCOTLAND

III WALES

IV N. IRELAND

PART I

I: ENGLAND

1. STEVENAGE (Hertfordshire)

Designated: 11 November 1946. *Area:* 6,156 acres plus 100
  added in 1967: total 6,256 acres
Population in 1946: 7,000
Planned population: 60,000, later increased to 105,000
Purpose: 'overspill' from London (distance 30 miles)

PLANS: The first tentative plan for Stevenage was drawn
up in 1945 by the Ministry of Town and Country Planning
while the Reith Committee was still sitting. It was revised
in 1949 by the Corporation's first Chief Architect, Professor
Clifford Holliday, and further revised in 1955 and 1966 by
his successor, Leonard G. Vincent. The original town plan
was divided into six neighbourhoods each for about 10,000
people, with adequate shops, primary schools, and other
facilities. One of these housing areas has subsequently been
enlarged to house some 20,000 people.

Running through the town is Fairlands Valley—a large
area of open space of which part is to be laid out as a
recreation area. Four hundred acres of industrial land on
the western edge of the town and an additional industrial area
to be built to the east will eventually provide employment
for up to 30,000 people.

Following the decision in 1966 to build for an increased
population, two new neighbourhoods are being added and
the town centre is being doubled in size. This attractive
centre, the first all-pedestrian shopping precinct in Europe
(see p. 123), with radio-controlled signs showing where
parking space is available, already includes a wide range of
civic, commercial, entertainment, and educational buildings,
and two eighteen-storey blocks of flats overlooking the
town-centre gardens. Plans for the future include an
ambitious arts centre and indoor sports centre.

Stevenage is also noted for traffic/pedestrian segregation in both the town centre and the newer housing areas, including a comprehensive system of cycleways.

PUBLICATIONS:

Stevenage New Town (D.C., 1949)

The expansion of Stevenage: a technical appraisal (D.C., 1963)

Stevenage Master Plan, 1966:

Volume I: Planning Proposals by Leonard G. Vincent, C.B.E. (D.C. 105s.)

Volumes II & III: Traffic Survey by E. C. Claxton, O.B.E. (D.C. 42s.)

Volume IV: Traffic Study: Technical Report (D.C. 20s.)

Stevenage Public Transport: Cost Benefit Analysis by Nathaniel Lichfield and Associates (D.C., 1970. 35s.)

Stevenage: a sociological study by Harold Orlans (Routledge & Kegan Paul, 1952)

The Arts in Stevenage by Sir William Emrys Williams, C.B.E. (D.C., 1963)

The Needs of Youth in Stevenage (Calouste Gulbenkian Foundation, 1959. 3s.)

Street Names in Stevenage by G. L. Lack (Stevenage Society, 1966)

The History of Stevenage by Robert Trow-Smith (Stevenage Society, 1958)

Hotels: Cromwell; Roebuck (Trust House Motel)

Chairman: Mrs E. Denington, C.B.E., HON. F.R.I.B.A., G.L.C.
General Manager: J. A. Balchin
Address: Swingate House, Danestrete, Stevenage, Herts. *Tel:* 3344

2. CRAWLEY (Sussex)

Designated: 9 January 1947. *Area:* 6,047 acres
Population in 1947: 9,000
Planned population: 50,000, increased in 1966 to 80,000
Purpose: 'overspill' from London (distance 30 miles)

PLANS: The first Master Plan in 1949 was by Anthony

Minoprio with modifications and extensions, as the town developed, by the Chief Architect, H. S. Howgrave-Graham. The old High Street, with its several sixteenth-century buildings and old coaching inn, has been carefully preserved, and linked to it by a pedestrian way is the new town centre with its spacious Queens Square and rose-lined Boulevard.

With the new development at Broadfield there will be eleven neighbourhoods, four of them beyond the pre-war by-pass road, each with its own shopping centre, primary school, and community buildings. There are no tall blocks of flats in Crawley, but one attractive three-to-four storey block—Deerswood Court—has been built round a group of trees at Ifield. No house is more than a mile from open country. A sports centre adjoins the new swimming bath, and the 210 acres of Tilgate Park, with its large lake, is now owned by the Urban District Council and open to the public.

The 350-acre industrial estate close to Gatwick Airport is noted for its many well-designed buildings and excellent landscaping.

A recent study indicates possible natural growth of the town to a population of up to 100,000.

PUBLICATIONS:

A Master Plan for Crawley by Anthony Minoprio (D.C., 1949)

Crawley Expansion Study by University of Sussex (West Sussex County Council, 1969)

The Development and Management of a New Town by R. M. Clarke (Chartered Institute of Secretaries, 1963)

The Use of Leisure in a New Town (W.E.A. (Crawley Branch), 1960)

Crawley: A Study of Amenities in a Town by G. Brooke Taylor (N.T.C., 1967. 12s. 6d.)

Hotels: George; Airport; Crawley Forest; Grange

Crawley Development Corporation was dissolved in 1962 and the assets were transferred to the Commission for the New Towns.

Chairman: Sir Henry Wells, C.B.E., D.LITT., F.R.I.C.S.

Secretary: F. Schaffer, LL.B.
Head Office: Glen House, Stag Place, London, S.W.I. *Tel:*
01–834–8034
Chairman of Local Committee: Robert May, O.B.E.
Manager (Crawley): R. M. Clarke, M.C., F.C.I.S.
Local Office: Broadfield, Crawley, Sussex. *Tel:* 26102

3. HEMEL HEMPSTEAD (Hertfordshire)

Designated: 4 February 1947. *Area:* 5,910 acres
Population in 1947: 21,200
Planned population: 80,000
Purpose: 'overspill' from London (distance 25 miles)

PLANS: A preliminary plan for Hemel Hempstead prepared
in 1947 by G. A. Jellicoe formed the basis of the Master
Plan adopted by the Corporation in 1951. A revised Master
Plan was adopted in 1961. There are ten neighbourhoods,
some of them quite small, divided from each other and from
the centre by landscaped valleys. The old High Street has
been preserved, and many of the buildings, some of which
date back to the sixteenth century, have been restored as
part of a 'face lift' carried out in association with the
Civic Trust, the local authorities, and the High Street
Association.

The new central shopping and civic area, Marlowes, was
built before pedestrian centres became fashionable. It is
$\frac{3}{4}$ mile long. The town centre is noted particularly for the
water gardens (see p. 122) and for the new Town Hall
and Pavilion. A large office block spans the road at one end,
and the new nineteen-storey Kodak head office building is
being built nearby.

The 231 acre industrial estate is linked to the London—
Birmingham motorway.

PUBLICATIONS:
Preliminary plan for Hemel Hempstead by G. A. Jellicoe
(D.C., 1947)
Master Plan for Hemel Hempstead (D.C., 1949)
Revised Master Plan for H.H. (D.C., 1960)
Films: The following 16-mm. films are available on loan,
free of charge, from the local office of the Commission:

'Home of Your Own' (800 ft.); 'New Town from Old' (475 ft.); 'The Queen Visits Hemel Hempstead' (400 ft.). *Slides and Photographs:* A representative selection is available on loan, free of charge, from the local office.

Hotel: Breakspear (Trust House Motel)

Hemel Hempstead Development Corporation was dissolved in 1962 and the assets were transferred to the Commission for the New Towns.

Chairman: ⎫
Secretary: ⎬ as under Crawley
Head Office: ⎭
Chairman of Local Committee: G. D. Hitchcock
Manager (Hemel Hempstead): Brigadier J. R. Blomfield, O.B.E., M.C., M.A., M.B.I.M.
Local Office: Swan Court, Waterhouse Street, Hemel Hempstead, Herts. *Tel:* 2222

4. HARLOW (Essex)

Designated: 25 March 1947. *Area:* 6,395 acres
Population in 1947: 4,500
Planned population: 90,000
Purpose: 'overspill' from London (distance 25 miles)

PLANS: Harlow is one of the few towns built entirely on 'green fields'. The old village has been preserved and improved and lies on the eastern edge of the town.

Sir Frederick Gibberd was appointed in 1947 by the Minister of Town and Country Planning to prepare the Master Plan, and he has remained throughout the consultant Architect-Planner. The town is designed in four main clusters of neighbourhoods separated by broad wedges of parkway, each cluster with its own neighbourhood centre and smaller sub-centres.

The town centre is mainly traffic-free, spaciously laid out, and with a wide range of shops and commercial buildings. The town has been particularly successful in attracting office development: several firms of international repute

265

now have their headquarters in or near the town centre. The Sportcentre (see pp. 149–50) is near by and a 168-acre park is in course of development. With a population of 90,000 it is expected that there will be employment for 40,500 people, with 20,000 employed on the two major industrial areas.

A survey in 1963 recommended expansion to a population of 125,000, but a decision has been held up to await the result of the inquiries into the siting of the third London Airport.

PUBLICATIONS:

Harlow Master Plan (D.C., 1949; revised ed., 1952. 13*s*. 6*d*.)

Living in Harlow (D.C., 1967. 2*s*. 10*d*.)

Harlow Sportcentre (D.C. 2*s*. 10*d*.)

History of Harlow (D.C., 1969: Hardback 28*s*. Paperback 16*s*.)

Welcome to Harlow (D.C. 1*s*.)

Neighbourhood Layouts (D.C. 2*s*. 10*d*.)

Dyelines of the Master Plan (D.C. 1*s*. 10*d*.)

Film: 'Faces of Harlow', 30-minute 16-mm. colour film, available for hire in Great Britain through Sound Services Ltd., Kingston Road, S.W.19 (£1. 12*s*. plus postage); and abroad (soundtrack in English, French, Hindi, Urdu, Malay) through Central Office of Information, Hercules Road, London, S.E.1. (Reference 300 1462–6)

Colourslides: Two sets of six colourslides at 10*s*. 6*d*. each set and a comprehensive set of 50 price £5 post free available from the Development Corporation at 1 Adams House, The High, Harlow, Essex.

Hotels: Churchgate (Old Harlow); Saxon Inn (Southern Way)

Chairman: Sir John Newsom, C.B.E., LL.D.

General Manager: B. Hyde Harvey, O.B.E., F.I.M.T.A., F.S.A.A., D.P.A.

Address: Gate House, The High, Harlow, Essex. *Tel:* 266621

5. NEWTON AYCLIFFE (County Durham)

Designated: 19 April 1947. *Area:* 865 acres plus 1,643 added
in 1966: total 2,508 acres
Population in 1946: 60
Planned Population: 10,000. Later increased to 20,000 and
now to 45,000
Purpose: to serve the nearby Industrial Estate

PLANS: Aycliffe, now named Newton Aycliffe to distinguish
it from the old village of Aycliffe a mile away, adjoins the
war-time Ordnance factory area, now converted to peacetime use.

The first plan for a town of 10,000 persons was drawn
up by the Grenfell Baines Group, but following the decision
to increase the size to 45,000 persons a report was prepared
for the Corporation by Edmund Wilford & Son with specialist advice on traffic problems from Professor Buchanan
and Dr Thomas Williams, and on landscape from Miss
Sylvia Crowe. The main principles of this report were
incorporated in a Master Plan prepared by the development
corporation and accepted in 1968.

The present development consists of six areas of houses
near the town centre, but the plan for the larger town
envisages another 6,870 houses with additional shops at
various places in the town for day-to-day needs. The existing shopping centre is being expanded to form the main
focus for the town by the addition of new shops together
with other major commercial, administrative and recreational
uses.

The Industrial Area (now under the control of the
Industrial Estates Management Corporation) with about
3,334,000 sq ft of factory space provides employment for
over 9,000 people and has been greatly improved in recent
years by the clearance of some of the war-time buildings
and by landscaping schemes.

PUBLICATIONS: *Master Plan Report* (D.C., 1968. 7s. 6d.)

Chairman: T. Dan Smith, D.C.L. (HON.)
General Manager: A. V. Williams, C.B.E., B.A.
Address: Churchill House, Newton Aycliffe, Co. Durham.
Tel: 2521

6. PETERLEE (County Durham)

Designated: 10 March 1948. *Area:* 2,336 acres plus 136
   added in 1965 and 313 in 1969: total 2,785 acres
Population in 1948: 200
Planned population: 30,000
Purpose: to meet local housing needs and diversify in-
   dustry

PLANS: Peterlee—named after Peter Lee, one of Britain's
most distinguished mining leaders—is on the Durham
coalfield and was designated following a suggestion that the
twenty-six mining towns and villages around the pitheads
should be replaced by a single new settlement that would
become a social and commercial centre. It would also enable
alternative employment to be provided for the men surplus
to the requirements of the mining industry and to the women
for whom at that time very little employment was available.
Both the plan and the programme of building have been
largely dictated by the need to extract the twenty-five
million tons of coal that lay beneath the site. A small area
only was left for support of the town centre, and all other
development is designed to allow for subsidence.

The Grenfell Baines Group prepared the final Master
Plan. There are six separate neighbourhoods, built mainly
on traditional lines; but the south-west area, for which the
artist Victor Pasmore was called in to collaborate with the
corporation's architects, broke new ground. More recent
development has concentrated on the Skarne system of
industrialized building.

The designated area includes two deep ravines known as
Castle Eden Denes that run down to the sea, and the area
is now declared a local nature reserve. Industry was slow
in coming, but the town is now a major growth point. By
1970 some 13,000 new jobs will be needed within a five-mile
radius, and the land added to the designated area in 1965
and 1969 is being used for manufacturing industry and for
the research and development centre that is being established in the town.

The design of the town centre went through many phases
but the final plans, drawn up in 1965 by A. T. W. Marsden,
Chief Architect, and R. G. S. Roberts, Chief Engineer, will

provide a modern, two-level, traffic-free centre in the best new town tradition.

PUBLICATIONS:
Farewell Squalor by C. W. Clarke (Easington R.D.C., 1946)
New Town Youth: leisure activities in Peterlee, by W. M. Morley (Easington R.D.C., 1966 2s.)
Master Plan (D.C.)
Town Centre Plan (D.C.)
Castle Eden Denes, Peterlee (D.C. 7s. 6d.)

Hotel: Norseman

Chairman: T. Dan Smith, D.C.L. (HON.)
General Manager: A. V. Williams, C.B.E., B.A.
Address: Shotton Hall, Peterlee, Co. Durham. *Tel:* 2301

7. HATFIELD (Hertfordshire)

Designated: 20 May 1948. *Area:* 2,349 acres
Population in 1948: 8,500
Planned population: 29,000
Purpose: to serve the nearby aircraft industry, diversify employment and take 'overspill' from London (distance 20 miles)

PLANS: The Master Plan for Hatfield, the smallest of the English new towns, was prepared in 1949 by Lionel Brett (Lord Esher). It provided for seven neighbourhoods and a new town centre. The centre itself was designed some years later, mainly by Professor Maxwell Fry, and is now being extended and modernized. He has also prepared the plans for redeveloping the old centre of the town. Two thirteen-to-fourteen storey blocks of flats and the local authority's striking new swimming bath are notable architectural features of the town centre.

The major employment is in the Hawker Siddeley Aircraft factory just outside the designated area, but half a million sq ft of new factory space within the town provides another 1,400 jobs.

Hatfield House, the 350-year-old home of the Cecil family, with its 1,500 acres of parkland, adjoins the town, and the house and the park are open to the public six days a week during the summer months.

PUBLICATIONS:
Outline Plan by Lionel Brett (D.C., 1949; reprinted 1957)

Hotels: Salisbury; Comet; Hatfield Lodge; Stone House

Hatfield Development Corporation was dissolved in 1966 and the assets were transferred to the Commission for the New Towns.

Chairman: ⎫
Secretary: ⎬ as under Crawley
Head Office: ⎭

Chairman of Local Committee: Dr W. A. J. Chapman, M.SC.(ENG.), C.ENG., F.I.MECH.E., HON.F.I.PROD.E.

Manager (Hatfield): Brigadier M. W. Biggs, C.B.E., M.A., M.I.C.E.

Local Office: Church Road, Welwyn Garden City, Herts. *Tel:* 28181

8. WELWYN GARDEN CITY (Hertfordshire)

Designated: 20 May 1948. *Area:* 4,318 acres
Population in 1948: 18,500
Planned population: 50,000
Purpose: 'overspill' from London (distance 22 miles)

PLANS: Welwyn Garden City, started by Ebenezer Howard and completed under the New Towns Act, is an outstanding example of the 'garden city' concept. The original plan was prepared in 1920 by the late Louis de Soissons and the firm of de Soissons, Peacock, Hodges, Robertson & Fraser have continued throughout as architectural and planning consultants.

The town centre, with its broad sweep of parkland and flower-beds and its Georgian-style buildings, has been declared a Conservation Area under the Civic Amenities Act; but changes are on the way. Multi-storey car parks, an improved road system, and a pedestrian shopping precinct are all included in the plans for improvement.

There are eight housing areas, some of which were built by the former garden city company between 1920 and 1937, and the last of which, at Panshanger, is now being built by the Commission for the New Towns.

The town is well equipped with open space (equivalent to 30 acres per 1,000 population). This includes the 17-acre Digswell Lake, which is open to members of a private society, the 180-acre Sherrards Park Wood, a golf course, and the Gosling Stadium, which is rapidly becoming a centre for international events.

PUBLICATIONS:

The Building of Satellite Towns by C. B. Purdom (Dent, 1925 & 1949. 25s.)

Site Planning at Welwyn Garden City by Louis de Soissons and A. W. Kenyon (Benn, 1927)

Master Plan by Louis de Soissons (D.C., 1949)

Digswell: 'a matter done': the Story of the Digswell Arts Trust (The Trust, 1957)

Hotels: Homestead Court; Treetops

Welwyn Garden City Development Corporation was dissolved in 1966 and the assets were transferred to the Commission for the New Towns.

Chairman: ⎫
Secretary: ⎬ as under Crawley
Head Office: ⎭

Chairman of Local Committee: S. R. Collingwood, J.P.

Manager (Welwyn Garden City): Brigadier M. W. Biggs, C.B.E., M.A., M.I.C.E.

Local Office: Church Road, Welwyn Garden City, Herts. *Tel:* 28181

9. BASILDON (Essex)

Designated: 4 January 1949. *Area:* 7,818 acres

Population in 1949: 25,000

Planned population: 50,000, later increased to 106,000 and now to 133,000

Purpose: 'overspill' from London (distance 25 miles) and redevelopment of shack areas

PLANS: At the time of designation the area included some 5,600 shacks, converted buses, railway coaches, or other temporary and sub-standard dwellings, with few roads, sewers, or other services. The development corporation have bought and demolished most of them, rehousing people where necessary in new dwellings, and are redeveloping the whole area.

The first Plan, prepared in 1950 by the then Chief Architect, Noel Tweddell, was revised in 1966 by the present Chief Architect, D. G. Galloway, to provide for the increased population. The town stretches for six miles from east to west, and eventually there will be twenty-four neighbourhoods of varying size, density, and design, with local shops, schools, and community buildings.

One of the most striking features of the spacious and impressive town centre is the fourteen-storey block of flats —Brooke House. The 350-acre Gloucester Park, which adjoins the centre, contains the new swimming pool and playing fields, an Arts Centre was opened in 1968, and there is a new golf course and a squash club a mile or so away. A private-enterprise sports and entertainment centre and hotel is also planned.

In the northern part of the town three industrial estates of over 400 acres will eventually provide some 25,000 jobs. The Ford Motor Company's tractor factory itself takes up a 100-acre site with an employment roll of nearly 3,000.

PUBLICATIONS:
Master Plan by Noel Tweddell (D.C., 1951)
Master Plan for 140,000 Population by D. G. Galloway (D.C., 1965)
Shopping—Work for Women—Leisure by Carole H. Byron (D.C., 1967. 21*s*.)

Chairman: W. M. Balch, F.R.I.C.S.
General Manager: R. C. C. Boniface
Address: Gifford House, Basildon, Essex. *Tel:* Vange 3261

10. BRACKNELL (Berkshire)

Designated: 17 June 1949. *Area:* 1,870 acres plus 1,426 added in 1961/2: total 3,296 acres

Population in 1949: 5,000
Planned population: 25,000, increased in 1961 to 60,000
Purpose: 'overspill' from London (distance 28 miles)

PLANS: In 1949 Bracknell—the name means 'a clearing in the wood'—was a small country town of 5,000 people. Because of local opposition the area originally proposed was much reduced and the first Master Plan by the corporation's former Chief Architect, E. A. Ferriby, proposed four neighbourhoods only, with a small new central shopping area adjoining the old High Street. When the designated area was extended for a much larger population the Plan was completely revised. Much of the old High Street has now been demolished, a new all-pedestrian town centre is being built, and five more neighbourhoods are being added.

A feature of all the housing areas is the careful preservation of mature trees. The three industrial areas, with a total of 243 acres, are also noted for their design and effective landscaping, and the town has proved particularly attractive to office organizations.

PUBLICATIONS:
Master Plan. Not published but print (scale $\frac{1}{5000}$) available on request
Bracknell Town Centre, 1963. (D.C. 2s.)
Bracknell (D.C. 5s.)
Household Survey (D.C., 1966)
Living alone in Bracknell's High Flats (D.C., 1967)
Wildridings: Social Survey (D.C., 1969)
The Sports Centre (Easthampstead R.D.C. 2s.)

Hotels: Admiral Cunningham; Royal Foresters (2 miles)

Chairman: C. D. Pilcher, C.B.E., F.R.I.C.S., F.A.I., J.P.
General Manager: J. V. Rowley, B.A.
Address: Farley Hall, Bracknell, Berks. *Tel:* 4511

11. CORBY (Northamptonshire)

Designated: 1 April 1950. *Area:* 2,494 acres plus 1,929 acres added in 1952–68: total 4,423 acres.
Population in 1950: 15,700

Planned population: 80,000
Purpose: to serve the steelworks, diversify industry and (later) 'overspill' from London (distance 80 miles)

PLANS: Corby was a small village until 1934, when a large new steelworks was built nearby by Stewarts & Lloyds Ltd. By 1939 the Company had built 2,329 houses for their work people.

The Master Plan of 1950 by Professors Holford and Myles Wright provided for a small new town centre, two new neighbourhoods, and the completion of existing housing areas in the south-east. With the large extension of the designated area a new Plan was prepared by John H. D. Madin & Partners. This expands the town centre considerably, making it all-pedestrian, and provides five more new neighbourhoods. Part of the building will be on land restored after opencast ironstone working.

Special care is to be taken to preserve Great Oakley Village on the outskirts, and the old Corby village has been protected and restored under advice from Misha Black. The 425 acres of land for industrial use will eventually provide some 14,750 jobs, in addition to the 12,600 in the steelworks.

Special features of the town are the 220 acres of Thorough-sale and Hazel Woods adjoining the town centre, and the Urban District Council's group of civic buildings built to the competition-winning design of Enrico de Pierio.

PUBLICATIONS:
Corby New Town (D.C., 1952. 7s. 6d.)
Corby New Town Extension: Second Master Plan by John H. D. Madin & Partners (D.C., 1965. 42s.)

Hotel: Strathclyde

Chairman: H. Chisholm, C.B.E., M.A., F.C.A.
General Manager: Brigadier H. G. W. Hamilton, C.B.E., B.A.(ENG.), M.B.I.M.
Address: Spencer House, Corporation Street, Corby, Northants. *Tel:* 3535

12. SKELMERSDALE (Lancashire)

Designated: 9 October 1961. *Area:* 4,029 acres plus 95
  added in 1969: total 4,124 acres
Population in 1961: 10,000
Planned population: 80,000
Purpose: 'overspill' from North Merseyside principally
  (distance 13 miles)

PLANS: Skelmersdale was the first new town to be designated in England after a gap of eleven years. The Master
Plan prepared in 1963 by Sir Hugh Wilson contains many
of the features of his plan for Cumbernauld. In particular,
the conception of 'neighbourhoods' is abandoned in favour
of fairly dense housing development connected through a
footpath system to a compact town centre. A network of
main roads and distributor roads with a limited number of
access points and a separate pedestrian system of footpaths
will ensure adequate and safe traffic circulation and a rapid
public-transport system. The town is under two miles east
of the M6, to which it is being directly linked. In the 1970s
this motorway standard link will be extended to the northern
end of Liverpool.

Great attention has been paid to landscape design in the
overall pattern of the town, and tree and shrub planting will
be on a generous scale. The old towns of Skelmersdale and
Up Holland will be redeveloped and integrated within the
framework of the larger town.

The first phase of the town centre is expected to be
completed in 1972. The commercial part will be fully
covered, and the design will allow complete separation of
pedestrians and vehicles.

Industrial development has been particularly rapid.
Although not initially in a Development Area, the grants
and allowances of the Local Employment Act applied
because the town took overspill from Merseyside (see p. 112).
Since the Industrial Development Act 1966 the new town
has been treated as if it were within the Merseyside Development Area.

PUBLICATIONS:
Skelmersdale New Town—Planning Proposals by Sir Hugh
  Wilson (D.C., 1964. 2 gns.)

Chairman: G. H. Heywood, F.R.I.C.S., F.A.I.
General Manager: R. W. Phelps, M.A.
Address: High Street, Skelmersdale, Lancs. *Tel:* Tawd
Vale 3131

13. TELFORD (Shropshire)

Designated: 16 January 1963. *Area:* 9,100 acres plus 10,143
added in 1968: total 19,243 acres
Population in 1963: 70,000 (including extension area)
Planned population: 220,000
Purpose: 'overspill' from Birmingham and the Black Country
(distance 30 miles)

PLANS: The town was named Dawley when it was first
designated, but with the inclusion in 1968 of Wellington
and Oakengates it was renamed Telford, after the famous
Scottish civil engineer who started his professional career
as an engineer in 1787 as surveyor of public works in
Shropshire. The Industrial Revolution began in the designated area at Coalbrookdale, where the first iron bridge in
the world was cast and built at Ironbridge over the River
Severn, which is the southern boundary of the New Town.
In the development of Telford over the next few decades
as a flourishing modern city large areas of land made derelict
in the early years of the Industrial Revolution will be
reclaimed.

The John Madin Design Group prepared the Structure
Plan. Within an urban motorway circling the city and a
grid pattern of access roads and pedestrian links, the town
will consist of 'clusters' of communities of about 8,000
people based on primary schools and small local centres.
Three such communities grouped together form a district
served by its own shopping, schools, welfare, and recreation
facilities. A 600-acre central park is to be created, a new
major town centre will be built, and also new industrial
areas. The aim is to provide for nearly 100,000 jobs by
1991.

Social and recreational needs have been the subject of a
special study, jointly with the local authorities, through an
advisory committee under the chairmanship of Mr J. C.

Cadbury. A £375,000 educational and recreational centre for dual use, jointly financed by the Corporation, local authorities, and others, is now being built by the Shropshire County Council.

PUBLICATIONS:

The West Midlands: a Regional Study by D.E.A. and W. Midland Economic Planning Council (H.M.S.O., 1965. 12s. 6d.)

Dawley, Wellington, Oakengates—Proposals for Development by John H. D. Madin and Partners (H.M.S.O., 1966. 25s.)

*The West Midlands—Patterns of Growth—*Report by West Midland Economic Planning Council (H.M.S.O., 1967. 8s.)

Telford Development Proposals by John Madin Design Group (D.C., 1969. Vol. 1, £3. Vol. 2, £2. 10s.)

Hotels: Charlton Arms (Wellington); Tontine (Ironbridge); Valley (Coalbrookdale)

Chairman: Sir Frank Price, Kt.
General Manager: E. Thomas, LL.B., L.A.M.T.P.I.
Address: Priorslee Hall, Telford, Salop. *Tel:* Oakengates 3131

14. REDDITCH (Worcestershire)

Designated: 10 April 1964. *Area:* 7,180 acres
Population in 1964: 32,000
Planned population: 90,000
Purpose: relief of overcrowding in the West Midlands

PLANS: The Master Plan by Sir Hugh Wilson and Lewis Womersley, in association with Michael Brown, landscape architect, contains many of the now familiar features of current new town thought—a ring road with special facilities for public transport and the housing areas and local shopping centres grouped along it 'like beads on a string' with footpath connections to the centre and elsewhere. In the first three housing areas 2,000 dwellings were either built or being built by 1969, and industrial development got off to a rapid start with nearly half a million sq ft of factory space.

The new town centre is to be built on the site of the old, with the ancient St Stephen's Church and green preserved as the focal point. The new arcaded shopping area will be at one level, and the civic, entertainment, sports, and cultural buildings will be grouped near by.

Many of the existing houses in the town are over eighty years old and the programme of building will include schemes of renewal or redevelopment that will progressively integrate old with new.

PUBLICATIONS:
Redditch New Town—Planning Proposals by Hugh Wilson and Lewis Womersley (D.C., 1967. 42s.)
Master Plan Brochure (D.C. 2s.)
Town Centre Plan Brochure (D.C. 2s. 6d.)

Hotels: Montville; Royal

Chairman: Sir Edward Thompson Kt., J.P., M.A.(ENG.)
General Manager: A. M. Grier, C.M.G., M.A.
Address: Holmwood, Plymouth Road, Redditch, Worcs.
  Tel: 64200

15. RUNCORN (Cheshire)

Designated: 10 April 1964. *Area:* 7,234 acres
Population in 1964: 28,500
Planned population: 100,000
Purpose: 'overspill' from Liverpool (distance 14 miles)

PLANS: Professor Arthur Ling's plan for Runcorn follows the linear pattern, with neighbourhoods, including shops and other services, linked by a separate public transport route that gives ready access to all parts of the town. The linear route, however, is in the form of a figure eight, with the town centre at the heart and open space, parks and playing fields flanking the whole of the housing areas. An 'expressway' for vehicles will encircle the whole town, with links to the shops, houses, and factories and to the motorway and the bridge over the Mersey and the Manchester Ship Canal.

The whole of the multi-deck town centre will be under cover, with bus access at shopping level. Civic buildings, entertainment and cultural facilities and offices are all included in this advanced plan. Pedestrian walks will link the centre to the 3,000 or so houses to be built near by.

Imperial Chemical Industries have been established at Runcorn for many years and are to build a new plant and research laboratories. Two new industrial areas are being established for other industry.

In the older parts of the town many of the houses are obsolete, and schemes of improvement or renewal will form part of the comprehensive programme.

PUBLICATIONS:
Runcorn New Town Master Plan by Prof. Arthur Ling (D.C., 1967. £3)
Runcorn New Town—illustrated brochure (D.C. 2s.)
Slides (1s. 6d. each); *Photographs* (10s. each)

Hotels: Wilsons; Old Hall (Frodsham)

Chairman: Vere A. Arnold, M.C., D.L., T.D., J.P.
General Manager: D. F. Banwell, L.A.M.T.P.I.
Address: Chapel Street, Runcorn, Cheshire. *Tel:* 4451

16. WASHINGTON (County Durham)

Designated: 24 July 1964. *Area:* 5,300 acres
Population in 1964: 20,000
Planned population: 80,000
Purpose: Tyneside and Wearside revival

PLANS: Washington, only six miles south of Newcastle upon Tyne and six miles from the centre of Sunderland, is to be developed as an integral part of the regional economy rather than a self-contained town. It was from this town that the grandfather of George Washington emigrated to America in 1656. The former family home, Washington Hall, has been restored and is under the care of the National Trust.

Much of the designated land shows the scars of a century of coal mining and heavy chemical industry. These are being energetically cleaned up, and a riverside walk on the banks of the Wear and a landscaped park along the Biddick Burn are planned.

The Master Plan by Lord Llewelyn-Davies, with Miss Sylvia Crowe as landscape consultant, is based on a very sophisticated transport system. A grid of urban motorways connecting the A1 and the Tyne Tunnel road will have fourteen connections to a system of secondary roads giving access to the housing, shopping, and industrial areas. But there will also be a complete and separate network of paths for pedestrians, to which the shopping centres and schools will be linked.

Within this framework the town is planned as a series of nineteen villages with shops, etc., each covering about a quarter of a square mile. Each village is being designed by a different team to ensure individual character.

There will be no less than six industrial estates, all linked to the A1 road and the freightliner rail service terminal at Follingsby.

The main shopping centre now being planned will include a wide range of civic, cultural and entertainment buildings, an Inland Revenue Computer Centre, a sports stadium, and swimming pool.

PUBLICATIONS:
Washington New Town: Master Plan and Report by Llewelyn-Davies, Weeks & Partners (D.C., 1966. £2. 10s.)

Chairman: Sir James Steel, C.B.E., D.L., J.P., F.B.I.M.
General Manager: W. S. Holley, A.D.K.(HON.)
Address: Usworth Hall, Washington, Co. Durham. *Tel:* 3591

17. MILTON KEYNES (North Buckinghamshire)

Designated: 23 January 1967. *Area:* 21,900 acres
Population in 1967: 40,000
Planned population: 250,000

Purpose: 'overspill' from London (distance 45 miles) and regional growth

PLANS: The area designated for this, the first new 'city' in Britain, includes the existing towns of Bletchley, Wolverston, and Stony Stratford and a number of smaller villages, of which Milton Keynes is one and which has been chosen to give its name to the city. It will be one of the aims of the new plan to protect these existing settlements and preserve their strong and independent sense of local community.

In an interim report by Llewelyn-Davies, Weeks, Forestier-Walker & Bor (in association with a wide range of other professional consultants), traffic and transport problems are seen as a dominating factor. A grid pattern of roads, one kilometre apart, is the basic concept, with computer-controlled traffic signals at junctions to generate waves of traffic. A 'small bus' system of public transport is recommended—eventually perhaps a 'dial-a-bus' system or if demand and technology permit a fixed track or guided system—to give ready access to all parts of the town.

Housing within the kilometre squares of 200–300-acre units (say 5,000 people) will ensure safety and adequate local social, etc., services, and the corporation are aiming at 50 per cent owner-occupation, with a wide range of choice. Some 2,000 acres will be reserved for industry, and leisure needs receive particular attention, with parks, woods, lakes, canal walks, sports centres, and golf courses all covered in the draft plan. Shopping needs are very fully analysed, but recommendations on the distribution of shops, in the light of rapidly changing retailing methods, have still to be made.

The Final Plan is expected early in 1970, but meanwhile a start has been made on the development of the industrial estates. The city is to become the Headquarters of the new 'Open University'.

PUBLICATIONS:
Milton Keynes: Interim Report by Llewelyn-Davies, Weeks, Forestier-Walker & Bor (D.C., 1969. 25s.)
Northampton, Bedford & N. Bucks Study (H.M.S.O., 1965. 25s.)

Chairman: Lord Campbell of Eskan

Managing Director (and Deputy Chairman: see Note 6 to
  Chapter 5): W. N. Ismay, B.SC., C.ENG., F.I.MECH.E.,
  F.I.W.M.

Address: Wavendon Tower, Wavendon, Nr. Bletchley,
  Bucks. *Tel:* Woburn Sands 3401

18. PETERBOROUGH (County of Huntingdon & Peterborough)

Designated: 21 July 1967. *Area:* 15,940 acres
Population in 1968: 84,000
Planned population: 190,000
Purpose: 'Overspill' from London (distance 72 miles) and
  regional growth, and creation of a new regional city as a
  counter-magnet to London.

PLANS: Peterborough, one of England's oldest cities, with a
cathedral dating back to pre-Norman times, was the first
large centre chosen for a major expansion under the
machinery of the New Towns Act. The designated area
includes the whole of the existing city, and the Development
Corporation and the County and City Councils are expected
to work in close partnership in planning and executing the
development programme. About 70,000 people will move
into the area by 1985, mainly from London, and the population is expected to grow to nearly 200,000 by the end of
the century.

An expansion feasibility study in 1964 by Sir Henry
Wells was followed in 1966 by a survey of possible expansion
areas and in 1968 by a draft plan for development drawn up
by Hancock and Hawkes, Planning Consultants. This
envisages four new 'townships', each of about 30,000 people,
built within a framework of motorways and linked by roads
and public-transport services.

The existing city centre will remain the regional shopping
and civic centre for the city, but with more shops, public,
commercial, and educational buildings. It will serve a
population in the new city and the rest of its dependent
sub-region of more than 400,000 in 1990.

Two new industrial areas are proposed near to the A1,
and the intention is that renewal of the worn-out old

housing areas of the city should proceed in pace with the building of the new.

A regional park is proposed in the valley of the River Nene, and the six old villages in the designated area will become conservation areas.

Industry already in the area includes the world's largest producer of diesel engines and other major engineering, brick-making and food-processing firms.

PUBLICATIONS:

Expansion Study by Henry W. Wells (M.H.L.G., 1964. 22s. 6d.)

Expansion of Peterborough by Hancock & Hawkes (H.M.S.O., 1966. 15s.)

Greater Peterborough (H.M.S.O., 1968. 85s.)

Draft Master Plan – Interim Policy Report (D.C., 1969)

Master Plan (D.C.—available early 1970)

Hotels: Great Northern; Bull; Angel

Chairman: Christopher T. Higgins

General Manager: Wyndham Thomas

Address: Peterscourt, Peterborough. *Tel:* 60311

19. NORTHAMPTON (Northamptonshire)

Designated: 14 February 1968. *Area:* 19,952 acres

Population in 1968: 131,000

Planned population: 300,000

Purpose: 'overspill' from London (distance 66 miles) and regional growth

PLANS: The designated area includes the whole of the county borough of Northampton, and, as in the case of Peterborough, the powers of the New Towns Act are being used to expand the town by a further 100,000 people by 1981, with an eventual population of 300,000.

The designation followed two preliminary reports to the Minister by Messrs Wilson and Womersley in which an area was recommended for designation. Some 1,300 acres were excluded from the final order, to meet objections at the local inquiry.

A linear form of development is envisaged, with two main expansion areas 2–3 miles wide, from Weston Favell to Great Billing, and southwards between Hardingstone and Wootton. Close on 2 million sq ft of shopping-floor space is planned. The Minister has stressed the importance of protecting the social life in the existing villages, and special attention will be paid to this.

The development is taking place as a partnership activity between the Development Corporation and the County Borough. The latter are primarily concerned with the redevelopment of the central area within the existing boundary, and the former with the new areas. Sharing of professional staff and other facilities has been arranged.

The first district plan, prepared by the consultants, for an area housing 2,500 people at Weston Favell is being discussed, and a start on the first housing scheme for 500 dwellings is planned for the summer of 1970.

PUBLICATIONS:

Northampton, Bedford and North Bucks: Study of inter-related growth (H.M.S.O., 1965. 25s.)

Expansion of Northampton (H.M.S.O., 1966. 13s. 6d.)

Northampton Planning Proposals by Hugh Wilson and Lewis Womersley (D.C., 1968. Main proposals 35s., appendices 45s.)

Master Plan (D.C., 1969. £2)

Hotels: Westone; Grand; Plough; Angel

Chairman: Sir William Hart, C.M.G.
General Manager: Dr John Weston
Address: Cromwell Street, Northampton, NN1 2LE. *Tel:* 30631

20. WARRINGTON (Lancashire)

Designated: 26 April 1968. *Area:* 18,650 acres
Population in 1968: 124,000
Planned population: 200,000
Purpose: 'overspill' from Manchester area (distance 18 miles)

PLANS: Warrington was the first new town to be designated to relieve overcrowding in the Manchester conurbation. The area, which almost adjoins that of Runcorn to the west, includes the whole of the Warrington county borough and a large area around. A further 40,000 people are expected to move in by 1981, and natural growth will take the town to well over 200,000 by the end of the century. Redevelopment or rehabilitation of much of the existing built-up area will be necessary, and this will be carried out, in co-operation with the local authorities, as part of an integral plan for the new town as a whole.

The Minister appointed the Austin-Smith, Salmon, Lord Partnership to prepare a preliminary report on possible areas for expansion. The same Consultants have prepared the Draft Master Plan, which is being considered in detail in the light of public comments which will be encouraged by meetings and exhibitions.

Meanwhile, on the instructions of the County Borough Council, the Consultants have prepared proposals for a new housing area for 7,500 people at Padgate and for a combined redevelopment/rehabilitation exercise in the Whitecross area. They have also prepared proposals for comprehensive central area redevelopment.

A linear park system is proposed along the waterways in the new town area, coupled with a policy of highway improvements, industrial relocation, and environmental improvements generally, with particular reference to derelict sites and atmospheric and water pollution.

PUBLICATIONS:

Expansion of Warrington. Consultants' Proposal for Designation (H.M.S.O., 1966. 12s. 6d.)

An Action Area Plan—Padgate (Warrington County Borough Council, 1969)

Whitecross Renewal Proposals (Warrington County Borough Council, 1969)

Primary Core Area Proposals (Warrington County Borough Council, 1969)

Warrington New Town. Consultants' Proposals for Draft Master Plan (D.C., 1969)

Hotels: Patten Arms; Old Vicarage; Hill Cliffe Hydro; Lymm

Chairman: C. Hamnett, J.P.
General Manager: D. J. Binns, LL.B.
*Address:*59–61 Sankey Street, Warrington, Lancs. *Tel:*33606

21. CENTRAL LANCASHIRE

Designated: 26 March 1970. *Area:* 35,225 acres.

The area finally designated in central Lancashire includes the whole of the county borough of Preston and stretches north into Fulwood and south to take in Leyland and Chorley. The population at that time was 250,000 and the proposal is to build for another 120,000, leaving the new city to grow to 430,000 by the end of the century.

The object is to provide a growth point for the economic revival of Lancashire and to help both with the 'overspill' problems of Manchester and Merseyside and the expected population growth in the region of over 2 million by the year 2000.

The obsolete development in the older parts of the towns presents an 'urban renewal' problem on which the development corporation (when appointed) will work in close consultation with the local authorities.

The area of over 41,000 acres originally proposed was reduced by nearly 6,000 acres following the local enquiry into objections.

PUBLICATIONS:
Central Lancashire – Study for a City (H.M.S.O., 1967. 42s.)
Central Lancashire New Town Proposals – Impact on N.E. Lancashire (H.M.S.O., 1968. 32s. 6d.)

II: SCOTLAND

1. EAST KILBRIDE (Lanarkshire)

Designated: 6 May 1947. *Area:* 10,250 acres
Population in 1967: 2,500
Planned population: 100,000
Purpose: 'overspill' from Glasgow (distance 9 miles) and North Lanarkshire

PLANS: East Kilbride, the first of the Scottish new towns, includes in the designated area over 2,000 acres intended as a 'green belt'. This general policy was recommended by the Reith Committee but became unnecessary after the Town and Country Planning Acts came into force in 1948.

The first tentative plan was prepared by the Department of Health for Scotland. This was developed into a full Master Plan by the development corporation (Chief Architect D. P. Reay), and was later extended to provide for another 15,000 people.

The plan is on 'garden city' lines, with five neighbourhoods and a sixth to be built later on for natural increase. The 44-acre town centre, made all pedestrian in 1960, gives shopping under canopies or in arcades, with the sloping footpath heated to avoid ice in winter; and a new 5-acre air-conditioned shopping unit is planned. Offices and sports, entertainment and cultural facilities and a new youth centre are included, and in the adjoining 10-acre park is an Olympic-length swimming pool of striking design.

Near by is an Inland Revenue computer centre, likely to employ up to 1,300 people. The four industrial areas with jobs for 15,000 people, include firms of world-wide repute.

PUBLICATIONS:
Mental Health and Social Adjustment in E. Kilbride by S. D. Coleman (Glasgow University, 1965)
The Plan that Pleased by Elizabeth B. Mitchell (Town and Country Planning Association, 1967)
Street Map, 1s. 3d.

Hotels: Bruce; Stuart; Torrane

Chairman: George Wallace, O.ST.J., J.P., S.S.C., F.INST.M.
General Manager: George B. Young
Address: Norfolk House, East Kilbride. *Tel:* 28788

2. GLENROTHES (Fife)

Designated: 30 June 1948. *Area:* 5,730 acres
Population in 1948: 1,150

Planned population: 95,000

Purpose: formerly to house-coal mining families, but now a growth point for diversified industry and 'overspill' from Glasgow.

PLANS: After the failure in 1962 of the new £14 million Rothes Colliery, Glenrothes, half-way between the Forth and Tay Road Bridges, made a remarkable recovery and quickly became a new industrial growth point for industry in Fife, and in particular for the electronics industry.

The original 1951 Outline Plan by the then Chief Architect and Planning Officer, P. Tinto, was for a population of 32,000 and was on traditional garden-city lines, but now that a population of 95,000 is envisaged a new Master Plan has been prepared by the Corporation's present Chief Architect and Planning Officer, M. C. Williams. A number of neighbourhoods or precincts, each with a primary school and a few shops and meeting rooms, are grouped around a compact town centre with the main shops, offices, civic and entertainment buildings. A 23-ft bronze sculpture 'Ex Terra' by Benno Schotz stands at the southern entrance to the town centre, which is completely roofed in glass. Two public parks and an eighteen-hole golf course are among the many amenities.

Approximately 1,000 acres are reserved for industrial development in five separate sites. Industrial plant and buildings qualify for grants and allowances under the Local Employment Acts and for relief of S.E.T. and payment of the Regional Employment premium. The town has its own licensed airfield suitable for executive and freight aircraft.

PUBLICATIONS:

Regional Survey and Plans for Central and South East Scotland by Sir Frank Mears (H.M.S.O., 1950)

Outline Plan Report (D.C., 1951)

Transportation Plan for Glenrothes by the Road Pattern Group (D.C., 1966)

Interim Planning Proposals: Phase 2 (D.C., 1966)

Shopping (D.C., 1967: further survey in preparation)

Master Plan (D.C., available 1970)

Glenrothes: its Environs in Days Gone By by W. G. R. Bodie (1960. 3s. 6d.)

Some Light on the Past around Glenrothes by W. G. R. Bodie
(1968. 12s. 6d.)
(Both available from 13, Barnton Park Gardens, Edinburgh
EH46 HL.)
Film: 'A New Day'—available from the Development Cor-
poration; also coloured slides.

Hotels: Golden Acorn; Rothes Arms

Chairman: Ronald R. Taylor
General Manager: Brigadier R. S. Doyle, C.B.E.
Address: Glenrothes House, North Street, Glenrothes, Fife.
Tel: 4343

3. CUMBERNAULD (Dunbartonshire)

Designated: 9 December 1955. *Area:* 4,150 acres
Population in 1955: 3,500
Planned population: 70,000
Purpose: 'overspill' from Glasgow (distance 15 miles)

PLANS: Cumbernauld, planned by Sir Hugh Wilson, then
Chief Architect and Planner to the Development Corporation, is probably the most controversial of all the New
Towns. 'There is nothing like it in Britain, or for that
matter in the world,' say the Development Corporation. The
most striking feature of this award-winning new town is the
Town Centre, which when finished will stretch for half a
mile along the brow of a hill and is planned on eight
enclosed levels with escalators, lifts, stairs and ramps
giving access from the covered bus stops and parking
spaces at the bottom up to the shops, hotel, restaurants,
cinema, bowling alley, ice rink, pubs, offices, town hall,
library, sports arena, and a dozen other facilities on the
floors above and to the maisonettes and penthouses at the
top.

Grouped around it, within easy walking distance, are
houses of above-average density and a few tall blocks of
flats, all designed to give maximum privacy and views across
the hills. There are houses at lower densities in three

'villages' separated from the main core by open spaces and woodland, and these have their own small shopping centres for daily needs. The character of the old Cumbernauld village has been retained with the commendation of the Royal Fine Art Commission.

Particular attention has been paid to landscaping, with half a million trees planted at various points throughout the town, and it is claimed that the elaborate road system, with its complete segregation of pedestrians, makes the town the safest in Britain.

Three main factory areas will eventually provide employment facilities for the planned population.

Because of the widespread interest in Cumbernauld, publicity literature is available in English, French, German, Dutch, Spanish, and Italian.

PUBLICATIONS: (available from the Information Centre, H4-14, Centre South, Cumbernauld)
Preliminary Planning Proposals (1958. 21s.)
1st Addendum Planning Proposals (1959. 21s.)
2nd Addendum Planning Proposals (1962. 21s.)
Retail and Service Trade Provision (revised 1964, 21s.)
Technical Brochure (10s.)
Household Survey and Report by University of Strathclyde (1967. 10s. 6d.)
Map of the town—1s.
Photographs (black and white) 5s. each; aerial photographs 6s. 6d. each
Colour slides 3s. 6d. each; set of 50 £8. 15s.
Film (in colour—35- and 16-mm.: 25 minutes) available 1970 in the United Kingdom from the development corporation and overseas from the Central Office of Information (address—see Stevenage).

Hotel: Golden Eagle

Chairman: Dame Jean Roberts, D.B.E., J.P., D.L.
General Manager: G. R. B. MacGill, C.B.E., C.A., F.I.M.T.A.
Address: Cumbernauld House, Cumbernauld, Scotland.
  Tel: 21155

4. LIVINGSTON (Midlothian and West Lothian)

Designated: 16 April 1962. *Area:* 6,692 acres
Population in 1962: 2,063
Planned population: 100,000
Purpose: 'overspill' from Glasgow (distance 29 miles) and
regional growth

PLANS: Situated on the motorway linking Glasgow and
Edinburgh, Livingston is well placed to become a centre of
rapid growth for new industry in the Lothians. In the plan
prepared by Peter Daniel, the development corporation's
former Chief Architect, a grid pattern of major roads linked
to the motorways divides the town into a series of districts
for residential and other development in which pedestrian
ways and underpasses will give protection from traffic. It is
a linear form of development capable of simple extension to
meet future needs.

The multi-level town centre will be developed in a valley
belt along the River Almond, flanked by open space but also
capable of growth. It will provide shopping, commercial,
entertainment, and recreational services for a wide surrounding area, linking nearby towns and villages into an
eventual community of 250,000 people.

Four industrial areas on the periphery are proposed, that
eventually, together with service industry and the distributive trades, will provide jobs for 45,000 people. The town
is proving popular with industrialists and by the end of 1969
over a million sq ft of new factory accommodation had
been occupied.

The first major house-building started at Craigshill,
mostly of industrialized building with components produced
at a factory close to the site. This project, together with the
schools, shops, health centre, and other facilities, is nearly
complete, and building has started in the Dedridge and
Bankton areas.

PUBLICATIONS:
The Lothians Regional Survey by Professors Sir Robert
Matthew, Percy Johnson-Marshall, and D. J. Robertson,
2 volumes (H.M.S.O., 1966. £7. 10s.)

291

Livingston New Town—Master Plan 1963 by Peter Daniel,
M.C.D., B.ARCH.(L'POOL), A.R.I.B.A., A.M.T.P.I., A.I.L.A.
(D.C. £2. 2s.)

Hotels: Livingston Inn; Golden Circle (2 miles)

Chairman: Wm. L. Taylor, J.P., B.L.
General Manager: Brigadier A. R. Purches, C.B.E., C.ENG.,
A.M.I.MECH.E.
Address: Livingston, West Lothian. *Tel:* 31177

5. IRVINE (Ayrshire)

Designated: 9 November 1966. *Area:* 12,480 acres
Population in 1966: 36,100
Planned population: 116,000
Purpose: acceleration of industrial development and 'over-
spill' from Glasgow (distance 25 miles)

PLANS: The designated area contains the two ancient towns
of Irvine and Kilwinning on the coast of the Firth of Clyde,
seven miles north of Prestwick International Airport.

Planning proposals were prepared in 1966 by consultants,
Hugh Wilson and Lewis Womersley, before the Corporation
was appointed in the latter half of 1967. These proposed a
linear development in a belt about 1 mile wide and 5 miles
long, away from the sea-coast and capable of further
expansion to the north.

In 1968 the Corporation concluded that because of
regional planning decisions, more accurate information
about demographic statistics, geological and other factors,
and mining subsidence, obtained since the planning proposals were prepared, they would need substantial revision.
Messrs Wilson and Womersley were recommissioned to
assist the Corporation's small planning staff in this work.
P.A. Management Consultants Ltd. and the Israel Institute
of Urban Studies were also commissioned to make a cost-
benefit analysis of the new proposals using a new technique
involving a mathematical model and a linear programme on a
large computer. An Interim Revised Outline Plan was published locally for public information and comment in

September 1969. This abandons the linear concept and provides for further expansion not only northwards but also to the east towards Kilmarnock, which is also expanding, and allows for an eventual population of 200,000, including that town. The new plan also seeks better to integrate the existing towns of Irvine and Kilwinning and to utilize the sea-coast location for a tourist and recreational development in the harbour and beach area. As well as increasing the available industrial area from about 700 to about 1,200 acres, four additional golf courses are proposed to add to the existing five in the designated area and the five more near by. With its relatively mild climate, five miles of excellent sandy beach, two salmon rivers, and sailing facilities, the town, in addition to facilitating the rapid acceleration of the existing industrial growth, already has over 2 million square feet of factory space and is likely to become a modern holiday resort, and to attract a much greater proportion of private property investment than have the earlier new towns.

Concurrently with the planning, the Corporation instituted some industrial and housing development both for sale and to let. The first houses were completed in August 1969, and it is expected that 540 will be completed by private enterprise and the various authorities in the twelve months to March 1970. The rate·of building is programmed to rise to 1,500 houses a year or more by 1973/4, with supporting industrial and commercial development.

PUBLICATIONS:

Irvine New Town, Planning Proposals by Hugh Wilson & Lewis Womersley (H.M.S.O., 1967. £2. 15s.)

Irvine New Town, Revised Outline Plan (D.C., 1969)

Hotels: Croft (Springside); Crown; Eglinton Arms; Grange; King's Arms; Redburn; Stanecastle; Victoria (Irvine); Winton Arms (Kilwinning)

Chairman: A. W. Hardie, E.R.D., F.A.C.C.A.
General Manager: Dennis Kirby, M.V.O., M.B.E.
Address: Perceton House, Irvine, Ayrshire. *Tel:* 4100

III: WALES

1. CWMBRAN (Monmouthshire)

Designated: 4 November 1949. *Area:* 3,157 acres
Population in 1949: 12,000
Planned population: 55,000
Purpose: to serve industry in the East Monmouth Valley

PLANS: The Master Plan prepared in 1951 by Minoprio, Spenceley & Macfarlane for a population of 35,000 followed the popular pattern of a town centre surrounded by a number of neighbourhoods, each with its own local facilities and small shopping centre. There was already industry in the valley, but a limited amount of additional employment, mainly in the distributive trades, has been provided on the 11-acre Grange industrial estate, and a 50-acre Avondale estate is being developed in the northern part of the town. The Plan was revised when the planned population was increased to 55,000 in 1962.

There is great variety in the design and layout of the houses, and particular attention has been paid to landscaping, with the planting of many thousands of shrubs and trees. There is some impressive engineering work, too, with seven new bridges crossing the river, two railways, and a canal.

The all-pedestrian town centre, designed mainly by Gordon Redfern, the former Chief Architect to the corporation, is the first such centre in Britain to have full district heating. It is ringed by a one-way traffic system, with multistorey and underground car parks for, eventually, 4,000 cars; the largest supermarket in Wales, with two-level shopping; Monmouth House, with 63,500 sq ft of sales space serviced from underground and fifty-six luxury flats above; Glyndwr House, with more shops and 18,000 sq ft of offices; and The Tower, a twenty-two-storey block of eighty-one small flats that also incorporates the district heating boiler and its 200-ft. chimney.

PUBLICATIONS:
Master Plan by Minoprio, Spenceley & Macfarlane (D.C., 1951)

Cwmbran, a pictorial brochure (D.C., 1968. 5s.)

Colour Slides: Set of 30 (primarily of planning and architectural interest), £3

Chairman: Rear-Admiral St John Micklethwait, C.B., D.S.O., D.L.

General Manager: J. E. McComb, C.B.E., D.F.C.

Address: Victoria Street, Cwmbran, Monmouthshire, NP4 3XJ. *Tel:* 2191

2. NEWTOWN (Montgomeryshire)

Designated: 18 December 1967. *Area:* 1,497 acres

Population in 1967: 5,500

Planned population: 11,000

Purpose: Mid-Wales revival

PLANS: With the object of improving the prosperity of Mid-Wales, consultants recommended a new town for 70,000 people centred on Caersws. They recognized, however, that it did not make sense in terms of Mid-Wales alone, and recommended that it should take 'overspill' from the Midlands—a suggestion that provoked a good deal of opposition from some Welsh quarters.

As a first step, therefore, the Government decided to adopt part of the recommendation by doubling the size of Newtown, a 700-year-old town in the area, with the object of providing jobs for about 1,600 men and 700 women by 1977. If the project is successful the wider object of the Caersws proposal is to be reconsidered. The corporation is called the 'Mid-Wales Development Corporation' and will be available to carry out other projects in other towns in Mid-Wales if called on to do so.

The professional staff of the Cwmbran Development Corporation are assisting in preliminary planning and design work, and the first development consists of one purpose-built factory of 30,000 sq ft and two advance factories of 10,000 sq ft, all on a new industrial estate at Pool Road, and the building of fifty-nine houses on the Corporation's 'Trehafren' housing estate at Llanidloes Road.

PUBLICATIONS:
Depopulation in Mid-Wales (H.M.S.O., 1964)
A New Town in Mid-Wales by Economic Associates Ltd.
 (H.M.S.O., 1965)
Wales—the Way Ahead (Cmnd. 3334: H.M.S.O., 1967)
Draft Planning Proposals (D.C., 1968)
Amendments to Draft Planning Proposals (D.C., 1969)

Hotels: Elephant and Castle; Bear

Chairman: Emrys Roberts, M.B.E., M.A., LL.B.
Secretary: D. P. Garbett-Edwards, F.C.I.S.
Address: Severn Street, Newtown, Montgomeryshire.
 Tel: 6241

IV: NORTHERN IRELAND

Two areas in Northern Ireland—Lurgan/Portadown and
Antrim/Ballymena—were among those recommended for expansion in Professor Robert H. Matthew's *Belfast Regional
Survey and Plan, 1962* (H.M.S.O., 1964). These two growth
points, together with Londonderry, are also key components of
the development strategy recommended by Professor Thomas
Wilson (*Economic Development in Northern Ireland*, H.M.S.O.,
1965). All these areas have now been selected for development
under the New Towns Act (N.I.) 1965.

The purpose is to promote economic growth, secure a more
uniform distribution of industry and population throughout the
province, and reduce the pressure of both population and
traffic on the Belfast Urban Area. All three proposed growth
points lie on the proposed regional motorway system at present
under construction.

The First Report on Lurgan/Portadown (now named Craigavon) and the Outline Plans for Antrim/Ballymena and Londonderry were prepared prior to designation by or through the
Ministry of Development and New Town Commissions were
then established to execute the plans. An Amending Act—the
New Towns (Amendment) Act (N.I.) 1968—enabling the 1965
Act to be applied to a County Borough, was necessary before

the Londonderry designation order could be made, covering both the former Rural District and the County Borough Area.

The Ministry has the power, subject to the approval of the Northern Irish Parliament, to dissolve the existing local authorities in the area and to confer municipal powers on the development commission. This has been done over the whole of the Londonderry area and over part of Craigavon. For accounting purposes, however, expenditure is divided between that spent on municipal account and that spent on development account. In the case of Londonderry, which is regarded as a special expansion rather than a strictly 'new town' operation, it is expected that the bulk of expenditure will be on municipal account rather than on development account.

Antrim and Ballymena are in the charge of a single development commission. The designated area of 400 sq miles includes both towns and the 10-mile stretch of land in between but it is not intended that the two towns should coalesce. They will retain their individual characters while playing a complementary role in the area which Professor Wilson's report regarded as a single complex.

1. CRAIGAVON (County Armagh)

Designated: July 1965. *Area:* 100 sq. miles
Population in 1965: 60,000
Planned population: 180,000

PLANS: The new city of Craigavon is named after the first Prime Minister of Northern Ireland.

The designated area is dominated by two existing towns or sectors, Lurgan and Portadown, each of 22,000 population situated some 5 miles apart and surrounded by a rural area which contains numerous small settlements. Within this context has emerged the concept of Craigavon as a 'rural city' with a dense linear core comprising the two existing sectors linked together by two new proposed residential sectors, each for about 20,000 population, and a proposed new city centre by 1981. Proposals for post-1981 development involve the establishment of two further sectors, each for 20,000 population at the western and eastern extremities of the existing town sectors. The new city centre will be a significant component in the plan, since it is expected to emerge as the focal point of activity and influence in the sub-region.

The plan envisages industrial development at five industrial estates and other smaller areas totalling 700 acres that will eventually provide jobs for about 21,000 people. On the southern shores of nearby Lough Neagh (the largest lough in the British Isles) a large-scale marina will make the town attractive to tourists.

In keeping with its role as a 'rural city', Craigavon is paying particular attention to landscape planning and tree planting.

PUBLICATIONS:

A New City in Northern Ireland: First Report on the Plan (H.M.S.O., 1964. 20s.)

Craigavon New City: Second Report on the Plan (H.M.S.O., 1967. 20s.)

Hotels: Seagoe (Portadown)

Chairman: S. J. McMahon, J.P.
General Manager: E. E. H. Cage, F.C.A., F.I.M.T.A., D.P.A.
Address: Craigavon House, Bachelors Walk, Portadown, Co. Armagh. *Tel:* 34221

2. ANTRIM (Co. Antrim)

Designated: 7 July 1966. *Area:* (with Ballymena) 400 sq. miles
Population in 1965: 7,000
Planned population: 30,000

PLANS: The Outline Plan for Antrim was prepared for a steering committee by a team from the Ministry of Development. It envisages a new road system connected to the motorway; neighbourhood development with local shopping centres and pedestrian ways passing over or under the main roads; 376 acres of additional industrial land; and, ultimately, an all-pedestrian shopping centre on the site of the present central area, with substantial redevelopment of obsolete property, and more public, commercial, sports, and entertainment buildings.

The existing Massereene Park in the town centre is to be protected and restored, recreational facilities on the northern shores of Lough Neagh are to be improved, and with these attractions and the surrounding wooded countryside, the town is expected to become a holiday and tourist centre.

PUBLICATIONS:
Antrim New Town: Outline Plan (H.M.S.O., 1965. 25s.)

Hotels: Halls; Dunadry Inn (nr. Templepatrick)

Chairman: H. A. Frazer, M.SC., F.R.I.C.S., F.A.I., J.P.
General Manager: G. R. Coles, D.I.C., B.SC.(ENG.), A.C.G.I.
Address: Thomas Street, Ballymena, Co. Antrim. *Tel:* Ballymena 3655

3. BALLYMENA (Co. Antrim)

Designated: 22 August 1967. *Area:* (with Antrim) 400 sq. miles
Population in 1966: 22,000
Planned population: 70,000

PLANS: The Ballymena Area Plan was also prepared for a steering committee by a team from the Ministry of Development. In addition to the town itself, the Plan includes a detailed survey of the possible expansion of four villages in the area— Ahoghill, Broughshane (of daffodil fame), Cullybackey, and Kells-Connor. A modern road system and pedestrian ways will form the framework within which 12,000 new homes, local shops, schools, four new industrial estates, and service industries will be built over the next fifteen years.

New shops and offices will be built in the central area, and the programme includes comprehensive redevelopment of much of the existing town, with more open space, parking facilities, public buildings and a sports forum. A landscaped recreational park and riverside walks are included in the plan and limited housing and industrial development in the four satellite villages.

PUBLICATIONS:
Ballymena Area Plan (H.M.S.O., 1966. 22s. 6d.)

Hotels: Adair Arms; Leighinmohr; Tullyglass House

Chairman: H. A. Frazer, M.SC., F.R.I.C.S., F.A.I., J.P.
General Manager: G. R. Coles, D.I.C., B.SC.(ENG.), A.C.G.I.
Address: Thomas Street, Ballymena, Co. Antrim. *Tel:* 3655

4. LONDONDERRY (County of Londonderry)

Designated: 5 February 1969. *Area:* 85,528 acres
Population in 1968: 81,000
Planned population: 110,000

PLANS: The Plan for Londonderry was prepared for the Ministry of Development by the James Munce Partnership. It contemplates the provision of 12,000 new jobs by 1981, equally divided between manufacturing and service industry, 9,600 new houses, including a major new residential area for 18,000 people at Ballyarnett/Shantallow, and a new road system that will take through traffic away from the central area of the city. Educational facilities will be expanded and recreational facilities will be improved by the creation of a sports complex, by increasing open-space provision in the urban area linked with landscaped pedestrian ways, and by opening up the riverside area.

Much of the existing city centre will be redeveloped, and the new housing development is intended largely for people displaced from the areas of unfit or obsolete housing that are to be replanned and rebuilt. In short, this is mainly an exercise in urban renewal—the first of its kind under new town legislation.

PUBLICATIONS:
The Londonderry Area Plan (H.M.S.O., 1968. 32s. 6d.)

Chairman: Brian Morton, F.A.I.
General Manager: G. J. Bryan, C.M.G., C.V.O., O.B.E., M.C.
Address: Guildhall, Londonderry. *Tel:* 5151

CHAPTER 2 – FOUNDATIONS

1. Broadcast to the French people, 21 October 1940.

2. Report of the Royal Commission on the Distribution of the Industrial Population, Cmd. 6153 – H.M.S.O., 1940.

3. See notes (8) and (15) below.

4. Report of the Committee on Land Utilisation in Rural Areas, Cmd. 6378 – H.M.S.O., 1942.

5. *The County of London Plan* by J. H. Forshaw and Patrick Abercrombie – Macmillan & Co. Ltd., 1943.

6. *Greater London Plan*, 1944, by Patrick Abercrombie – H.M.S.O., 1945.

7. Lords, 26 February 1941, cols. 507–8.

8. Uthwatt (I).

9. Lords, 17 July 1941, cols. 849–54. See also Chapter 7, pp. 68–9 and 72.

10. Lords, 11 February 1942, col. 752; Commons, 11 February 1942, col. 1531.

11. Minister of Town & Country Planning Act 1943. In 1951 the name was changed to Minister of Housing & Local Government. In Scotland the Planning Minister is the Secretary of State for Scotland and in Wales (since 1965) Secretary of State for Wales.

In October 1969 the Department of Local Government & Regional Planning was created to co-ordinate the planning work of the Ministries of Housing and Transport and to take over the planning functions of the former Department of Economic Affairs.

12. Uthwatt (F), para. 136; T.C.P. (Interim Development) Act 1943.

13. Uthwatt (F), para. 145. The powers in the T.C.P. Act 1944 were repealed and re-enacted on an extended basis by the T.C.P. Act 1947. See also Chapter 17, pp. 247 and 253–4.

14. Financial Memorandum to T.C.P. Bill (1944). The limitation on the powers of the local authorities was repealed by the T.C.P. Act 1947 and provision was also made in that Act for financial help on 'blight'. The grant provisions are now contained in ss. 7–8 of the Local Government Act 1966 and the relevant grant Regulations (S.I. 1968 No. 189) which enable up to 50 per cent grant to be paid towards net expenditure on development, redevelopment, or the provision of open space. See also Chapter 17, pp. 253–4.

15. Uthwatt (F), pp. 31–56. See also Chapter 7, pp. 70–2.
16. *The Control of Land Use*, Cmd. 6537 – H.M.S.O., 1944.
17. Commons, 8 May 1946, col. 1107.

CHAPTER 3 – POWERS

1. Progress Report of the Ministry of Town & Country Planning 1943–51, p. 22, Cmd. 8204 – H.M.S.O., 1951.
2. N.T.R. (1).
3. N.T.R. (2).
4. N.T.R. (F).
5. See Chapter 7, pp. 68–9 and Note 17.
6. See Chapter 5, p. 37.
7. See Chapter 15, pp. 213–16.
8. Commons, 8 May 1946, cols. 1149–56 and 5 July 1946, cols. 2533–5.
9. Commons, 5 July 1946, col. 2538.
10. Commons, 5 March 1946, cols. 189–92.
11. Commons, 12 March 1946, col. *198*.

CHAPTER 4 – DESIGNATION

1. In England, the Minister responsible for new towns is the Minister of Housing & Local Government; in Scotland, the Secretary of State for Scotland; in Wales, since 1965, the Secretary of State for Wales. (Northern Ireland is subject to separate legislation—the New Towns Act (Northern Ireland) 1965—under the Minister of Development of the Government of Northern Ireland.)
2. N.T. Act 1965, sec. 1 and First Schedule.
3. Rollo *v.* Minister of Town & Country Planning (1947), 45 L.G.R. at p. 648. (See also Note 11 below.)
4. For a typical order, see S.I. 1967, No. 1100 (Peterborough).
5. N.T. (No. 2) Act 1964 (now sec. 53 (4) of the N.T. Act 1965).
6. Commons, 27 November 1967, cols. 171–97.
7. *Stevenage: a sociological study of a new town* by Harold Orlans – Routledge & Kegan Paul, 1952.
8. Franklin and Others *v.* Minister of Town & Country Planning (1947), 45 L.G.R. 130, 243, and 581; [1947] 2 All E.R. 289; [1948] A.C. 87 H.L.

9. *Crawley Observer*, 13 and 20 August 1965. This quotation is from a series of weekly articles (6 August 1965–1 October 1965) by Mr Stanford who was for many years a member, and later deputy chairman, of the Crawley Development Corporation. This is about the only contemporary account, written 'from the inside', of the problems of the early days of new towns. Mr Stanford carried the story up to October 1949 and died before he was able to deal with the later stages of the corporation's work in Crawley.

10. Ibid., 3 September 1965.

11. Rollo *v.* Minister of Town & Country Planning (1947), 45 L.G.R. 640; 46 L.G.R. 114; [1948] 1 All E.R. 13.

12. Fletcher *v.* Minister of Town & Country Planning (1947), 45 L.G.R. 649; [1947] 2 All E.R. 496.

13. *The Expansion of Ipswich* – H.M.S.O., 1966.

14. *Expansion of Ipswich: Comparative Costs* – H.M.S.O., 1967.

15. *Agriculture and Urban Growth* by G. P. Wibberley – Michael Joseph, 1959; *Land for New Towns* by Robin H. Best – Town & Country Planning Association, 1964. See also 'Extent of Urban Growth and Agricultural Displacement in Post-war Britain' by Robin H. Best, *Urban Studies*, February 1968.

16. P.A.C. 1966–7, Minutes of Evidence Q. 1128.

17. M.H.L.G. Circular 73/65 – H.M.S.O.

18. P.A.C. 1966–7 5th Report paras. 101–106. Minutes of Evidence Q. 1123–1217; 1967–8, Minutes of Evidence Q. 2492–2525.

CHAPTER 5 – CORPORATION

1. In Northern Ireland (where the title is 'development commission') the Ministry of Development have power, with the approval of Parliament, to confer on the commission all the powers of a local authority.

2. Town & Country Planning (New Towns Special Development) Order 1963. S.I. 1963, No. 1142 (re-enacting previous order made under the 1947 Act).

3. N.T. Act 1965, Second Schedule.

4. House of Commons Disqualification Act 1957.

5. M.H.L.G. Press Release, No. 200, 20 August 1965.

6. The Milton Keynes Development Corporation is excep-

tional in having a full-time deputy chairman who is also the 'Managing Director'. In the case of the Commission for the New Towns (see Chapter 15) the staff is headed by the Secretary, with a Manager in each town.

A brochure is being prepared outlining the jobs available in new towns. See also the *Directory of Opportunities for Graduates*.

7. The south-west area of Peterlee. See Appendix, p. 268.

8. *Principles of Estate Management* by Michael Thorncroft, B.Sc. (Est. Man.), A.R.I.C.S., A.A.I., p. 365 – Estates Gazette Ltd., 1965.

9. Report of Ministry of Housing & Local Government 1959, p. 135 (Cmnd. 1027).

10. See Chapter 14, pp. 192–4.

11. R.D.C. 1950, pp. 103–4. Sir Ernest Gowers was Chairman of the Harlow Development Corporation from 1947 to 1950.

12. R.D.C. 1949, pp. 39 and 58. Sir Thomas Bennett was Chairman of the Crawley Corporation from 1947 to 1960 and also of the Stevenage Corporation from 1951 to 1953.

13. N.T.R. (1), para. 11; N.T.R. (F), paras. 283–93.

14. Conference on 'Social Facilities in New and Expanded Towns', organized by the Town & Country Planning Association, 29 June 1967.

CHAPTER 6 – PLAN

1. References to all the Master Plans are given in Part I of the Appendix.

2. *Planning for Sport* – Central Council of Physical Recreation, 1968. See also the detailed analysis in 'Open Space in New Towns' by F. T. Burnett, *T.P.I. Journal*, June 1969.

3. N.T.R. (F), paras. 43–4.

4. *Design of Dwellings* (Dudley Report) – H.M.S.O., 1944.

5. N.T.R. (F), para. 43.

6. *The Needs of New Communities*. Report of sub-committee of the Minister's Central Housing Advisory Committee – H.M.S.O., 1967.

7. See Chapter 10, p. 124.

8. *Cumbernauld: a Household Survey and Report*, Occasional Paper No. 1 – University of Strathclyde, 1967. But Dr Ferdynand Zweig, in a report commissioned by the Urban Research Bureau (to be published 1970), is rather more critical.

9. A lengthy analysis of the 'linear city' can be found in the *Northampton, Bedfordshire and N. Bucks Study* – H.M.S.O., 1967.

10. *Town Planning* by Thomas Sharp – Penguin Books, 1940.

11. *Traffic in Towns* – H.M.S.O., 1963. Shortened edition, Penguin Books, 1964.

12. Redditch Master Plan, p. 8.

13. Runcorn Master Plan, p. 18.

14. Corby Master Plan, p. 122.

15. R.D.C. 1964, p. 220; 1968, p. 400.

16. For an extensive study of mass transit methods, see also *Manchester Rapid Transport Survey* – Manchester City Council, 1968.

17. *Milton Keynes: Interim Report.*

18. The term Mark I, Mark II, etc. was first applied to new towns (per Maurice Brown, *T.P.I. Journal*, January 1966) by a leader writer in the Edinburgh *Evening Despatch* as long ago as 25 October 1946. He urged, with commendable foresight, that the brave new town ideas should not be too rigid and that each new town should benefit from the lessons of experience learned from its forerunners.

19. *A Runaway World*, Reith Lectures 1967, by Edmund Leach – B.B.C., 1968.

CHAPTER 7 – LAND

1. N.T. Act 1965, secs. 7–8 and Third Schedule.

2. N.T. Act 1965, sec. 18 (2).

3. Commons, 5 July 1946, col. 2559.

4. N.T. Act 1965, sec. 11.

5. See p. 75.

6. N.T. Act 1965, sec. 6 (3).

7. Agricultural Holdings Act 1948.

8. Agriculture (Miscellaneous Provisions) Act 1963, sec. 22.

9. Agriculture (Miscellaneous Provisions) Act 1968, sec. 9.

10. T.C.P. Act 1944, incorporated in N.T. Act 1946 and re-enacted in N.T. Act 1965.

11. Acquisition of Land (Authorisation Procedure) Act 1946.

12. N.T. Act 1965, secs. 15–17, now repealed and replaced by T.C.P. Act 1968, sec. 30. Where entry on the land takes place before payment of compensation, interest is payable from the

date of entry at a rate fixed from time to time by the Treasury. In 1969 this rate was increased to 9½ per cent (Acquisition of Land (Rate of Interest after Entry) (No. 2) Regulations 1969, S.I. 1969, No. 896).

13. Compulsory Purchase Act 1965, Sched. 2.

14. Lands Clauses Consolidation Act 1845.

15. Acquisition of Land (Assessment of Compensation) Act 1919.

16. Uthwatt (I); T.C.P. Act 1944, secs. 58 (2), 60 (3).

17. Acquisition of Land (Increase in Supplement) Order 1946, S.R. & O. 1946, No. 1163.

18. Report of the Royal Commission on the Distribution of the Industrial Population, paras. 250–6, Cmd. 6153 – H.M.S.O., 1940.

19. Uthwatt (F), paras. 18–28.

20. Uthwatt (F), paras. 49–52.

21. See Note 16 to Chapter 2.

22. Commons, 26 February 1952, col. 121. (The final figure was £387 million: see Report of Central Land Board, 1958–9.)

23. Earl Fitzwilliam & Wentworth Estates Company *v.* Minister of Housing & Local Government [1952] A.C. 362, [1952] 2 All E.R. 509.

24. Progress Report of the Ministry of Town & Country Planning 1947–50, pp. 12–13, 36, Cmd. 8204 – H.M.S.O., 1951.

25. P.A.C. 1950–1, Q. 6595 et seq. See also Report of Central Land Board for 1949–50, para. 32.

26. An account of the Mr Pilgrim tragedy is given by Harold Macmillan in his memoirs *Tides of Fortune* – Macmillan & Co., 1969.

27. Report of Ministry of Housing & Local Government 1950–4, p. 82, Cmd. 9559.

28. T.C.P. Act 1953.

29. T.C.P. Act 1959, secs. 5–8 (now Land Compensation Act 1961, secs. 17–20).

30. T.C.P. Act 1959, sec. 9 (now Land Compensation Act 1961, First Schedule.)

31. Commons, Standing Committee D, 10 February 1959, col. 621.

32. N.T. Act 1966, sec. 2.

33. *Compensation for Compulsory Acquisition and Planning Restrictions*, Appendix 1—Chartered Auctioneers & Estate Agents' Institute, 1968.

34. Commons, 29 January 1947, col. 980.

35. Explanatory and Financial Memorandum to Land Commission Bill (1965).

36. *A Selection of Unit Costs in Public Expenditure* – H.M.S.O., 1968.

37. Co-operative Permanent Building Society Bulletin, No. 83, February 1968.

38. *The Times*, 20 September 1968.

39. *The Property Boom* by Oliver Marriott – Hamish Hamilton, 1967; Pan Books, 1969.

CHAPTER 8 – HOMES

1. *The Guardian*, 4 July 1967. The R.I.B.A. awards were to: 1st Thomas Simey (Redditch) and 2nd George Oldham (Runcorn).

2. M.H.L.G. circular 58/64.

3. *Capital Investment in 1948*, Cmd. 7268 – H.M.S.O.; N.T.R. (F), p. 60.

4. *Houses 1952: Houses 1953:* M.H.L.G. circulars 38/51 and 37/52 – H.M.S.O.

5. R.D.C. 1957, p. 48.

6. *Architectural Review*, July 1953.

7. Ibid.

8. *Town & Country Planning*, March 1954.

9. *Land for New Towns* (see Note 15 to Chapter 4).

10. See, for example, *Family and Kinship in East London* by Michael Young and Peter Willmott – Penguin Books, 1962.

11. Gardens vary from about 300 sq ft to 800 sq ft. Higher rented houses do not necessarily have larger gardens but in some towns plots of $\frac{1}{4}$–$\frac{1}{2}$ acre can be bought by those wishing to build to their own design. See also the inconclusive comments about gardens at p. 191 of *Planning for Leisure* by K. K. Sillitoe – H.M.S.O., 1969.

12. *Homes for Today and Tomorrow* – H.M.S.O., 1961.

13. See Chapter 14, p. 199.

14. P.A.C. 1967–8, Minutes of Evidence Q. 2553. See also P.A.C. 1968–9, Minutes of Evidence Q. 2413–2440.

15. M.H.L.G. Circular 31/69.

16. Civil Appropriation Accounts 1966–7 (Classes VI–XI) p. v, – H.M.S.O., 1968.

17. P.A.C. 1967–8, Third Report, paras. 193–8, Minutes of

Evidence Q. 2526–2641, 3349–3633; P.A.C. 1968–9, Minutes of Evidence Q. 3575–3587.

18. *The Times Special Supplement on Industrialised Building*, 12 January 1967.

19. Report of the Inquiry into the Collapse of Flats at Ronan Point, Canning Town – H.M.S.O. 1968.

20. See Chapter 13, pp. 165–6.

21. R.D.C. 1950, p. 56; 1957, p. 161.

22. R.D.C. 1955, p. 219; 1956, pp. 230–1; 1965, p. 210.

23. R.D.C. 1966, p. 137.

24. The N.T.C. abolished these restrictions in 1967 (Report of N.T.C. 1968, p. 11).

25. *The Ownership & Management of Housing in the New Towns* by J. B. Cullingworth and V. A. Karn, p. 141 – H.M.S.O. 1968.

26. N.T.R. (2), paras. 15–20.

27. N.T. Act 1946, sec. 5.

28. Town Development Act 1952, sec. 18.

29. Leasehold Reform Act 1967, sec. 19. The N.T.C. are proposing a scheme of management for the towns under their control (Report, 1968, p. 11). So also are the Cwmbran and Stevenage Development Corporations.

30. Report of the Committee on Positive Covenants affecting Land (Chairman, Lord Wilberforce), Cmnd. 2719 – H.M.S.O., 1965.

31. *Architects' Journal*, 29 November 1967.

32. *Estates Gazette*, 9 September 1967.

CHAPTER 9 – JOBS

1. See Chapter 3, p. 17.

2. Census 1961, Workplace Tables (England & Wales) – H.M.S.O., 1966. An analysis of the 1961 census information is given by Audrey A. Ogilvie in 'The Self Contained New Town', *Town Planning Review* April 1968; republished in 1968 as 'Building Research Station Current Paper 56/68'. See also Sample Census 1966, England and Wales, Workplace and Transport Tables – H.M.S.O., 1968 and the detailed study in *London's New Towns: a study of self-contained and balanced communities* by Ray Thomas, P.E.P., 1969.

Travel to work information needs careful analysis to avoid

wrong conclusions. Thus Hatfield was built for people working in the nearby aircraft works and Corby for those working in the steel industry, both just outside the designated area. Some commentators therefore conclude that the towns are no longer self-contained!

3. See Note 2 to Chapter 2.

4. T.C.P. Act 1962, sec. 38 (re-enacting T.C.P. Act 1947, sec. 14 (4)). See also S.I. 1963, No. 1142; S.I. 1965, No. 1659; Local Employment Act 1960, sec. 21; Control of Office and Industrial Development Act 1965, secs. 19–20; Industrial Development Act 1966, secs. 22–26. Control over the distribution of industry was transferred in October 1969 from the Board of Trade to the Ministry of Technology.

5. R.D.C. 1949, p. 70.

6. P.A.C. 1950–1, Fourth Report, paras. 102–4.

7. P.A.C. 1951–2, First Report, Appendix p. xxix.

8. Commons, 27 November 1967, col. 194.

9. Commons, 5 February 1969, col. 533.

10. *The Intermediate Areas* (Cmnd. 3998). – H.M.S.O., 1969.

11. Commons, 24 April 1969, col. 671.

12. *N.T. Acts: Accounts 1967–8* – (H.C. Paper 153 of 1968–9); P.A.C. 1968–9, Third Report, paras. 171–179; Minutes of Evidence Q. 3588–3769.

13. Mineral Workings Act 1952. The Corby Development Corporation are among those entitled to claim from the fund if they carry out any restoration work themselves.

14. R.D.C. 1964, p. 129; 1967, p. 120. A full account is given in the report of the investigation under the Companies Act 1948, *Cadco Development Ltd.*, etc. – H.M.S.O., 1966.

15. The main inducements offered in Development Areas are (*a*) grants of 25 per cent of the cost of a new building (up to 35 per cent in some cases); (*b*) grants towards initial expenditure in setting up in or transferring to the area; (*c*) investment grants of 40 per cent—sometimes higher—on new plant and machinery.

16. Finance Act 1963, sec. 15 (6). This section was applied to Skelmersdale, but under the Industrial Development Act 1966 the new town is now regarded as within the Merseyside Development Area.

17. Control of Office and Industrial Development Act 1965. The Act applies to office buildings over 3,000 sq ft in Greater London and over 10,000 sq ft in outer London, Birmingham, the South-East and the East and West Midlands. (S.I. 1965,

No. 1564; S.I. 1966, No. 888; S.I. 1967, No. 1087; S.I. 1969, Nos. 173 and 174.) The control, until October 1969 exercised by the Board of Trade, is now transferred to the Ministry of Housing & Local Government.

18. See also Chapter 13, p. 164 and Note 6.

CHAPTER 10 – SHOPS

1. For an exposition of Reilly's Law see *Principles of Estate Management* by Michael Thorncroft, pp. 224–5 – Estates Gazette Ltd., 1965; and for an example of the modification made in new town calculations, see *Expansion of Northampton: Planning Proposals*. All the recent Master Plans contain a very detailed analysis of future shopping needs.

2. N.T.R. (F), para. 136.

3. Ibid., paras. 144–6.

4. *The Planning of Shopping Areas* – Retailers' Advisory Committee, May 1947.

5. R.D.C. 1954, p. 374.

6. R.D.C. 1958, p. 352.

7. Copies of the Jury's Report on Stockholm, Tapiola, and Cumbernauld (reprinted from *A.I.A. Journal*, July 1967) are available from the Reynolds Metals Company, P.O. Box 2346, Dept. A.D., Richmond, Virginia 23218.

8. Food & Drugs Act 1955, Part III.

9. See article by J. G. Pease in *Law Quarterly Review*, vol. 32, pp. 199–207.

10. Lord FitzGerald in Gt. Eastern Rly Co. *v.* Goldsmid [1884] 9 A.C. at p. 964.

11. See, for example, *Basildon: Shopping—Work for Women—Leisure*, by Carole H. Byron, p. 108 – Basildon Development Corporation, 1967.

12. *Planning and the Shopkeeper* by Gillian M. Pain – Barrie & Rockliff, 1967.

13. While this book was in the Press revised Regulations were made enabling shop-window advertisements to be challenged if they are prejudicial to amenity or safety.

CHAPTER 11 – SERVICES

1. N.T. Act 1965, secs. 3 (2) and 34; Water Acts 1945 and 1948. For a typical order see S.I. 1965, No. 1924 (Runcorn).

2. R.D.C. 1962, p. 235.

3. Local Government Act 1966.

4. Commons, 19 December 1968, col. 1088.

5. The 1958 birth-rate in Peterlee, for example, was 35·4 per 1,000 and in Harlow 20·4 per 1,000, compared with 16·4 in England and Wales. This does not mean that new town families are larger than elsewhere. It is entirely due to the age-grouping in the towns. For the age-groups concerned the birthrate was around the national level.

6. A list, as in 1969, of the number of hospital beds in the areas in which the English new towns are situated was given in reply to a Parliamentary Question (Commons, 31 March 1969, cols. *18–19*).

7. N.T.R. (F), para. 177.

8. For a detailed account of the Harlow health services, see R.D.C. 1966, pp. 196–202. Dr Patricia Elliott succeeded Lord Taylor as Medical Director in 1967.

9. *Reports from General Practice No. IV* – College of General Practitioners (1966); *The Provision of General Medical Care in New Towns* – Office of Health Economics (1967).

10. Ministry of Health circular to local authorities, No. 7/67, dated 21 April 1967. See also Commons, 2 February 1968, cols. *432–3*. A £72,000 Health Centre for five doctors and a dentist has been built in Livingstone in Scotland.

11. N.T.R. (F), para. 24 and pp. 74–7.

12. R.D.C. 1950, pp. 12–13; 1951, p. 13.

13. *Climate for Living* by Anthony Tucker – Macdonald & Co., 1967.

14. Full technical details of this coaxial cable were given in Parliament by the Postmaster General (Commons, 16 April 1969, col. *270*).

15. 'Are Special Powers Needed?' by A. W. Thomas (later Manager and Chief Engineer, Hemel Hempstead, Commission for the New Towns), *Journal of the Institution of Municipal Engineers, January* 1967.

16. 'Signs in a New Town—How Crawley solved its Sign Problems' by H. S. Howgrave-Graham (Chief Architect, Commission for the New Towns) – *Sign World*, September–October 1967.

17. *Municipal Journal*, 25 April 1969, p. 1030. Mr Gazzard was for some time Chief Architect to the Aycliffe and Peterlee Development Corporations, and is now Director of Development

at Killingworth, the town being built by the Northumberland County Council under the powers in the Town & Country Planning Acts for dealing with areas needing 'comprehensive development'.

18. R.D.C. 1948, p. 65.

19. R.D.C. 1957, p. 285.

20. *Architects' Journal*, 13 December 1967.

CHAPTER 12 – LEISURE

1. *Community Centres* – H.M.S.O., 1945.

2. *The Needs of Youth in Stevenage*, Calouste Gulbenkian Foundation, 1959.

3. A standard of six acres of open space per 1,000 population is recommended by the National Playing Fields Association and in the Ministry's Technical Memorandum No. 6. But see also page 52 and Note 2 to Ch. 6.

4. R.D.C. 1964, p. 215.

5. The stadium was named after the first Chairman of the Development Corporation, Mr R. G. Gosling, who died in 1958.

6. 'Recreation Facilities in a New Town' by Dan Waldorf, *Official Architecture & Planning*, November 1966.

7. *Journal of the Town Planning Institute*, April 1968, p. 153.

8. *The Times*, 8 May 1968.

9. See Note 2 above.

10. *The Arts in Stevenage* by Sir William Emrys Williams, C.B.E. (formerly Secretary-General of the Arts Council of Great Britain) – Stevenage Development Corporation, 1963.

11. Licensing Act 1949, repealed by the Licensed Premises in New Towns Act 1952 (now consolidated in the Licensing Act 1953).

12. *Basildon: Shopping, Work for Women, Leisure*, p. 68 see Note 11 to Chapter 10.

13. See page 152.

14. R.D.C. 1950, p. 185. Many years later, the development corporation in fact set up a new social relations department.

15. The financial implications are discussed in Chapter 14, pp. 205–9.

16. *Crawley: a Study of Amenities in a New Town* by G. Brooke Taylor – N.T.C., 1966.

CHAPTER 13 – PEOPLE

1. *Report of Working Party on Social Workers*, p. 183, H.M.S.O., 1959.

2. R.D.C. 1966, p. 330.

3. See Note 9 to Chapter 4.

4. R.D.C. 1957, p. 286.

5. See Part I of Appendix, p. 266.

6. See Chapter 9, pp. 114–15. Details of the Industrial Selection Scheme and of the linkage with certain exporting areas are given in M.H.L.G. Circular No. 29/53.

7. Commons, 8 May 1946, cols. 1089–90.

8. R.D.C. 1954, p. 247. See also *New Communities in Britain* by J. H. Nicholson – National Council of Social Service, 1961.

9. N.T.R. (F), paras. 22–5.

10. 'Urban Sociology' by Ruth Glass, *Current Sociology*, No. 4 1955, pp. 14–19.

11. 'The New Towns & London's Housing Problem', *Urban Studies*, February 1966, and 'Social Class and the New Towns', *Urban Studies*, February 1968, by B. J. Heraud, Senior Lecturer in Sociology, North West Polytechnic, London.

12. 'British Town Planning: One Ideology or Three' by D. L. Foley, *British Journal of Sociology*, 1960.

13. 'Migration to Eight New Towns in 1966', by A. J. Kellaway, *T.P.I. Journal*, May 1969.

14. R.D.C. 1961, p. 236.

15. Based on figures for the four new towns in Hertfordshire. See also R.D.C. 1959, p. 283.

16. *Crawley Observer*, 8 March 1968. See also Third Annual Bulletin on Narcotics published by United Nations.

17. *Evening News*, 13 December 1967.

18. *Town & Country Planning*, April 1968, p. 198.

19. Based on Registrar-General's Statistics for 1966.

20. Report of the Ministry of Housing & Local Government 1960, p. 96, Cmnd. 1435.

21. Mrs M. Glanville of Hatfield in a letter to *Woman's Own*, 16 December 1967; *D. Telegraph*, 3 September 1964.

22. *Mental Health and Environment in a New Town* by Lord Taylor and Sidney Chave – Longmans, 1964.

23. *The Evolution of a Community* by Peter Willmott – Routledge & Kegan Paul, 1963.

24. *Daily Mirror*, 13 February 1967, in an interview with Paula James.

25. See Note 10 to Chapter 8.

26. R.D.C. 1962, p. 269.

27. Letter to *The Times*, 2 October 1968, from L. E. White, Liaison Officer of the Harlow Development Corporation.

28. *T.P.I. Journal*, March 1967.

29. Speech to Annual General Meeting of Town & Country Planning Association, 29 April 1968.

30. *The Death and Life of Great American Cities*, by Jane Jacobs – Penguin Books, 1964.

31. 'Major changes in Environmental Form required by Social and Psychological Demands' by Christopher Alexander, Associate Professor, University of California. *Second International Symposium on Regional Development*, Tokyo, September 1968.

32. 'Sociological Background of Urban Planning' by Eiichi Isomura, Professor of Tokyo University. Ibid.

33. 'A City is not a Tree' by Christopher Alexander – Kaufmann International Design Awards, 1965. Originally published in the American journal *Architectural Forum* and reprinted in *Design*, February 1966.

34. Letter from R. A. Barker in *Hemel*, 2 December 1966.

CHAPTER 14 – MONEY

1. N.T. Act 1965, sec. 45 (1) which applies only to the N.T.C. (see Chapter 15). Any surplus in the hands of a development corporation will normally be used to finance further development.

2. R.D.C. 1968, pp. 334–5. See also p. 125.

3. *Architects' Journal*, 7 February 1968.

4. Commons, 20 February 1969, col. 914.

5. Explanatory and Financial Memorandum to New Towns Bill 1946.

6. P.A.C. 1948–9, Minutes of Evidence Q. 2725.

7. N.T. Act 1969. The figures relate to Great Britain and do not include Northern Ireland.

8. Commons, 19 December 1969, col. 1619.

9. *N.T. Acts: Accounts 1967–8*, H. C. Paper 153 of 1968–9.

10. See New Towns Acts of 1952, 1953, 1955, 1958, 1959, 1964, and 1966.

11. P.A.C. 1950, Minutes of Evidence Q. 795–821.

12. P.A.C. 1950, Fourth Report, para. 107.

13. P.A.C. 1950–1, First Report, Appendix p. xxii.

14. Commons, 31 March 1952, col. 1312.

15. Commons, 11 Nov. 1966, col. 1740. See also Chapter 4, p. 27.

16. P.A.C. 1957–8, Minutes of Evidence Q. 912.

17. N.T. Act 1965, sec. 4 (1).

18. N.T. Act 1965, secs. 6 (1) and 42 (3).

19. See Note 2 to Chapter 5.

20. See Chapter 8, pp. 89–91.

21. P.A.C. 1950, Minutes of Evidence, Q. 949.

22. P.A.C. 1957–8, Minutes of Evidence, Q. 925–6.

23. R.D.C. 1968, p. 213.

24. *The Civil Service*, paras. 188–91, Cmnd. 3638 – H.M.S.O., 1968.

25. Advances made before 1 April 1967 were repayable by sixty yearly instalments.

26. P.A.C. 1957–8 Minutes of Evidence, Q. 970–1.

27. N.T. Act 1965, sec. 44 (1) as amended by the National Loans Act 1968. For an explanation of the functions and relationships of the National Loans Fund and the Consolidated Fund see *Government Accounting*, H.M.S.O., 1968.

28. R.D.C. 1962, p. 285; R.D.C. (Scotland) 1968, p. 66; see also Note to Appendix, Part III.

29. Subsidy in respect of houses built by N.T.C. is paid only in respect of a limited number of Old People's Dwellings.

30. Housing Subsidies Act 1967 ss. 1–2. The calculation of subsidy on houses completed during any financial year is based on the difference between 4 per cent and a 'representative rate of interest'. Separate 'representative rates' are fixed each year for the new towns in England and Wales and in Scotland based on the average rate for all new town borrowings during the previous financial year. For houses built during 1969/70 the rate was 8·21 per cent for England and Wales and 8·15 per cent for Scotland. (Housing Subsidies (Representative Rates of Interest) Orders 1969 – S.I. 1969, Nos. 1003–4).

31. The additional subsidy, payable for sixty years, is £34 per annum for each thousand pounds per acre over £4,000, rising to £40 per acre for each thousand pounds over £50,000 per acre (Housing Subsidies Act 1967, sec. 10).

32. The additional sixty years' subsidy is £8 per annum for

each dwelling in a four-storey block of flats, £14 p.a. for five storeys and £26 p.a. for six or more storeys (Housing Subsidies Act 1967, sec. 4).

33. Housing Subsidies Act 1967, sec. 13.

34. N.T. Act 1965, sec. 42 (2); Housing Subsidies Act 1967, s. 16.

35. Rents of local authority dwellings in 1968 ranged from ten shillings to over £8 a week (exclusive of rates). *Housing Rent Statistics* – I.M.T.A., 1969.

36. Housing Subsidies Act 1967, sec. 18; N.T.C. Report 1969, p. 3.

37. See Note 25 to Chapter 8.

38. *Statistics on Incomes, Prices, Employment & Production*, published periodically by Dept. of Employment & Productivity – H.M.S.O. The *average* weekly earnings in April 1969 for men over 21, including bonus and overtime and before tax deduction, was £23. 18s. 5d (D.E.P. Press Notice 29 July 1969.)

39. N.T. Act 1965, secs. 3 (3) (*b*) and 35 (3) (*b*).

40. Ellis *v.* Ruislip–Northwood U.D.C., [1920] 1 K.B. at p. 370.

41. Lords, 16 July 1959, col. 115; Commons, 29 October 1966, col. 1647.

42. Commons, 28 October 1966, col. 1583.

43. Quoted in 'Local Authorities and Development Corporations' by C. W. G. T. Kirk (Town Clerk, Hemel Hempstead), *Town & Country Planning*, January 1953.

44. Commons, 1 December 1958, cols. 958–9.

45. Report of N.T.C. 1968, pp. 19–20.

46. *Town and Country Planning*, January 1968, pp. 42–4.

CHAPTER 15 – COMMISSION

1. The figures quoted are for Crawley, as given in Report of N.T.C. 1966, p. 5. See also Fig. 2 at p. 171.

2. N.T.R. (2), paras. 82–6.

3. Uthwatt (F); see also Chapter 2, pp. 11–12 and Chapter 7, pp. 71–2.

4. See Note 16 to Chapter 2.

5. See Chapter 7, p. 74.

6. Land Commission Act 1967.

7. N.T. Act 1964, sec. 15 (1).

8. Commons, 4 July 1946, cols. 2376 et seq.

9. Ibid.

10. Commons, 1 December 1958, cols. 843 et seq.; Standing Committee D, 9 April–14 May 1959; Commons, 30 June 1959, cols. 249–389; Lords, 7, 16, and 20 July.

11. *Labour's Housing Policy*, p. 17 – Labour Party, 1957.

12. *The Future of the New Towns* – Labour Party, 1959.

13. N.T. Act 1965, sec. 36.

14. House of Commons Disqualification Act 1957; New Towns Act 1959, Sch. 1, para 1 (10).

15. Speech at Redditch, 20 July 1965 – M.H.L.G. Press Release, No. 200.

16. Speech at Stevenage, 1 July 1967: N.T.C. Report 1968, p. 19.

17. See Note 25 to Chapter 8.

18. N.T.C. Report 1969.

19. N.T.C. Report 1965, pp. 27–8. See also Report 1967, pp. 5–6.

20. See Chapter 14, p. 202.

21. Quoted in Cullingworth Report (see Note 25 to Chapter 8), pp. 81 and 156–7, from a report (unpublished) of a teach-in at Harlow on 18 June 1967.

22. Report of Royal Commission on Local Government in England, Cmnd. 4039–40 – H.M.S.O., 1969.

CHAPTER 16 – ACHIEVEMENT

1. For a detailed study of housing progress in Europe see *The Government of Housing* by Professor D. V. Donnison – Penguin Books, 1967.

2. *The City in History* by Lewis Mumford, p. 594 – Penguin Books, 1967.

3. Commons, 25 February 1952, col. 724.

4. *The Ministry of Housing and Local Government* by Evelyn Sharp, G.B.E. p. 166 – George Allen & Unwin, 1969.

5. Commons, 28 November 1957, col. 1310.

6. *The Planning of a New Town* – L.C.C., 1961.

7. See Note 11 to Chapter 6.

8. Details are given in Part I of the Appendix.

9. *Central Lancashire: study for a city; Central Lancashire new town proposal: impact on N.E. Lancashire*, by Robert Matthew,

Johnson-Marshall & Partners in consultation with Economic Consultants, Ltd. – H.M.S.O., 1967 and 1968. (At the time of going to press no decision had been announced on the draft Designation Order for Central Lancashire. See also p. 286.)

10. *The Ashford Study* by Colin Buchanan & Partners. H.M.S.O., 1967.

11. *Expansion at Ashford: an appraisal of its impact on East Kent* – Kent County Council, 1968.

12. See Chapter 4, pp. 32–3.

13. *East Anglia: A Regional Appraisal* – East Anglia Consultative Committee, 1969.

14. *Llantrisant: Prospects for Urban Growth* by Colin Buchanan & Partners – H.M.S.O., 1969.

15. *South Hampshire Study* by Colin Buchanan & Partners, in association with Economic Consultants Ltd. – H.M.S.O., 1967.

16. *Humberside: A Feasibility Study*, by the Central Planning Unit of the Department of Economic Affairs – H.M.S.O., 1969.

17. *Tees-side Survey and Plan: Policies and Proposals* by Hugh Wilson and Lewis Womersley – H.M.S.O., 1969.

18. The Tayside Report is being prepared by the Tayside Economic Planning Consultative Group, and the Severnside Report by the Central Unit for Environmental Planning.

19. *Journal of Administration Overseas*, January 1969.

20. For an account of foreign achievements see Chapter 13 and Appendix I of *The New Towns, the Answer to Megalopolis* by Sir Frederic Osborn and Arnold Whittick – Leonard Hill. Revised edition 1969.

21. *Through the Great City* by Anthony Bailey, p. 31 – Macmillan, N.Y., 1967 (quoted in *Urban and Rural America: Policies for Future Growth*. Report A.32 of the Advisory Commission on Intergovernmental Relations, Washington, D.C., 1938).

22. Oakley Garden Village, Wimborne. Design by Leonard Vincent and Raymond Gorbing & Partners, consultants to Stevenage Development Corporation of which Leonard Vincent was formerly Chief Architect (*The Times*, 1 November 1968).

23. See Note 39 to Chapter 7.

24. Report of Public Record Office 1967, p. 6 – H.M.S.O., 1968.

25. See Note 20 above.

CHAPTER 17 – FUTURE

1. Commons, 7 March 1968, cols. *145–6*.
2. Commons, 6 November 1961, col. 650.
3. Commons, 18 March 1968, cols. *43–4*.
4. *The Future of Development Plans* – H.M.S.O., 1965.
5. See Chapter 2, p. 11.
6. *Town & Country Planning*, Cmnd. 3333, p. 6 – H.M.S.O., 1967.
7. *Planning and People* – H.M.S.O., 1969.
8. Commons, 8 May 1946, col. 1108.
9. See Note 5 to Chapter 2.
10. Commons, 20 November 1967, col. *257*.
11. *The Deeplish Study: improvement possibilities in a district of Rochdale* – H.M.S.O., 1066.
12. Commons, 18 June 1968, col. 901. The new Chair of Environmental Studies at London University, which combines planning, architecture, and sociology, is a step in the right direction.
13. See Note 10 to Chapter 9.
14. *The Guardian*, 7 March 1967.

INDEX